(CONVERGING
MOVEMENTS)

CONVERGING MOVEMENTS

Modern Dance and Jewish Culture

at the 92nd Street Y

NAOMI M. JACKSON

. . .

WESLEYAN UNIVERSITY PRESS

MIDDLETOWN, CONNECTICUT

WESLEYAN UNIVERSITY PRESS

Middletown, CT 06459

© 2000 by Naomi M. Jackson

Printed in the United States of America

5 4 3 2

First Wesleyan paperback 2002

Originally produced in hardcover in 2000 by
Wesleyan/University Press of New England,
Hanover, NH 03755

Library of Congress Cataloging-in-Publication Data

Jackson, Naomi M.

Converging movements : modern dance and Jewish culture
at the 92nd Street Y / Naomi M. Jackson.

p.   cm.

Includes bibliographical references (p.) and index.

ISBN 0–8195–6419–2 (cl.); ISBN 0–8195–6420–6 (pa.)

1. Modern dance—Social aspects—New York (State)—New York.

2. Jews—New York (State)—New York—History—20th century.

3. United States—Civilization—Jewish influences.

4. 92nd Street Y (New York, N.Y.)—History.

I. Title: Modern dance and Jewish culture at the 92nd Street Y.

II. Title.

GV1783 .J33 2000

792.8'089'92407471--dc21   00–011313

FOR MY PARENTS, SARAH & ANTHONY

CONTENTS

ILLUSTRATIONS

ACKNOWLEDGMENTS

First and foremost I would like to thank Steven Siegel, Archivist and Library Director of the 92nd Street YM-YWHA, for his ongoing patience, assistance, and support. The staff of the Dance Collection at the New York Public Library, especially Pat Rader and Karen Nickeson, also played an invaluable role in assisting me with my research.

Also of great importance to my work has been Nathan Kolodney, who not only gave me insight into his father, William's brilliance but combines in himself the intellectual, artistic, and socially conscious characteristics that are the hallmark of the Jews about whom I write. My conversations with Nathan, along with those with Carl Urbont, acted as a continual reminder of the power of this strand of American Jewry, with its sensitivity to the particular Jewish experience along with general humanist values, as expressed in the realm of art and ideas.

Important individuals who graciously answered my many questions and provided helpful insights into the Y's historic role include Judith Brin Ingber, Ayalah Goren, Jill Gellerman, and Larry Warren. I would also like to thank all those who shared with me their extensive memories and knowledge about the Y: Maurice Bakst, Bonnie Bird, Eva Desca, Felix Fibich, Joan Finkelstein, Lee Freeson, Elaine Genkins, Ruth Goodman, Martha Hill, Omus Hirshbein, Rima Kolodney, Marie Marchowsky, Sophie Maslow, Bernice Mendelsohn, Freema Nadler, Joe Nash, Edna Ocko, Janet Soares, Eugenie Schein, Nona Schurman, Sybil Shearer, Manon Souriau, Carl Urbont, Edith Valentine, Lucy Venable, Ethel Winter, and Charles Woodford. I would also like to thank Nona Schurman's dancers who so kindly demonstrated for me, and the family of Lillian Shapero, who passed on valuable materials to me without hesitation.

Marcia Siegel, Barbara Kirshenblatt-Gimblett, Richard Schechner, Barbara Browning, Ellen Graff, Joel Gereboff, Barbara Palfy, and Lynn Garafola all gave valuable feedback at various stages of the research. In addition, *Dance Chronicle* published an earlier version of the chapter on the birth of the Y, and George Dorris gave helpful recommendations.

I would also like to acknowledge the Lucius Littauer Foundation and the Memorial Foundation for Jewish Culture in New York for their financial assistance during the early stages of my research.

Finally, everlasting gratitude goes to my friends and family for their constant love and support, especially my parents, Sarah and Anthony, and my brother Tim.

N. M. J.

(CONVERGING MOVEMENTS)

Precisely because we believe that the Jews
constitute a liminal border case, neither inside nor outside—or,
better, both inside and outside—they have the capacity to open up
multicultural theory in new and interesting ways.
David Biale, Michael Galchinsky,
and Susannah Heschel[1]

INTRODUCTION

Democracy, Diversity, Dance, and the

Jewish Encounter with America

· · ·

The Ninety-Second Street Young Men's and Young Women's Hebrew Association (familiarly referred to as the 92nd Street Y or simply the Y), which stands at the corner of Ninety-second Street and Lexington Avenue in New York City, marks the intersection of two historical trajectories: it is a symbol of the accomplishments of American Jewry, and it is a reminder of the remarkable achievements of modern dance. Initially a community-oriented institution that catered to a local membership, from the mid-1930s through the 1950s the Y was a major home for dance in New York. The Y's active Dance Center offered classes in technique, choreography, and appreciation and an extensive performance series featuring both prominent and lesser-known dancers. Among the famous works premiered on the Y stage were Anna Sokolow's *Rooms* (1955) and Alvin Ailey's *Revelations* (1960). In 1945, Doris Humphrey was named director of the Dance Center and was active in overseeing many of the program's affairs until her death in 1958.

The 92nd Street Y's influential and pioneering work in the contemporary arts is widely recognized. During this century the institution's Kaufmann Auditorium became known as a celebrated concert hall, where the Budapest String Quartet performed, along with Isaac Stern, Nathan Milstein, Rudolf Serkin, Nadia Reisenberg, and other distinguished soloists. The Y is also remembered as the place where Dylan Thomas's *Under Milk Wood* received its American premiere in May 1953 by staff members of the Y, who proved

The 92nd Street Y Today.
92nd Street YM-YWHA Archives.

Kaufmann Concert Hall, 1970s.
92nd Street YM-YWHA Archives.

themselves talented actors. T. S. Eliot, Robert Frost, William Carlos Williams, and W. H. Auden, among others, read their work at the Y, and the renowned playwright Arthur Miller made appearances there well into the 1990s.

Despite this rich history little has been written about how or why the arts program developed and exactly what it signifies for dance history or the fields of Jewish, American, and cultural studies.[2] Although numerous generations have flocked to the Y to attend the concerts, poetry readings, and lectures, many have remained unaware of the Y's Jewish affiliation, let alone known of the institution's original and lasting contributions to American culture. Meanwhile, scholars struggling with the meaning of postmodernism and multiculturalism have yet to benefit from examining the Y and its richly conceived conceptions of identity, ethnicity, and community, which might greatly contribute to current debates in the humanities.

The following study aims to redress this imbalance by considering the initiation, growth, and broader significance of the Y's dance component at the

Kaufmann Concert Hall.
92nd Street YM-YWHA Archives. Photographer: Steve Williams.

height of its fame, from the 1930s through the 1950s, both by considering what happened at the Y with its dance programming (the historical question) and what this can tell us about the way we might reconceptualize dance and Jewish and American history (the historiographic question). The work challenges standard modern dance history as a genealogy of great individual American innovators. Instead, the case of the Y situates modern dance at the heart of the Jewish encounter with America, revealing that not only were specific institutions central in validating and stabilizing the form but also that diverse individuals and ethnic groups, especially Jews, contributed to shaping contemporary American dance. Such a perspective suggests that struggles over the meaning of American culture that occurred during the 1930s and 1940s involved what might today be called multiculturalism.

This book, therefore, not only strives to right the historical record, but it also highlights, as much as possible, the theoretical issues raised by the material. While I hope that the story of the Y evokes the excitement of the institution as a long and active gathering place through dance, it is my primary intent to foreground the details of the programming and their implications for our understanding of American culture, both past and present. The rest of the opening chapter consequently lays out in broad brush strokes how the

particular way that Jewishness was defined, spoken of, and performed at the
Y, in relation to American culture, affected both the evolution of American
Jewry and the modern dance world. I also consider how what happened at
the Y foreshadowed many of the concerns surrounding diversity today and
how it provides a possible model for thinking (and dancing) about multiculturalism in today's context.

• • •

WHY THE Y?

One of the first questions that springs to mind when considering the vast
legacy of dance at the Y is, why did it occur there, at an institution founded
in 1874 by prominent German Jews intent on promoting harmony and good
fellowship among Hebrew young men? The answer lies in the particular historical moments in which certain Jews and modern dancers found themselves in the 1930s and 1940s. The Jews who frequented the Y at that time
were mostly affluent and middle-class, from both German and Eastern European backgrounds, who lived in the ethnically mixed surrounding area of
Yorkville or in new Jewish neighborhoods that had sprung up in the 1920s in
Queens, the Bronx, and Brooklyn.[3] For second- and third-generation
women and men from these communities there was a strong desire to be engaged in general American life yet retain a link to Jewish culture. What this
translated into was a particular manifestation of Jewishness in which traditional sources of identification, such as religion and custom, were largely replaced by institution, constituency, association, and patronage.[4] Within the
walls of the Y, one studied, socialized, attended recitals, and danced with
other Jews. At the Y the use of leisure time became the primary means of
maintaining Jewish solidarity within the new urban American context.
Moreover, and most interestingly, at the Y hundreds of Jews found a comfortable way to manifest their Jewishness, largely through participation in
nonparochial American culture. While sectarian programming did occur
and was treated with great seriousness, central emphasis was placed on designated "general" activities. For the Y's members, expressing one's Jewishness through the general, contemporary arts became the acceptable and preferred way of being Jewish in America.

In some ways, taking part in the art world was a means of displaying upward mobility and acceptance into genteel middle- and upper-class American
life. However, the Y's Jews were far from being involved in a simple assimila-
tion process. Rather, along with other minorities from socially conscious

backgrounds, they were passionately engaged in redefining these entities, even as they joined them. Theirs was an active reshaping of art and society in line with long-held progressive and humanistic views rooted in the moral tenets of the Jewish religion as well as Jewish trends since the Haskalah, a period in Jewish history known as the Jewish Enlightenment, when Jews began transferring their intellectual and creative energy away from religion to contemporary arts and ideas.[5] Overall, taking classes and attending lectures and performances on the contemporary arts allowed Jews to actively participate in and contribute to the making of modern American culture while evolving definitions of ethnicity within the Jewish community that would allow them to retain specific group identification.

Meanwhile, modern dancers in the 1930s were struggling to gain respectability. Faced with poor performance conditions and overall lack of facilities, many dancers were searching for new places to teach and perform. Unlike classical music, for instance, which was already an established discipline with a set of accepted performers, repertories, and stages, in the 1930s modern dance was striving to find institutional bases beyond the individual studios of its founders. While Martha Graham, Doris Humphrey, Charles Weidman, Hanya Holm, Helen Tamiris, Esther Junger, and Sophia Delza were already establishing themselves as serious exponents of the modern dance, there were many others eager to present work, such as Anna Sokolow, Edna Guy, Eleanor King, and Lillian Shapero. For all these dancers, a dance center in a prestigious institution would come as a welcome offer.

The easy convergence of modern dance and Jewish culture at the Y consequently occurred for a variety of reasons. For the Y's Jewish members and modern dancers of the time there were ideological as well as practical reasons for a smooth merging of interests. Both, for instance, shared a humanistic outlook on the role of the arts in modern life. Influenced by the various progressive movements of the time, they thought the arts and humanities uplifted men's souls, making them better individuals and citizens in a democratic society. Jews at the Y were seeking fulfillment through contemporary art, and many modern dancers saw themselves as providing just such emotional and spiritual nourishment to themselves and their followers. On the practical level, many early modern dancers needed decent stages on which to perform their work and audiences to view it. As of 1930 the Y had the institutional support to offer both. Since its inception the Y had provided a wide range of educational activities to its members. During the early 1930s in particular the Y boasted elegant modern facilities and proved itself committed to classes in philosophy, music, art, drama, and dance, along with more standard recreational activities involving sports and physical fitness.

The Y's long-standing support of progressive education provided the foundation for an extensive cultural program. However, it was the effort of one man, William Kolodney, who was educational director of the Y from 1934 to 1969, that brought about the specific meeting of the dance and Jewish communities that proved so fruitful. Under Kolodney's guidance the basic interests of the Y's progressive leadership were focused and expanded into a full-fledged program of classes and performances that emphasized contemporary

William Kolodney, 1954.
92nd Street YM-YWHA Archives.

art and ideas. It was as part of this broader program that dancing made its first large-scale appearance at the Y in the mid-1930s and remained of central importance throughout the next two decades. Kolodney's role in the establishment and direction of the Y's cultural program, including the dance component, remains fascinating and complex. With a strong background in education, psychology, and Jewish center work, he was a remarkable individual of great intelligence and integrity. His choice of advisers, teachers, and performers was dictated by a variety of concerns that grew from his being a lover of art, a social activist, an entrepreneur, and a leader of Jewish causes. These concerns included his basic belief that the arts enrich the human spirit, his interest in things contemporary, his desire to promote the less- as well as more-established artists, and his wish to foster creativity in Jews.

Kolodney's manifold concerns were united by an overarching desire to bring together the Jewish and non-Jewish worlds. He fervently believed that within the American context, with its potentially pluralistic society, this difficult act of integration could be achieved with joy and mutual benefit. Repeatedly, his message was that non-Jewish and Jewish creativity could be synthesized to improve everyone's experience. As Carl Urbont, a longtime executive of the Y, observed, "Kolodney was a unique man. There are relatively few people in the community who have the knowledge and the interest and commitment that Kolodney had both to the universal as well as the Jewish as sources of human enrichment."[6] To this end, Kolodney brought to bear his business acumen and talent for traversing borders. To carve out a special niche for the Y, he assessed the tastes of the Jewish community and matched them with the needs of the wider artistic community. In terms of dance this meant recognizing an interest in modern dance on the part of young, predominantly female Jews and being aware that, in the broader dance world, modern dance was a struggling art form, lacking institutional support and recognition. Here was a golden opportunity to fill a gap in the general culture and satisfy a sector of the Jewish community. The result of Kolodney's efforts was the successful establishment of the Dance Center and a performance series featuring many famous dancers.

· · ·

REDEFINING MODERN DANCE

If the intersection with contemporary art was to help to define the nature of American Jewry, the reverse was also true. Kolodney, along with the Y's audiences, teachers, and students, helped to broaden modern dance to embrace

diversity in terms of ethnicity, race, age, experience, and stylistic experimentation. This was achieved through the Y's long sponsorship of young performers, European-trained dancers, dancers of different ethnic origins—
Hispanic, African American, and most particularly, Jewish—and dancers
who largely operated outside New York City. Many members of the Jewish
community drew on the universalistic discourse of modern dance, which
implied that an individual could transcend his or her particular circumstances to make statements of universal significance, to make a space for one-
self and other minorities and underrepresented performers in the dance
world. At the same time, the commitment of those individuals to Jewish concerns and to a progressive ideology of tolerance and egalitarianism led them
to challenge the narrowly formalist definition of modern dance that was frequently advanced by the more established wing of the dance community, as
represented by the critic John Martin and the dancers who are now considered the "Big Four," namely, Martha Graham, Doris Humphrey, Charles
Weidman, and Hanya Holm, thereby helping to reframe modern dance as a
more inclusive practice.

The role played by the Y in the dance world, however, was far from
straightforward, reflecting the frequently liminal status of Jews as both insid-
ers and outsiders in American culture. Pulling the Y to the center of what has
since come to be viewed as the mainstream modern dance world (associated
most closely with Martin and Graham) was the Y's close and long-standing
relations with its key players. At the beginning of his tenure at the Y, Kolodney recognized his limited knowledge about dance. His desire to present the
best and most powerful in the field led him to search out Martin, followed by
the composer Louis Horst (who was closely connected to Martha Graham)
and Doris Humphrey as advisers. As is well known, these individuals were
central creators and propagators of early modern dance, active in many aspects of its development.

Martin and Horst in particular were conservative forces at the Y and elsewhere, pushing for the establishment of general principles and the creation
of standards for modern dance and championing a limited number of choreographers as reaching those standards, notably Graham, Humphrey, and
Weidman. As third- and fourth-generation Americans, these dancers fit well
with Martin's framing of modern dance as pure, nonethnic, and generically
American (ballet, it might be noted, was linked with Italians and Russians) in
a way that masked difference while implicitly favoring white Anglo-Saxon
choreographers. The subtly racist aspects of Martin's conceptualization were

most evident in his problematic distinction between modern and so-called ethnic dance and in his reviews of black dancers, as revealed in recent studies of this period.[7]

A number of factors pushed the Y to the margins of general dance activity. The Y's location outside the downtown theater district meant that it did not receive the same recognition as a Broadway venue, and most of its dance performances were not reviewed in the daily newspapers, a severe limitation for many dancers. The Y's perceived status as a sectarian, recreational institution also made it suspect to secondary consideration, being viewed by some as too low-key and, for those aware of its origins, "too Jewish." The opinion was hinted at by the booking agent Frances Hawkins, who angrily wrote to Kolodney concerning the loss of money on performances by Lincoln Kirstein's newly established Ballet Caravan after it appeared at the Y in the late 1930s. She claimed, "I think that in a downtown theatre the same size as the Kaufmann Theatre, I could schedule even two performances for the Caravan and sell out both of them. The Kaufmann Auditorium is inaccessible and it is not associated in peoples' minds with professional dance performances." Hawkins further attacked the Y's policy of closing for the Jewish Sabbath, claiming: "Saturday is almost the only day when many people have the time to make the journey up to the Auditorium to buy tickets in advance and on Saturdays you are closed until late in the afternoon. If people do not have their tickets in advance and anything comes up that promises entertainment closer to home they are very apt not to make the journey up to 92nd and Lexington."[8]

Most significantly, the Y's particular way of conceiving of Jewishness, as a synthesis of the "general" and "particular" in a manner that retained the integrity of people's differences, led to the support of individuals and policies that fostered programming not quite in accord with the interests of Martin and his followers. Kolodney's own varied set of interests were central in the promotion of young and ethnically diverse dancers. Others, like Humphrey, frequently encouraged individual expression at the Y during her years there as a teacher and artistic director of the Merry-Go-Rounders, a company for children developed in the 1950s. The celebrated Jewish modern dancer, Pauline Koner, recalls Humphrey sending her a congratulatory note after one of her concerts in 1945; as a result of this interaction, Humphrey started working with Koner on a project they called choreographic direction, in which they collaborated to create original works.[9]

The Jewish dancers, in particular, who were featured on the Y's stage were a constant challenge to the potential ethnocentrism and racism of the dominant discourse of modern dance. Sophie Maslow, for instance, represented a generation of Jewish dancers from poor Russian-Jewish backgrounds, whose leftist orientation led them to embrace the democratic promise of the modern dance movement. She not only assumed the acceptance of Jewish dancers as valid artists but also hired black dancers to perform in her pieces when it was a far from common occurrence. The New York premiere of *The Village I Knew,* for instance, which focused on Jewish experiences in a shtetl in tsarist Russia, took place at the Y in 1951 and had two black dancers in the cast — Ronne Aul and Donald McKayle. Others from similar backgrounds, especially Anna Sokolow, enjoyed long associations with the Y and similarly used black dancers over the years, including Alvin Ailey. Sokolow's early revolutionary Dance Unit performed at the Y in the 1930s, and she later premiered a number of major works on its stages, including those that focused on the horrors of oppression, as with *Dreams* in 1961.

The important role played by working-class dancers in the making of American modern dance has recently gained recognition with the publication of Ellen Graff's *Stepping Left: Dance and Politics in New York City, 1928–1942* (1997) and Mark Franko's *Dancing Modernism/Performing Politics* (1995). Both writers have persuasively shown that a large number of dancers with left-wing leanings existed in the late 1920s and 1930s, and that these dancers challenged the dominant discourse promulgated by Martin (which emphasized the abstract, personal nature of modern dance) by linking dance to social and political causes. Graff also notes the fact that "the single most important distinction between choreographers allied with bourgeois dance and those allied with workers' dance" was the Eastern European Jewish origin of dancers on the left. It was the daughters of poor Jewish immigrants who led the challenge; and in their attempt to make a place for themselves in America they used working-class ties to bridge racial, religious, and gender differences and fought to enlarge the definition of modern dance to make room for themselves and others (especially African Americans) who similarly lacked a place in standard American mythology. Significantly, many of these women simultaneously formed the backbone of the early schools and companies of Graham, Humphrey/Weidman, and Holm, illustrating the way in which Jews shifted back and forth between the roles of insider and outsider in the dance world.[10]

This study contributes to such a revisionist history of American dance by drawing out more of the complex and important ways in which Jews intersected with the making of contemporary art generally and modern dance specifically in New York City. Clearly, the Y was one of numerous institutions where Jews played an active part in supporting the arts, each with its own particular agenda and lesser or greater consciousness of expressly Jewish concerns. In the 1930s, union halls embraced many Jewish left-wing artists, and Yiddish theaters like Maurice Schwartz's Yiddish Art Theatre provided opportunities for Jewish dancers. Throughout the period, the New School for Social Research and the Neighborhood Playhouse were extremely influential, and there were dance schools such as the New Dance Group that catered to adults interested in modern dance. In the late 1950s and 1960s the Jewish Museum became a major promoter of contemporary art in New York City. In 1957 the museum put on an exhibition entitled *Artists of the New York School: Second Generation*, featuring twenty-three young painters, including Helen Frankenthaler, Jasper Johns, Robert Rauschenberg, and George Segal. This was the first of numerous exhibitions to feature young avant-garde artists who later became highly successful.[11]

In the case of the 92nd Street Y, one sees the convergence of Jews from various backgrounds and the significance of their contribution as enacted in a space whose very purpose was to promote the creation of a vibrant contemporary Jewish-American culture. Significant changes occurred in the contemporary dance scene and Jewish life throughout the period, and it is possible to observe some general trends at the Y. The presence of Jews from working-class backgrounds, for instance, one of the driving forces in the debate over the nature of modern dance in the 1930s, as discussed above, was primarily manifested through performances on the institution's stage by artists like Maslow and Sokolow. At the same time, the middle-class and affluent Jews, who made up the main membership of the Y (as staff, students, and audience members), were equally important in shaping the evolution of dance throughout the period owing to their patronage of the form. Often less stridently political and more directly engaged in a process of smooth integration into existing American life than were their working-class brethren, these Jews were nonetheless committed to nondiscriminatory practices and to making contemporary dance as inclusive as possible. Kolodney's programming vision, for instance, made the Y for many years *the* main stage for African Americans to present their work, from Katherine Dunham in the late 1930s to the historical debut performances by Alvin Ailey in the late 1950s. This aspect of the Y's history has gained increasing visibility, largely through recent attempts to document African American contributions to

American dance, such as John O. Perpener III's "Seminal Years of Black Concert Dance" (1992) and Jennifer Dunning's biography, *Alvin Ailey: A Life in Dance* (1996).[12]

Moreover, Jewish patronage at the Y played a central role in developing an educated audience for modern dance in New York that helped the genre evolve. The extensive program of classes and lectures, such as the critic Walter Terry's Dance Lab, which ran from 1947 to 1963, resulted in the creation of a highly informed Jewish public that was well versed in a broad range of movement styles. A large number of patrons of the Y repeatedly showed up at the Sunday afternoon recitals until they became articulate in interpreting and assessing work by radically different artists. As a reviewer of one Y dance recital in 1941 observed, "It was an audience equipped with the necessary knowledge of technique, familiar with the interpretive method, and thus able to analyze and discuss the performance intelligibly and intelligently."[13] Some of these individuals became lifelong supporters of dance, sending their children to take classes in the future. Others were stimulated to become performers themselves, adding to a growing number of Jewish artists and intellectuals working in the city.

Between the audiences and dancers, policies and presentments, studying the history of dance at the Y in many ways allows us to rethink our conception of both the modern and the subsequent era of postmodern dance, which began in the 1960s and has continued through the 1990s. While standard histories of American dance see a radical divide between the two movements, with postmodern dance bursting onto the scene with the work of the Judson Dance Theater in the early 1960s, it may be that there is a greater connection than previously thought. Today, one of the most visible dimensions of postmodern culture is the movement toward multiculturalism, which challenges the priority of a monolithic identity in American history, highlighting racial as well as ethnic diversity and claiming public resources on behalf of these groups. The Y's long patronage of Jewish, African American, and out-of-town dancers, among others, foreshadowed many of the current effects and questions of multiculturalism in the postmodern dance world in terms of both policy and style. The choreography of young, lesser-known artists of all kinds appearing at the Y was often innovative, involving a combining of different movement traditions. Analyzing their legacy can help us to better understand current choreographers' fascination with stylistic fusion as well as lead to a greater awareness of the continuity of the democratic tradition in American dance.

• • •

BEING JEWISH IN AMERICA

What it means to be Jewish is certainly a complex question and one that is increasingly answered by looking at particular people and communities as ever-shifting lived realities rather than at Jewish religion and law. Today there is a growing body of literature that considers Jewish identity as a social construction from the perspective of ethnography, gender, and performance studies. In her fascinating study, *People as Subject, People as Object: Selfhood and Peoplehood in Contemporary Israel* (Dominguez, 1989), Virginia Dominguez critically analyzes the dynamic processes through which Jewish culture and identity are constructed, disseminated, and maintained in Israel. Like cultural anthropologists Stuart Hall and James Clifford, Dominguez sees group identities as produced, revised, represented, and perpetuated through discursive practices. In the case of Israel, Dominguez reveals the conflicting and competing discourses and ideologies, from the more dominant words and practices of the Ashkenazic elite to the more excluded Sephardic communities composed of immigrants from North Africa and the Middle East. Other writers who reflect the new ethnographic and performative approaches to questions of Jewish identity include Barbara Kirshenblatt-Gimblett, Jack Kugelmass, and Daniel Boyarin and edited collections of essays such as Steven Kepnes's *Interpreting Judaism in a Postmodern Age* (Kepnes, 1996).

Examining the ways in which Jewishness was constructed at the Y illuminates how one prominent sector of American Jewry came to define itself during this century. In particular, the close intersection of Jewish concerns with those of the dance world between 1935 and 1960, a period spanning the Second World War and the establishment of the state of Israel, offers insight into the way many American Jews related to modernism, Zionism, and the changes of the postwar era. Their responses can be seen in the ways they chose to dance: whether they consistently chose to express themselves through nonsectarian dance styles, through modern dance with a Jewish twist, or through Israeli folk dance. In each case, the dancing provided an aesthetic mediation through which sponsors, artists, and their audiences negotiated their relationship to their Jewish identity.

The Y, for instance, was, throughout the 1950s, the American home of Israeli folk dance, as disseminated and theatricalized through the efforts of Fred Berk. At the Y, Israeli folk dance symbolized Israel and a unified Jewish people, with dances like Berk's *Holiday in Israel* (1952) idealizing "the land," rustic simplicity, and the joy of existence. Such a view suited the desire on the part of many American Jews to retain a strong cultural connection with Israel without necessarily making aliyah (settling there). At the Y, young Jews could passionately experience the "Israeli spirit" and rejoice in the euphoria of the creation of a state that assured them they were no longer members of an uprooted, persecuted people. At the same time, they celebrated from a comfortable, middle-class distance in the well-maintained halls of the Y, confirming postwar Jews' rootedness to American society and their own successful cultural life within America.[14]

Most evident, however, is the way Jews at the Y remained in a flexible relation to their Jewish identity throughout this period, moving between a more and less conscious connection to themselves as a distinct community. Which position was taken was closely tied to the social and political climate of the times and the seeming threat to Jewish survival. For many Jews in the pre–Second World War period, for instance, a time of relative freedom and opportunity, any conscious awareness of their Jewish identity was secondary to their embracing of general American culture. The young Jews flocking to the Y's programs yearned to participate in modern life. As Sophie Maslow once described it, "We could feel life changing around us and new things happening in the arts, and we wanted to be part of that future."[15] As the atrocities of the war became evident, however, administrators, artists, and intellectuals who had previously stood aloof from their Jewish identity began to shift programming and artistic content to reflect a new commitment to Judaism. Once again, Maslow gives characteristic voice to this sentiment when she claimed, "This horrible experience [Holocaust] made me realize that as much [as] I thought I was American, I was just as much Jewish ... I then wanted very much to do something Jewish."[16]

It was, in fact, the way in which modern dancers like Maslow gave expression to their hopes and dreams which beautifully captures the predominant way that Jewishness came to be defined in America, especially in the postwar period. In their dances traditional sources of identification (Jewish history, community, religion, and custom) were combined with modernist influences that encouraged individual freedom, artistry, and female expression. Anna Sokolow's dance *Kaddish*, for instance, performed at the Y in 1946, illustrates the trend. In the original choreography, Sokolow wrapped tefillin (Orthodox Jewish prayer boxes) around her head and arm, imitating a daily practice of highly religious men in Jewish religion. Meanwhile, the movement was intense and individualistic, consisting of halting, rigid steps, spins, and reaches upward. In the dance one can see that Sokolow reveled in the mystical spiritualism of an imagined Jewish tradition, while marking the distance from the very same Jewish heritage. For nothing could be farther from Jewish tradition than a woman dancing around a stage in bare feet wearing tefillin. Rather, the dance was embodying a new form of Jewishness mediated by the views and conventions of contemporary dance. As such, it appeared as an important locus for the liberation for Jewish women from the hold of traditional law and to a great extent foreshadowed feminist developments that were to occur only in Reform and Conservative circles after the 1960s.[17]

Works like *Kaddish* suited the deeply felt need of American Jews after the war to create images of a positive Jewish identity that were uplifting, timeless, and spiritual yet largely purified of any negative associations with the Old World, immigrant life, or actual Orthodoxy. This argument has been made by Barbara Kirshenblatt-Gimblett in her introduction to Mark Zborowski and Elizabeth Herzog's *Life Is with People*, the first major anthropological study of Eastern European culture, originally published in 1952. Observing that the book "represents a turning point in the relationship of American Jews to their Eastern European past,"[18] she writes: "Created in the wake of World War II, *Life Is with People* encouraged its readers, demoralized by the annihilation of European Jewry, to take pride in the distinctiveness of their heritage. Attempts to minimize Jewish difference had failed to stem anti-Semitism. The task, now a sacred duty, was to recover the inner life of East European Jewry, its values and the distinctive culture they animated."[19] Kirshenblatt-Gimblett then proceeds to draw on the work of Eric Hobsbawm who, in *The Invention of Tradition*, has argued that "traditions" that appear or claim to be old are often quite recent in origin and sometimes invented. By "invented" Hobsbawm refers to a process of formalization and ritualization, characterized by reference to the past.[20]

In her reflections on *Life Is with People,* Kirshenblatt-Gimblett shows how Eastern European life was construed in a very particular way by many American Jews in the postwar period. Her argument is that Zborowski and Herzog constructed or invented a particular heritage by searching for something essentially Jewish, identifying it with the shtetl and then imbuing the shtetl with timeless, endearing qualities, such as warmth, group solidarity, and affirmative joy in being Jewish. This configuration of the shtetl, she argues, neither matched the reality of the heterogeneous nature of the settlements in which Eastern European Jews lived nor, one might add, acknowledged the negative aspects of such a lifestyle, including the repression of women.[21]

Similar to *Life Is with People*, many pieces by modern dance choreographers presented rather idealized, nostalgic commemorations of Jewish life by locating Jewishness in the Bible and in the religious world of the shtetl. Like Zborowski and Herzog's community, they narrowed "to the world of Sholom Aleichem, the world of our fathers . . . an exclusively Jewish world, a vanished world."[22] Maslow's *The Village I Knew* was just such a work, based as it was on the stories of Sholom Aleichem. It depicted quaint interactions among basic characters, combining exaggerated, mimelike gesture with folk dance steps and periodic technical dance movements.

Analysis of dances like *The Village I Knew* reveals that modernist tenets and conventions were extremely compatible with the new conception of Jewishness. While some Jews of the postwar period might not have realized that they were searching for a quintessential Jewish mode of expression that transcended a specific time and place, modern dancers were propelled in that very direction by the theories they espoused. Specifically, modern American Jews' quest for an essential, timeless Jewishness rooted in a heartwarming "folk" community fit beautifully with modern dancers' tendency to search for underlying essences and their fascination with the common man.

It is important to realize, however, that while idealization of the common man, or folk, emerged in modern dance in the late 1930s with dances like Graham's *American Document* (1938) and Agnes de Mille's *American Suite* (1939), such convictions were particularly embraced by Jewish modern dancers as a way of making room for themselves and other poor and overlooked members of society. As Graff notes in *Stepping Left*, as Jews and blacks, in particular, joined together in the larger class struggle to fight social oppression, they inadvertently also challenged the supremacy of white Protestant bodies (such as Graham's) that strode to subsume every other identity within their representations. Graff's analysis of Sophie Maslow's Americana dances, like *Dust Bowl Ballads*, convincingly shows that in such dances a "kind of revisionist account of American history" was being displayed, which made a place for "not only the descendants of the Mayflower but all the tired, hungry, and poor who had arrived since then."[23] Such dances broadened the notion of "the people" to include all Americans and, in so doing, made modern dance in general more conscious of issues of diversity.

The new concept of Jewish identity, however, did not go unchallenged, as different factions of the Jewish community consistently fought against it. Following the Second World War, for example, the 92nd Street Y's policies were challenged by members of the Jewish establishment, who felt they were too assimilationist. This was particularly notable in the 1948 *JWB Survey,* supervised by Oscar Janowsky, a professor of history at the City College of New York, for the Jewish Welfare Board. The report consisted of interviews with members of Jewish community centers throughout the country as well as observations of some of the centers' activities. The final document upheld the mission of Jewish institutions to devote primary attention to Jewish content and criticized adult education programs of a nonsectarian nature.[24] In the eyes of the report's supporters, continuance of such general programs as Kolodney's at the 92nd Street Y could easily lead to a negation of the unique Jewish spirit and the eventual end of a distinct Jewish presence in America.

Such reactions mark the presence of different interpretive communities engaged in constructing notions of self and society through distinct practices and master narratives. For more observant, traditional American Jews, the various influences present in works by Jewish modern artists and dancers lay together very uncomfortably, revealing the disjunction between religion and custom on the one hand and contemporary values on the other. Meanwhile, for the progressive Jewish viewers of the 1940s and 1950s, for whom the Y was a core disseminator of their values, the combination appeared not only seamless but also highly satisfying and fulfilling. The aestheticization of the religious and folk dimensions of Jewish experience and its articulation through the powerful, increasingly liberated female body expressed well the lived reality of the modern American Jew.

• • •

JEWS, DANCE, AND A MULTICULTURAL IDEAL

In *Insider/Outsider: American Jews and Multiculturalism* (1998), the editors David Biale, Michael Galchinsky, and Susannah Heschel pose the question, how might the Jewish experience challenge the conventional polar opposition of a majority "monoculture" and a marginalized "multiculture"?[25] They observe that many people have become disillusioned with the current way that multiculturalism is realized, where the effort to restore the voices of history's victims has sometimes led to the status of victim valorization for its own sake and where an exaggerated politics of identity has increasingly denied the possibility of uniting with others of different backgrounds. They write: "With the breakdown in communication and even in the belief in the

universality of language, all that is left sometimes seems to be dogmatic political correctness."[26] Their hope is to contribute to a growing number of
writers who do not reject the desire to create a true multiculture, "but instead
try to see beyond present multicultural politics toward a more inclusive vision of an America in which particularity and universalism are not contradictory goals but rather poles in a fruitful dialectic."[27] Within this discussion,
Jews are presented as providing a valuable perspective, living, as they have for
centuries, as both insider and outsider, as a distinct people living in interaction and struggle with other cultures and as a group whose identity has always been an indeterminate composite of so-called religious, ethnic and national dimensions.

The Jewish encounter with America, in particular, presents interesting insights into the multicultural debate, since Jews often led the challenge to a
monolithic conception of American identity at the beginning of this century, when the ideas of melting pot and cultural pluralism were being hotly
discussed. This challenge in many ways consisted of enlarging the conception of whiteness to make room for themselves as a distinct people, along
with other peoples of color, for Jews were initially considered nonwhite and
were accepted as white only following the Second World War, as anti-
Semitism and formal discrimination waned and Jews became economically
successful.[28] The drive to envision an America in which Jews and other ethnic
groups might be both integrated and still retain their distinctiveness was
driven by a dual consciousness on behalf of Jews: the awareness of themselves as the discriminated "other" of millions of years and the hope that the
golden New World would finally mean acceptance as part of the majority.
Thus, as Biale notes in "The Melting Pot and Beyond: Jews and the Politics of
American Identity," a great deal of the discourse about America as a melting
pot or pluralistic nation of cultural minorities was "originated by Jews to address the particular situation of Jewish immigrants. Jews therefore not only
adapted to America but also played central roles in shaping the definitions of
their adopted country."[29]

The Y stands as a marker of such a leadership role during the first part of
the century in the shaping of a pluralistic, egalitarian America. From
Kolodney's carefully articulated conceptions of the Jewish place in America to
the performed ideals of Maslow, the Y was a central institution in New York
where an attempt to retain ethnic/racial distinctiveness was combined with
the desire to unify and integrate. This was achieved by a complex of factors
that included the flexible approach taken to asserting Jewish uniqueness;[30] the

locating of Jewishness more in association and constituency and in numerous constructions of Jewishness than in a single, all-encompassing definition
based on religion or custom; the embracing of the discourse of modern,
democratic America, which promised the ability to transcend one's own particularity to appreciate/produce art and ideas; and the active commitment of
its leaders and members to diversity. All these aspects, and undoubtedly
more, were significant in the Y's success.

No doubt, the Y's heyday, especially in relation to the dance world, occurred before the radical movements of the 1960s, when the civil rights movement led the change in consciousness that created multiculturalism in its
present theoretical and political forms. The Y, as such, functioned within a
context in which ethnic/religious difference was still more or less regarded as
a private affair, with the public ideal remaining a homogenized culture based
on Anglo-Saxon history, art, and mythology. Within this context, the Y's Jews
clearly positioned themselves to try to work with this particular model of cultural pluralism as successfully as they could. As rapidly rising members of society, both economically and socially, they were benefiting from this view of
America and were not intent on overthrowing it. Those who wish to dismiss
the long-term significance of the Y would be quick to make this observation,
perhaps even arguing that their desire to become "white" actually led many
American Jews to be racist and sexist and, with their success in achieving their
goal in the postwar era, to misunderstand the value of multiculturalism in its
present form.

Dispelling reductive, subtly anti-Semitic interpretations of Jewish activities at the beginning of the century are the kinds of insights that emerge from
such particularized studies as the history of dance at the 92nd Street Y during
its heyday. This research articulates and traces a potential multicultural ideal,
in which unity is created between different individuals and groups through
passion for the arts and ideas. It demonstrates how this approach encourages
the maintenance of different experiences while allowing people to celebrate a
shared excitement at exploring the nature of contemporary life. And it gives
voice to the success of the enterprise as echoed in the expressions of euphoria
of the manifold non-Jews as well as Jews who have passed through the Y's
doors. As dancer and educator Bonnie Bird put it in an interview, "The
amount of people who came and went happily in that institution was *truly*
amazing."[31] Indeed, it is ultimately these voices, with their intelligence, creativity, and passion, that make it possible and indeed necessary to write about the
important contribution of Jews to American life in the twentieth century.

*They [Jewish community centers] all aim to aid
in the adjustment of Jewish life in America. They seek to achieve
this adjustment by various means, but all based on the utilization of the
leisure time of the Jewish constituency, through wholesome participation
in educational, recreational, and social activities.*
Harry L. Glucksman[1]

(1)

JEWS & AMERICAN CULTURE

The 92nd Street Y and William Kolodney

· · ·

The Y currently located at Ninety-second Street and Lexington Avenue is the
largest and oldest continuously operating YM-YWHA in the United States. The
history of the organization reveals the extent to which its particular conception of Jewishness laid the groundwork for the establishment of a center for
dance in the 1930s. At the Y, institutional control of leisure time was used as
the means to bind the Jewish community together. However, within its walls,
Jewishness was often defined by constituency, association, and patronage
rather than manifestly Jewish content. Although sectarian programming occurred, the emphasis was on general cultural and educational activity. Interest in such programming evolved in line with widespread progressive thinking in arts and adult education circles regarding the cultivation of the
individual within an American democracy. A humanistic perspective viewed
the arts as enriching the lives of modern men and women, making them better citizens and members of society. Such a view was refashioned in the Jewish context, with a view toward stimulating individual growth, providing institutional support for activities that would otherwise draw people to venues
outside the Jewish community, and creating a vital communal cultural life
that would help to sustain Jewish life within America.

Of all the Y's personnel, William Kolodney most concentrated attention on contemporary art and education and its special significance for the regeneration of American Jewry within the context of a community center. He articulated the broader rationalizations for strong arts and humanities programs at the Y, which proved sympathetic to the needs and values of many intellectuals and artists, both Jewish and non-Jewish, including practitioners of the emerging modern dance.

• • •

THE CREATION OF THE YMHA

The 92nd Street YMHA was founded in 1874 by predominantly German Jews prominent in the professional and business life of New York City.[2] Their aim was to establish a Jewish youth and education center for the cultural and intellectual advancement of young men, and in the first official declaration of their association, the founders documented their intent "to promote harmony and good fellowship among Hebrew young men, and to unite them in an organization tending to improve their social, moral and mental condition."[3] The first permanent quarters for the association were located at 112 West Twenty-first Street, where a small house was rented in September 1874; but in less than two years the association was ready for a larger residence, and in April 1876 a lease was taken on a building at 110 West Forty-second Street. This facility contained a gymnasium, bowling alleys, reading room, and club and class rooms, which allowed the institution to expand and develop its programming over the next ten years.

From early on, the YMHA offered young Jewish men a mixture of educational and cultural activities. There were debates and lectures on historical, scientific and literary subjects, along with free classes in German, Hebrew, French, phonography, music, bookkeeping, and freehand drawing.[4] Music and vocal recitals, along with recitations, offered the membership a taste of assorted "entertainments." Unlike later in the Y's history, no clear distinction was made among the different activities; they were offered together as a collection to prospective members.

The emphasis on nonsectarian programming derived in part from the Y's leaders, who were mostly men from the well-established New York German-Jewish community and as such integrated socially into American society, while retaining ties to the Jewish life through service organizations like the Y.[5] They spoke English, assumed American manners and attire, and were well educated. At the same time they lived within predominantly Jewish neigh-

borhoods, frequently associated with other Jews, and were connected to the
Jewish community through various philanthropic and volunteer endeavors.
Oscar Solomon Straus, for instance, one of the Y's founders, studied law at
Columbia University and went on to become a prominent diplomat and pol-
itician. A native of Rhenish Bavaria, he enjoyed broad literary and historical
interests as well as commitment to Jewish causes, becoming the first president of the American Jewish Historical Society in 1892 and a founder of the
American Jewish Committee in 1906. Straus and his friends were interested
in achieving what they considered a successful synthesis of Jewish and American interests. They consequently supported a program that would educate
Jewish youngsters in subjects of importance to the general population while
allowing them to study and socialize with other Jews.[6]

Other influences on the programming derived from the Y's close affinity
to Jewish youth organizations previously operative in America, such as the
Jewish Literary Association established in Philadelphia in 1850 and earlier
Young Men's Hebrew Associations, the first of which appeared in Baltimore
in 1854. Members of these groups met to discuss current affairs and assemble
for cultural events. As socioliterary associations for native-born, middle-
class, and affluent urban adolescents of German background, such organizations represented an attempt to maintain Jewish solidarity within the new
American context. Use of leisure time to focus these efforts was one particular response to modernization that rapidly gained in popularity as more traditional ties to Judaism by way of religious observance were increasingly
abandoned.

Concurrently, the Y in certain ways mirrored the coinciding work of the
Young Men's Christian Association, first founded in England in 1844 and in
North America in 1851 (when a branch was opened in Boston). The YMCA was
dedicated to the moral and intellectual development of young Christian men,
with an evangelical emphasis. While the organization focused on Sunday
schools and Bible classes, it also opened libraries and introduced educational
programs. In the late 1850s, for instance, branches of the YMCA in New York
and Brooklyn offered classes in music, foreign languages, and gymnastics.[7]

The YMCA and the YMHA were participating in a broad social movement
sweeping America at the time, whose followers sought to cultivate the individual and improve communal life of ordinary men and women through
physical fitness, art, and education. This thrust for change included the
parks and recreation movement, the public library movement, and the arts
and adult education movements. Each of these found their roots in the

nineteenth century and continued to expand their influence with the assistance of prominent philanthropists and private institutions like the YMHA. One of the best-known examples of this larger trend was the Chautauqua Literary and Scientific Circle, which brought entertainment and culture to rural America in the late nineteenth century. The original Chautauqua began after the Civil War as an assembly for the training of Methodist Sunday school teachers and church workers at Chautauqua Lake in New York state. The program then broadened to include general education and popular entertainments aimed to "take people on all sides of their natures, and cultivate them systematically, making men, women and children everywhere more affectionate and sympathetic . . . more intelligent and thoughtful as students in a universe of ideas."[8]

It was within the context of this broader social transformation, along with the more unique needs faced by adjustments to American life occurring within the American Jewish community, that the Y initiated and continued its programs. Over the next decade the Y relocated to other sites in the city, continuing to build a reputation and participate in the "cultivation" of America's Jewish youth through fitness programs, the arts and education. In 1886 a small building was rented at 721 Lexington Avenue, near Fifty-eighth Street, where activities of the association were carried on for the next nine years. During this time, along with its regular recreational programming, the association offered public lectures and courses in Jewish subjects and oversaw large-scale celebrations of the Jewish holidays like Purim and Chanukah at outside locations such as the Metropolitan Opera House, Chickering Hall, and Terrace Garden.[9]

While the Y continued with its earlier projects, the 1880s witnessed a slight shift in the institution's agenda. The first part of the decade saw the commencement of Russian-Jewish refugees pouring into America, escaping persecution and poverty at home. In an attempt to assist these new immigrants, the Y, along with other Jewish agencies, undertook some of the work of helping people settle into their new country of citizenship. In 1882–83 the association established a downtown branch where English-language classes were held and an employment bureau and library were made available to the newcomers, along with rooms for lectures, forums, and recitals.

The Y's overall breadth and excellence in programming, along with its assistance with immigrants, helped to distinguish the association as a significant force among more influential members of the Jewish community. In 1898, when the success of the Y's programming again generated increased demand for larger facilities, Jacob Schiff, a New York banker who was one of the most generous philanthropists in the early twentieth century, came to the rescue. Schiff, a German Jew originally from Frankfurt am Main, was so impressed with the work of the Y that he provided it first with a home at 861 Lexington Avenue, near Sixty-fifth Street and then in 1900 donated a new building at Ninety-second Street and Lexington Avenue that was "commensurate with the services the Association was rendering to the Jewish community."[10] This building was to become the main home of the Y until 1928, when it was torn down and replaced with a new facility.

Schiff chose the Ninety-second Street site because he believed it was well situated in the heart of the growing uptown Jewish community. He wrote to the Y's president of the time, Percival S. Menken: "In making selection of this location, I have been led by the fact that the large mass of the Jewish population of this city in the up-town districts is at this time, and will for many years be, centered in the district East of Fifth Avenue, between 50th Street on the South and 150th Street on the North, so that the location selected represents as nearly as possible the heart of this district, while to the Jewish population located West of Central Park the 86th Street surface railroad line affords the means of easy communication with the location."[11]

Schiff's choice placed the institution in an area increasingly inhabited by prosperous Jews, assuring that it would largely serve upwardly mobile Jews rather than poorer immigrants from the Lower East Side. As early as the Civil War, German Jews had begun to populate the East Side, and during the 1880s and 1890s this population was greatly enlarged by a new wave of affluent German Jews settling in the region between Fiftieth and Ninetieth Streets. At that time, smaller contingents of their brethren also began to settle farther north, in the upper-class neighborhood of Harlem, north of Central Park, and the well-situated brownstone homes west of Central Park.[12]

However, the new site was not without its shortcomings. By 1859, Yorkville, which was the area centered at Eighty-sixth and Third Avenue, was predominantly German. Although this situation began to change in the 1880s, when Irish as well as Jews began to move into the area, many of the shops, restaurants, and bakeries in the heart of the area remained German-owned. This caused problems in the 1930s, when the German American Bund, situated on Eighty-sixth Street, held Nazi rallies and Jews living in the area found themselves the target of vandalism and other forms of anti-Semitism. During the turn of the century, however, Schiff's choice of site seemed to have little effect on the Y's popularity. Through these years the Yorkville neighborhood became more ethnically diverse, with Hungarians, Czechs, Slovaks, and Italians moving into the area, making Yorkville an active and exciting part of the city. The Y's membership steadily grew as the institution attracted young Jewish men from the surrounding streets and, as Schiff had foreseen, from other predominantly middle- and upper-class Jewish neighborhoods in New York.

During the first couple of decades of the twentieth century, the association proceeded to offer a more comprehensive program of activities to its membership. The Y's work became increasingly defined through the establishment of committees made up of members of the board of directors. When the Y moved into its new home at Ninety-second Street, a Class Committee was formed, which oversaw all the courses, including those in athletics, as well as Hebrew and Jewish history. In 1906 these activities came to be called the Educational Department, showing the extent to which the educational program had become a significant force within the Y. The move into the new building in 1900 also prompted an expansion of religious activities and the formation of a standing Committee on Religious Work. The first chairman was Dr. F. de Sola Mendes, rabbi of Temple Shaaray Tefila, a Reform synagogue then located on Eighty-second Street on the West Side. The committee's initial responsibility was to plan High Holy Day services, which proved a great success. Friday night services were also organized, and in the spring of 1904 the Y held its first community seder on Passover.

Mention of the Y's expanding religious program raises questions concerning the Y's religious affiliation. A problematic issue throughout its history, the Y's leaders ranged in their level of personal observance while making sure a link was maintained between the Y and religious institutions and practices. The tendency of the Y was (and is) to associate itself with progressive-minded members of the Conservative and, occasionally, Reform movements. When rabbis were required to lead services and establish Hebrew schools and other religious programs, they were often drawn from Conservative synagogues in the surrounding neighborhoods. In general, the Y tried to avoid promoting any one branch of the religion, instead focusing on basic aspects of religious practice (like attending High Holy Day services) and encouraging participation in worship as part of its broader educational and recreational programming.

The Y's particular approach to Judaism was given shape by the institution's close association with Dr. Mordecai Kaplan, a theorist and rabbi of the early twentieth century whose ideas highly motivated the Y's leadership. Kaplan assisted in hiring the Y's first religious director, Rev. Adolph Coblenz, in the summer of 1912; and in 1913 he was elected to the Y's board of directors, where-upon he was immediately named chairman of the Committee on Religious Work. Kaplan helped to oversee the committee's activities until 1919, when he resigned from the Y to pursue other opportunities. Even so, he continued to give periodic speeches at the institution and affect its course of action.

Kaplan was born in Lithuania and came to the United States at the age of eight. He attended the College of the City of New York and Columbia University and received his rabbinical degree in 1902 from the Jewish Theological Seminary of America. In 1909 he became principal of the Teachers Institute of the seminary and proceeded to hold various posts there over the years, at the same time remaining active as a community leader. According to his biographer, Mel Scult, "Kaplan was concerned with the 'thinness' of contemporary religious life."[13] Whereas traditionally Jewish life had been bound up with the community as a whole, in the context of modern, democratic society, religious life had become detached and made into a sometime activity. Kaplan felt this situation was dangerous and needed to be reversed. Scult states, "Kaplan believed that Judaism would survive only if Jews have a life together other than just praying together: Community precedes religion and gives rise to it."[14]

To help to restore the energy to Jewish life in America, Kaplan believed it was necessary to create institutions where Judaism could be kept alive in all its aspects. In 1916 he conceived of the "synagogue-center" as a multifaceted institution that would meet the physical, educational, and social demands of a person, along with his or her spiritual needs. Kaplan argued that "whatever helps to produce creative social interaction among Jews belongs to the category of Jewish religion, because it contributes to the salvation of the Jew."[15] In 1918 Kaplan proposed four activities for such a center: worship, study, social service, and recreation. In planning for a community-based revival of Jewish life, Kaplan conceived of the synagogue-center as a neighborhood institution. He argued that the synagogue should be an institution providing services to all Jews, stating that it "must not be monopolized by a particular congregation. It must belong to the entire Jewish community." He emphasized that "all Jews to whom it is accessible should resort [to it] for all religious, cultural, social and recreational purposes."[16]

While debates existed over the extent to which "Jewish" activities should be included in the programming, Kaplan's ideas appear to have been greatly influential in the case of the 92nd Street Y, which in many ways aimed for a similar kind of multiple-purpose space and lack of congregational affiliation that Kaplan promoted.[17] Like many others of their generation, the Y's leaders participated in a widespread attempt on the part of the New York Jewish community to implement some of Kaplan's ideas to a lesser or greater extent.[18] Religious leaders and social and community workers were seeking ways to create an institution that would ensure Jewish survival within America, and it seemed that some kind of broadly conceived Jewish center was a good way to achieve this goal.

The popularity of the 92nd Street Y and other centers was evident in the expansion of these organizations. In 1916, Felix Warburg, the president of the Y, proposed the formation of a Federation of Charities, which would become the fiscal agency for the Jewish philanthropic organizations in New York. As a result of his perseverance, the Federation for the Support of Jewish Philanthropic Societies was founded in 1917 as a central fundraising agency for New York Jewish organizations. The federation provided an annual subsidy to the Y, which was then augmented through donations by board members and income generated from membership fees. (This funding method continued throughout the century and became an important means, from the mid-1930s on, of subsidizing the cultural programming.) The Jewish Welfare Board (JWB), also founded in 1917, merged in 1921 with the National Council of Young Men's Hebrew and Kindred Associations (which dated back to 1910). The JWB helped the Y and other institutions in their programming and long-term development through their publications and lecture bureau.[19]

As Jewish community organizations grew stronger, larger social changes were taking place that would have an effect on the Y. During the first two decades of the twentieth century, high immigration from Eastern Europe had focused the New York Jewish community's attention on newcomers' needs. This influx was drastically retarded in the 1920s, when a series of quota acts restricted the number of immigrants to the United States. The most severe of these was the Johnson Act of 1924, which limited yearly immigration to a total of 154,000 and gave overwhelming preference to immigrants from Northern and Western Europe. New ways of setting the quota meant that only about six thousand immigrants could be admitted yearly from Poland, two thousand from Russia, and seven hundred from Romania.[20]

The reduction of Jews entering New York meant that the Y could fully attend to the needs of the new generation of affluent and middle-class Jews of both German and Eastern European heritage, which was quickly rising in number.[21] During the 1920s and 1930s, the expanding subway system made it possible for Jewish families to leave the crowded Lower East Side and Harlem in search of a higher standard of living. By the 1930s, almost 80 percent of the city's Jewish population lived in the Bronx and Brooklyn, while Manhattan housed about 16 percent in select enclaves. During these decades the older split between uptown and downtown Jews faded as Eastern European Jews became more successful and the two groups increasingly lived side by side. Second- and third-generation Jews lived in growing communities in upper Manhattan, Brooklyn, the Bronx, and Queens.[22] Yorkville, which surrounded the Y and housed about 4 percent of New York's Jews in the 1930s, along with the Upper West Side, were the most elite Jewish districts in Manhattan. Washington Heights, meanwhile, was a middle-class area that attracted successful Jews who wanted to move out of Harlem, and in the 1930s, they were joined by German-Jewish refugees who created their own special subcommunity. Brooklyn's new Jewish neighborhoods included the affluent Flatbush and more middle-class Eastern Parkway and Borough Park neighborhoods, while financially secure Jews in the Bronx lived in the western section of the borough on the Grand Concourse.

Beth Wenger stresses, in *New York Jews and the Great Depression*, that "in New York's upper-class and solidly middle-class Jewish districts, the Depression's impact was seldom visible on neighborhood streets."[23] Whereas the Depression hit poorer Jewish neighborhoods much more severely, in Manhattan especially, the wealthier Upper East and West Sides were little affected by it. Wenger observes that the Upper West Side, in particular, with its population of upwardly mobile Eastern European Jews, prospered and expanded through the Depression years. With ten synagogues and many kosher butchers, bakeries, and restaurants, the "area surrounding Central Park West demonstrated few visible effects of the economic crisis."[24] In fact, the Jewish population in the area increased throughout the decade as many Jews achieved financial success and moved into the area. These newcomers had the economic resources to attend concerts and to send their children to expensive summer camps and after-school programs.

In the 1920s and 1930s, consequently, it was a mixture of Eastern European and German Jews from these growing Jewish middle-class and affluent neighborhoods who traveled to the 92nd Street Y to take advantage of its recreational programming. During this time, life at the Y revolved around the gym and pool, overseen by an Athletics Committee created in 1921, and numerous clubs that brought together young men in their leisure time. The clubs were made up of groups of boys who spent time together, whether to play basketball, hike, or stage a chess tournament. They were amateur in nature and mostly functioned as a way of making friends and having fun. The Educational Department also offered classes in vocational subjects, along with "cultural activities of an informal nature."[25] Courses included bookkeeping, history, stenography, piano, violin, and voice. Throughout the 1920s the Religious Committee oversaw a limited amount of programming, mostly consisting of Sabbath services and High Holy Day observances, with some courses on Jewish history and the Bible.

As the 1920s came to a close, it became clear that the existing building could not meet the demands of the membership. The most pressing of these concerned housing, since many young men who came to the city to study or work needed a place to live, and there was currently no adequate structure

The 92nd Street Y, 1930.
92nd Street YM-YWHA Archives. Photographer: N. Lazarnick.

Theresa L. Kaufmann Auditorium, 1930.
92nd Street YM-YWHA Archives. Photographer: A. N. Russoff.

that could accommodate them. In May 1927, a drive for funds began for a new building to replace the structure donated by Schiff twenty-seven years earlier. The old building was demolished in 1928, and for two years the YMHA resided with the YWHA on 110th Street. The Young Women's Hebrew Association was founded in 1902 as a sister institution to the Y and since 1914 had been located at 31 West 110th Street.[26]

In 1930 the new building opened at 92nd Street with a modern gymnasium, pool, classrooms, dormitory, and fully equipped, elegant theater.[27] The dormitory contained two hundred rooms, accommodating 278 young men. The theater was named the Theresa L. Kaufmann Auditorium, after the late wife of Henry Kaufmann, who had donated $200,000 to have it built.[28] Kaufmann, an immigrant from Germany, had arrived in the United States in the nineteenth century and run a successful department store business in Pittsburgh. By the 1920s he was dividing his time between Pittsburgh and New York, where he became a major donor to the YMHA building fund in 1927. The wonderful modern facilities made possible an extensive new program of educational, cultural, social, religious, and athletic activities. For the first time, many of the spheres of the Y's activities were defined and given official status. A religious department was established with a full-time director, a physical education department was created, and the Educational Department was expanded to include an art department and a drama department. The Music Department, which had been founded in the fall of 1917, continued as an independent entity.[29]

. . .

GENERAL AND "JEWISH" PROGRAMMING AT THE Y

The subdivision of the Y's activities had an extremely significant role in determining the nature of the Y's future educational programming. Until the late 1920s, no clear-cut distinction was made in the Y's internal documentation between classes of a "general" nature and those with "Jewish" content. The Educational Department had often overseen the former, and what was then called the Religious Committee the latter. With the opening of the new building, however, this perspective shifted as the Y's administrative staff began to distinguish consistently between "general" and "Jewish" programming.[30] The change is clearly marked in the writings of Herman Jacobs, who designed the Y's courses and lectures, and of Rabbi Henry M. Rosenthal, who headed the Religious Department. In his "Memorandum on Educational and Cultural Program" of August 1930, Jacobs outlines a series of lectures and he remarks, "This series must exclude from its list Jewish speakers on Jewish questions, since a separate major series of Jewish lectures is to be offered under the auspices of the Department of Religious Activities. In other words, this Forum will present eminent authorities and speakers on general themes." Later, in describing his plans for the Y, Jacobs continues: "As in the case of our program of monthly lectures, we are limited in the realm of classes and courses to a few of general cultural interest, to the exclusion of any work in Jewish studies. According to the plan, any work to be offered in Jewish history, customs and ceremonies, Jewish philosophy, Jewish current problems, world Jewish movements, theories of Jewish survival and the like, will be presented under the auspices of the Department of Religious Activities."

Such a clear distinction between the kinds of programming was supported by statements of the Religious Department. A report from September 1930, for instance, indicated that Rosenthal, who was a recent graduate of Columbia University and the Jewish Theological Seminary, "has spent considerable time in making contacts with the members with the hope of developing interest in Jewish activities." The report continues that Rosenthal "is

Audience at the Theresa L. Kaufmann Auditorium, 1950s.
92nd Street YM-YWHA Archives. Photographer: G. D. Hackett.

organizing classes in Hebrew, Jewish history and Jewish literature, discussion groups, Friday evening services and lectures."

In this way, specifically "Jewish" programming was placed under the jurisdiction of the Religious Department, and the Educational Department was left to focus on programs of a "general" nature, with little or no direct relation to Jewish themes or issues. Although Jacobs and Rosenthal did state their commitment to support each other's efforts, this division was very important for determining the direction the educational programming would take throughout most of the decade and into the future, namely, focusing on activities of a nonsectarian nature. For it was owing to such a distinction that a program of contemporary arts—specifically, modern dance—would eventually flourish at the Y.

It would be misleading however, to associate this division of interests as meaning that the Y lacked commitment to Jewish life. While this was frequently the perception and the cause for ongoing debate within religious and community center circles over the appropriate mission of the Y and other centers like it, the institutional naming of parts of the Y as Jewish or general masked the larger reality, namely, that, at the YMHA, Jews found a comfortable way to express their Jewish identity in numerous ways, ranging from the less to the more consciously sectarian. Moreover, the choice to frame Jewishness largely through association and patronage, and through participation in nonparochial American culture, was in itself a distinguishing aspect of their identities as modern New York Jews. Unlike some people of the period, such as those who followed Felix Adler's Ethical Culture movement and largely rejected their Jewish ties, most Jews committed to the Y retained a strong connection to their ethnicity/religion.[31] That connection just happened to be manifested in a modernized form.

• • •

CULTIVATING THE INDIVIDUAL THROUGH THE ARTS AND EDUCATION

With its newly defined mandate for nonsectarian programming, the Y's Educational Department saw the commencement of the most active era yet in the institution's history. The new theater and classrooms spawned a surge of interest, on the part of the Y's leadership, in developing a dynamic general educational program open to both women and men.[32] In May 1931 the Membership Committee of the Y reported that "the chief field for pioneering activity among the membership in the future lies in the field of the cultural program." And the September 4, 1931, issue of the *YMHA Bulletin* carried a front-page headline boldly proclaiming the new approach: "Staff Plans Adjustment of All Departments; Creative Cultural Activity to Be Fostered."

The Y's revitalized enthusiasm for adult education and the arts was spearheaded by Jacobs, who had graduated from New York University and was currently completing his master of science at Columbia. The philosophy underlying the new approach was laid out by him in 1930 in his proposal to Jack Nadel: the philosophy was "to be found in the spirit and purpose of Adult Education as exemplified in the writings of such persons as John Dewey, Eduard C. Lindeman, Everett Dean Martin, Joseph K. Hart, and Professor Mordecai M. Kaplan."[33] Jacobs went on to explain: "For if we have properly evaluated their contribution to modern thinking and education, Adult Education means for us a system and course of behavior practiced by individuals eager to make their education coterminous with life, eager to become enriched through their study, by being sensitized to new forces, or to new aspects of old forces as presented by the teacher and the group, and by contributing, out of their own experiences and in terms of their own unique personality, to the thinking of the entire group of which they are a part." Jacobs's writing indicated that the Y was directly in keeping with contemporary trends, as the late 1920s and early 1930s witnessed a flowering of the various adult and arts education movements begun in the late nineteenth century. There was a surge of activity in both general and Jewish circles, as teachers, community workers, and theorists began to write and speak about the importance of new developments. Herman Jacobs, along with others at the Y, was eager to implement the current ideas and help to shape the future direction of adult education in America.

Each of the men mentioned by Jacobs—Dewey, Lindeman, Martin, Hart, and Kaplan—were leaders in the adult education movement and saw the uplift of the individual as a key component in improving modern democratic life. John Dewey was undoubtedly the most famous, writing and teaching on a diverse range of issues concerning philosophy, psychology and education. Lindeman, Hart, and Martin, on the other hand, focused largely on adult education, exploring the meaning of a liberal education and its effect on people's ways of thinking and behaving. In the 1920s, Kaplan further developed ideas on adult education in the context of the Jewish encounter with America. Their theories influenced the leaders at the Y in the early 1930s and later appear in the work of William Kolodney, the successor of Herman Jacobs and the major force at the Y from 1934 onward.

Dewey's interest in education began during his years at the University of Michigan, where he was appointed as an instructor in philosophy and psychology in 1884. He believed that most schools were failing to adjust to current findings of child psychology and to the needs of a changing democratic social order. Over the next several decades, as he moved to the University of Chicago (1894) and Columbia University (1904), Dewey developed a philosophy of education that would remedy these problems and allow for reform in the educational system. Dewey's resulting view of education is based on an understanding of democracy, not as a mere form of government but as a mode of association that provides the members of a society with the opportunity for maximum experimentation and personal growth. Within this context, education's aim is to assist in the realization of such growth and the achievement of individual maturity. This, in turn, allows for increased social efficiency and harmony. Regarding the education process itself, Dewey believed that it must begin with *experience* and focus on the *total* student, or whole personality, in his or her endeavors to adjust to the environment. Dewey's writings on education, including *The School and Society* (1899), *The*

Child and the Curriculum (1902), and *Democracy and Education* (1916), laid out the central tenets of his philosophy. These were that the educational process must begin with and build on the interests of the child, that it must allow room for the interplay of thinking and doing in the classroom, and that the school's goal is the maturation of the child in all aspects of his or her being.

Dewey's ideas strongly affected educational theory and practice in the United States. They became the basis of the progressive movement in education, which stressed the student-centered rather than subject-centered school and education through activity rather than the formal lecture format. This movement advanced relatively slowly during the first decades of the twentieth century. During the 1920s, however, Dewey's work spread rapidly, influencing many aspects of education, including the more specialized fields of adult and art education.

The social psychologist Everett Martin writes in *The Meaning of a Liberal Education* (1926) that "adult education is now becoming an important interest in American life."[34] He notes that higher branches of learning are being pursued by many people outside regular educational institutions: "Perhaps at no time since the thirteenth century has the desire for knowledge nearly approached a mass movement."[35] Martin's aim is to examine what an educated person is like and what adult education consists of. Far from being information, skill, or propaganda, he argues, education is a "spiritual revaluation of human life" through which a person is liberated and enriched. He asserts: "It is sought to make of adult education something which will . . . lift men's thought out of the monotony and drudgery which are the common lot, to free the mind from servitude and herd opinion, to train habits of judgment and of appreciation of value, to carry on the struggle for human excellence . . . to dispel prejudice by better knowledge of the self, to enlist all men, in the measure that they have capacity for it, in the achievement of civilization."[36]

Eduard C. Lindeman, in *The Meaning of Adult Education* (1926), also criticizes any formalized, mechanical process that refuses to recognize the higher goals of education. He asserts that the purpose of adult education is "to put meaning into the whole of life"[37] and stresses the need for full self-expression of the total personality through activities that are not standardized but highly creative. These include the arts, which can help to lift us above the monotonous necessities into the realm of pure joy. Both Lindeman and Joseph Hart, in his book *Adult Education* (1927), similarly stress the higher goals of the educational process and the special role played by the arts in achieving these. According to Hart, this is because the arts are the "creative expressions of the human spirit at various stages of this [life's] adventure."[38] Lindeman notes in particular that "games, dancing and the drama," which involve motion and active participation, "furnish the best opportunities for bringing forth values which are susceptible of vivid enjoyment."[39]

These writers were by no means alone in seeing a special role played by the arts in the new philosophy of education. By the early 1930s the benefits of arts education were being widely commented on. The *Proceedings of the Seventy-First Annual Meeting of the National Education Association of the United States*, held in Chicago in 1933, includes such articles as "Art Training in Preparation for Adult Leisure" and "Enrichment of Adult Life thru Art." Here educators argued that "at no time has the responsibility for providing for the enrichment for adult life been as great as now. How are we going to enrich the lives of those who are already educated but who cannot find avenues of expression in their vocations? . . . Creative art must be emphasized."[40] Another writer extolled the virtue of the arts for self-improvement, stating "I have recently read the statement that 'a man cannot grow to his height without self-knowledge.' Cultivating the tastes is a progressive revelation of one's own powers."[41]

While ideas such as these were being articulated in general circles, they were also finding a new formulation and strong advocate in Mordecai Kaplan.[42] Through the 1920s Kaplan continued to encourage Jewish community leaders to focus on the needs of the entire individual, with a special emphasis on serious educational pursuits.[43] He argued that, "institutions like the synagogue, the Communal Center, and the YMHA . . . should regard it as their main task not merely to edify or amuse him, but to stimulate his mental and moral growth and widen the horizon of his inner life."[44]

During the 1920s and 1930s, Kaplan founded Reconstructionism, which holds Judaism to be human-centered rather than God-centered. He and his followers believed that Judaism is an evolving civilization whose standards of conduct are established by the Jewish people and that, like any other civilization, it comprises a culture, a language, and a social organization as well as a religion. For Kaplan, education and the arts were central to building the vibrant and fully developed Jewish civilization he envisaged. In his celebrated work, *Judaism as a Civilization* (1934), he explained, "A civilization cannot endure on a high plane without the preservation and cultivation of its arts."[45] Kaplan proceeded to stress the importance of incorporating elements of drama, dance, and music in prayer as well as in other aspects of Jewish life. To

him, these were creative expressions of Jewishness that were just as important
as more traditional Jewish practices in helping to preserve Judaism.[46]

The work of Kaplan, like that of Dewey, Lindeman, Martin, Hart and others, provided to a large degree the philosophical justification for the leaders
of the 92nd Street Y to implement a newly expanded cultural program in the
early 1930s. Within this larger context, the arts were recognized by many of
the Y's leaders as an important aspect of adult education that required further exploration. The staff observed that the current membership displayed
"mediocre interests and capacities." Nonetheless, they aimed to "refine these
interests and make them serve as stepping-stones to higher interests."[47] As a
direct result of the opening of the new building in 1930, the Educational Department was expanded to include in-depth unit courses on current trends
in different fields (such as psychology and philosophy) as well as to establish
an art department and a drama department under its auspices.

• • •

EARLY DANCE AT THE Y

Dance began at the YMHA as a part of the new cultural policy. A Report of the
Department of Education, November 1930, announced that the Y had "just
inaugurated a new activity in the form of dancing of the sort that is done in
recitals." Classes began under the direction of the Jewish dancer Benjamin
Zemach, a performer and choreographer who had worked with the Habima
theater group in Moscow and traveled to America in the 1920s to find greater
artistic freedom and opportunity. Since arriving in New York, he had performed in the Yiddish theatre and become involved with productions at the
Neighborhood Playhouse, an active center of dance and drama overseen by
the Jewish sisters Irene and Alice Lewisohn.[48] At the Playhouse, Zemach performed with Martha Graham, Charles Weidman, Doris Humphrey, and Mi-
chio Ito and created several solo concert pieces. Zemach's performance style
was highly expressionistic, using exaggerated gestures and elaborate stage
makeup. He drew heavily from stories by Jewish writers and fictionalized life
situations, with a strong reference to Chassidic lifestyle.[49] One of his favorite
characters was a religious Jew who gradually becomes more enraptured as he
begins to pray, swaying ecstatically and lifting his arms heavenward. In New
York, Zemach's work drew high praise, and he was marked as an innovator to
be watched and encouraged.[50]

During the 1930–31 season (seasons at the Y normally running from October to May), Zemach offered classes for beginners, intermediate, and ad-

Benjamin Zemach, early 1930s.
92nd Street YM-YWHA Archives. Photographer: Maurice Goldberg.

vanced students as well as a performing concert group geared toward dance based on Jewish themes. By June 1931 he was striving to establish an official dance department and asking for $1,000 as a director's salary "to provide instruction in pantomime and aesthetic dancing for the members, to contribute to the holiday celebrations and other public occasions of the program, and to offer one or two complete programs of dance-concerts during the year."[51] Although members of the Y's Cultural Activities Committee appeared interested in his request, it was ultimately denied. After a lengthy discussion in April 1932 "it was the sense of the meeting that the expenditure involved did not warrant the creation of this department."[52]

Meanwhile, perhaps as a result of the lack of serious support and of better opportunities on the West Coast, Zemach pursued his career in Los Angeles the following year. Therefore, despite plans for him to teach at the Y, no dance classes were offered in 1931–32; Zemach taught and choreographed in California. In the fall of 1932, however, another teacher was hired by the Y, Matilda Naaman, who had an eclectic training in various dance techniques, including experience in staging dances for Maurice Schwartz, the director and leading actor of the Yiddish Art Theatre.[53] Her course descriptions demonstrate a strong influence of emerging modern dance practice, stating, for example, that "Miss Naaman's technique is built on an understanding of anatomy in relation to movements and the projection of movement in relation to the emotions. The work in these courses is modern in the sense that its movement derives from the life and rhythm of our times."[54] A photograph from a recital program reinforces the notion that Naaman was strongly influenced by early modern dance. Five women are grouped together in bold formations. Three are balanced on the balls of their feet while leaning backward, while the other two stand with legs spread open in a wide lunge, arching back. The dancers create clear, angular lines in space, and display qualities of strength and control. The severity of their expressions as they concentrate in these positions also reflects a close connection with the work of other early modern dancers.

The progressive philosophy of the Y continued to provide the broad setting in which dance first occurred at the Y, and in the fall of 1933 the Y's commitment to this outlook was again made clear through its hiring of the educator Samuel Richard Slavson to make a study of the possibilities of applying the principles of progressive education to the general field of Jewish Center work.[55] This study was regarded as an experiment, possibly leading to some aspects of progressive education being "further developed at Y.M.H.A.s and Jewish Centers."[56] A report on the Y's programs in December 1933 was quick to point out that "a large portion" of the activities recommended by Slavson "had always been a part of the 'Y' Program." What his proposal was doing, therefore, was simply suggesting the further development of certain activities at the Y, in the realm of arts and crafts and in creative dramatics and music.

MATILDA NAAMAN

presents her group in a

PROGRAM OF DANCES

Saturday Evening, February 10, 1934
at 8:45 o'clock

Theresa L. Kaufmann Auditorium
Lexington Avenue at 92nd Street

AT THE PIANO—GENEVIEVE PITOT

1. Two Studies—
   (a) .... *Without Music*
   (b) .... *Genevieve Pitot*
   (GROUP)

2. Figures at Night ....*Nathan Novick*
   (GROUP)

3. Insouciance.................*Bartok*
   (SYLVIA AVERBUCK)

4. Pastoral ....*Casella*
   (STELLA SANDERS)

5. Hebrew Patterns—
   (a) Consolation ....*Saminsky*
   (b) Exaltation.................*Engels*
   (GROUP)

6. In Modo Esotico.............*Casella*
   (GROUP)

7. Procession of Exiles ....*Kodaly*
   (GROUP)

8. Prairie Wind...... ....*Bartok*
   (SYLVIA AVERBUCK)

9. Mountain Songs —
   Carl Sandburg's American Songbag
   (GROUP)

10. Marcato ....*Genevieve Pitot*
    (GROUP)

There will be an intermission after the 5th number

Dancers: SYLVIA AVERBUCK, STELLA SANDERS and Gladys Rappoport,
Beatrice Schindler, Eva Saper, Gwendolyn Liss, Silvia Berman

Dances created and directed by Matilda Naaman

Matilda Naaman Recital Program, 1934.
92nd Street YM-YWHA Archives.

In both cases the advice was for the young people to create original art, songs, poems, and plays and to develop initiative, self-reliance, and the ability to help themselves instead of relying entirely on adults.

Matilda Naaman remained at the Y until 1935 and, similar to Zemach, ran the classes at little cost to the YMHA, using the students' fees to cover her teaching. Her work drew recognition from other Y personnel, as seen in a report of the Department of Education in January 1933, which remarks: "Our classes in dancing, under the direction of Mathilda Naaman, despite the absence of advertising and promotion work, have been increasing. A group of the best students is rehearsing for a recital to be given later this season. This group has really been developed by the sheer personal effort and fine teaching of Miss Naaman. It merits all the encouragement which the Association can offer." In May, it was observed that "the recital presented by part of this group on Sunday . . . was a genuinely artistic success and indicates the high potentialities of the Department. We recommend that it be continued."[57]

The praise of Naaman's work, as well as Zemach's, illustrates the 92nd Street Y's early support of contemporary dance. The Y provided space for the dancers to teach and offered them performance opportunities in terms of recitals and holiday celebrations. Naaman and Zemach were both able to find Jewish students who were eager to learn about dance and who attained a certain degree of technical proficiency. In a review of a performance of Naaman's students in 1934, the observation was made that "although one or two of the dancers were still a trifle 'green,' the group as a whole exhibited a commendable facility of movement and demonstrated the result of what is evidently very intensive and intelligent training on Miss Naaman's part."[58]

• • •

WILLIAM KOLODNEY:
INTELLECTUAL, ADMINISTRATOR, VISIONARY

During Naaman's tenure at the Y a change in leadership occurred that had far-reaching consequences for the entire arts programming. William Kolodney was hired in October 1934 as the educational and club director, replacing Herman Jacobs, who had recently become assistant director of the Bronx YMHA. Kolodney was recommended by Harry Glucksman, a long-standing member of the Y and outstanding figure in Jewish Center work who had known him for ten years, and was wholeheartedly approved by the executive director, Jack Nadel.[59] Kolodney was a medium-sized man with short-cropped hair and glasses, and clear blue eyes which literally sparkled when he

William Kolodney, ca. 1934.
Courtesy of Nathan Kolodney.

laughed. Slim and "aesthetic"-looking in his younger and midyears, he became slightly more rounded, with pure white hair in his late fifties and six-
ties. To most people he appeared modest, calm and dignified, with an unas-
suming, soft-spoken manner. His more immediate colleagues and family
members knew him as a man of great passion who was extremely dedicated
to his family, job, religion and improving the wider society. He was a perfec-
tionist for whom meaning lay as much in details as in conception and inspiration. Jacobs, who had known him for some fifteen years at the time of the
changeover, described him as "an outstanding worker in the field [of Jewish
center work] . . . a man of very high intelligence, rare sensitivity [and] . . . a

discriminating and highly analytical mind."[60] For Kolodney's son, Nathan, it was "people's sense of his passion and strength coupled with his gentleness and lack of vindictiveness that made it possible for some of his strongest opponents to yield and for some of his greatest supporters to be effective."[61]

Kolodney shared many of the progressive values and ideals of his colleagues at the Y, including a strong commitment to adult education and the arts and recognition of the importance of such a program within the context of a Jewish institution. At the same time, Kolodney went far beyond those who preceded him in terms of rationalizing and implementing these ideals. He alone was responsible for expanding the program, raising its quality, and opening the Y to a greater involvement with the non-Jewish community. Each of these factors made possible a major cultural program focusing on contemporary ideas and art and led to several generations of people traveling to the Y for classes and performances. In this way, Kolodney's efforts firmly established the larger frame within which the Dance Center eventually originated and developed.

In 1935, shortly after his arrival, Kolodney proposed that the Y offer a major new assortment of educational activities including a lecture series on art, current events, books, and famous individuals; seminar courses on contemporary philosophy and sociology; and lecture discussion courses on literature, psychology, music, and drama. In addition, Kolodney outlined plans for the Art and Drama Departments and the establishment of a performance series—the Major Subscription Series—of significant proportions. A Dance Center to consist of classes in various kinds of modern dance, with Graham, Humphrey, Weidman, and Holm, also was proposed. These were the first of many changes in the Y's offerings; for the next thirty-five years, Kolodney continued to develop and expand the educational program at the Y, until his retirement in 1969.

Kolodney's professional experience demonstrates his prior commitment to the arts and education within the Jewish center context. Before coming to the Y he had worked as the educational director and assistant to the executive director at the YMHA in Pittsburgh between 1925 and 1931. There he had also implemented an extensive educational and cultural program, consisting of classes, lectures, and performances. Before holding that position, Kolodney had been the director for the Extension Department of the Bureau of Jewish Education and executive director of the Y, in Elizabeth, New Jersey.

Kolodney's upbringing provides an important key to understanding his later commitment to adult education. Born in Minsk, Russia, on October 12, 1899, Kolodney moved to the United States with his family in 1903. In 1918 he received a diploma from the Teachers Institute of the Jewish Theological Seminary. From there he went to New York University, where he received his B.S. degree in pedagogy in 1922. From 1922 to 1925 he studied psychology and education at Columbia University. Although he left New York to assume the position in Pittsburgh, Kolodney continued to work on his thesis, "Philosophy of Adult Education."[62] In 1950, after many years of Jewish center work, he received his Ed.D. degree from Columbia's Teachers College.

Kolodney stated in an interview soon after arriving at the Y: "After all, Mr. [Herman] Jacobs and I are of the same school of thought and have had similar educational backgrounds."[63] Kolodney's training shows he was exposed to the progressive ideas in education generally and Jewish education in particular, of the early decades of the century. Kaplan, for instance, taught at the Jewish Theological Seminary from 1909 on, becoming dean of the institution in 1931, and Dewey taught at Columbia through the 1920s, offering many courses on educational psychology. At both institutions, Kolodney became familiar with their work and theories on adult education and the arts. Kaplan's ideas, particularly on the need to reconstruct spaces in America that reinterpreted the traditional role of the synagogue as a house of spirituality, study, and community, shaped the direction in which Kolodney wished to take Jewish expression. If Kolodney, like many other intellectual/spiritual Jews, "could not feel comfortable within the contemporary American synagogue or temple, he tried to recreate the ethos of the synagogue at the Y. It was there that he hoped to reconstruct what some Jews had sacrificed in a rejection of the enlightenment, and others had lost to the distortions of a misdirected modernity. It was his teacher, Mordecai Kaplan—the founder of Reconstructionism—who strengthened his belief that this could and must be done."[64]

What Kolodney culled from his early training, as well as his years of programming experience at the Pittsburgh Y, may be found in his yearly proposals for the 92nd Street Y. These were written at the beginning of each fall and outlined his intentions for the upcoming season. Intended to be read by the board of directors, these proposals often included a statement of the philosophy of the program and a description of the intended courses. Kolodney also wrote reports, periodically during the year, that examined the progress of his plans and sometimes included statistics regarding class and recital attendance.

. . .

EDUCATION AS (JEWISH) RECREATION

The writings from 1935 and 1936 outline Kolodney's early arguments for establishing a strong educational program in a Jewish recreation center. He asserts that first and foremost such a program should exist because there is a
long tradition in Jewish life of people being interested in study and the pursuit of knowledge for its own sake. He writes: "Contrary to popular impression . . . our movement started as an educational institution and not as a
gymnasium. This program was the outgrowth of the Jewish historical tradition of learning."[65] Kolodney continued to argue that there was a significant
number of Jewish youth in the community whose "chief means of recreation
was in the field of the fine-arts, and in education generally." At the moment,
however, these young Jews usually went to places "indifferent or inimical to
Jewish group life" to satisfy this particular need. The creation of a strong educational program at the Y was consequently required to draw these young
people into a positive Jewish setting and concurrently satisfy their need for
intellectual and creative stimulation.

The tone of Kolodney's early writing suggests that he felt the need to *de-
fend* an educational program at the 92nd Street Y, as if one did not already
exist there. This is because his vision, although grounded in the same progressive philosophical tradition as the Y, was far more expansive than what
had come before, consisting not of a few classes or teachers but a wide array
of courses, lectures, workshops, and performances. In Kolodney's eyes, despite its higher ideals, the existing leadership behaved as if the Y's main purpose was recreational in the most common sense of the term, namely, to provide pleasurable means of filling people's leisure time through play and
sport. To Kolodney this meant that the Y staff regarded the association's social and athletic programs as central and its educational and cultural programming as secondary. This perspective seemed to be reflected by the Y's
youthful male membership, which, despite the recommendations for greater
cultural activity in the early 1930s, appeared most involved in activities that
revolved around the gym.

Kolodney was the first person in the Y's history to so rigorously advocate
the rightful place of education within a recreational context. With his rationalizations, he attempted to establish a continuity with Jewish practices in the
distant past and constantly referred to the so-called ancient roots of Jewish
interest in learning while drawing attention to the many people who currently

enjoyed the arts in their leisure time. He wrote that "educational recreation is taken seriously by a good part of the population, and . . . there are some members who are almost as devoted to the pursuit of philosophy, literature, art and the drama as some are to athletic activities"; and elsewhere, "Our forefathers studied for the joy of it and not for university credits. We are trying to revive this ideal."[66]

In later years, Kolodney articulated his beliefs more thoroughly and with a more obvious grounding in progressive educational theory. In his 1950 dissertation for Columbia University's Teachers College, "History of the Educational Department of the YM-YWHA," he presented the origin and evolution of his program at the 92nd Street Y, with a discussion of the philosophy underlying his efforts.[67] In the dissertation, Kolodney asserts that current Jewish recreational interest in the arts and education is largely the result of a transference of attention away from religion: "A small but significant part of the second and third generation of Jews in this country that formed the nucleus of the Jewish intellectual leadership have transferred their interest from knowledge of a religious nature to knowledge of general interest, particularly in the abstract fields such as the liberal arts."[68]

Kolodney also more fully explores the general conditions of modern society that make adult education such a valuable activity within a recreational setting. He claims that industrialization has forced man to specialize in one form of activity and conform to a uniform mode of production and consumption. The result is that daily labor is exhausting and highly stressful, involving only a limited part of a human being. For Kolodney, a recreation program seeks to relax the individual, and "provide freedom from tension."[69] Relief is achieved, however, only by immersing the "whole personality" of the individual in an activity like the arts because "surface interests contribute to boredom and fatigue while true relaxation can come only from the most intense absorption in one or more activities such as art, music, drama, or poetry, since interest on this level involves the total personality over a long period of time."[70]

Kolodney's wording here clearly evokes the work of John Dewey—with the stress on the engagement of the "total personality" and the growth of the individual. It also draws on the theories of Eduard Lindeman and Joseph Hart in stressing the special role played by the arts in adult education; and like Everett Dean Martin, Kolodney felt deeply that the arts enrich the human spirit. Kolodney's final argument was that the arts provide nourishment to the inner life of the individual in a contemporary world devoid of myth and religion: "Even if there are no scientific or moral certitudes as there seem to have been in a previous age . . . the hunger for beauty and for truth is enduring. It is in this area that adult education can meet most effectively the needs of every individual to live in a world of his own making."[71]

In 1935 this fervent belief in the importance of adult education and the arts led Kolodney to propose an enlargement of the educational program at the 92nd Street Y and to seek a new standard for the work being done there. Kolodney firmly believed in excellence, in which the depth of the educational experience was more important than its length or breadth. He wrote that "a quality program is the only kind of program that will bring to us those Jewish young men and women who seek recreation, through education and the fine arts." He continued, "We find frequently that if educational activities are presented on the highest level, people in substantial numbers are willing to pay a moderate fee, and, on the other hand, when they are presented on a low or mediocre level, people will not accept them even though they are free."[72] In July 1936, Kolodney further insisted, "The general attitude towards the entire program is that it must sink or swim on the basis of authenticity of content, method, scholarship and learning. . . .There will be no retreat to superficiality and statistical illusions that characterize adult education in this country."[73]

· · ·

NONSECTARIAN PROGRAMMING AND MOVING
BEYOND THE JEWISH COMMUNITY

Kolodney's desire to expand the program and to raise its quality were two significant changes in the existing Educational Department. Taken together, they implicitly indicated a third alteration that was also to have a profound implication for the future direction of the program. This was the notion that the Y should increasingly reach beyond the Jewish community in developing its prestige. The idea of an educational program of general activities at the Y was nothing new, as the Y had already distinguished between activities with content of a specifically "Jewish" or a "general" nature. Once again, what was different was how Kolodney expanded the idea of a general educational program and how he rationalized his efforts. Examining the educational programming before Kolodney arrived, it appears that, although many of the courses did not necessarily contain Jewish subject matter, it was taken for granted that such classes were largely taught by Jews for Jews. This was certainly the case in dance, where Zemach and Naaman taught classes attended by Jewish students. Kolodney altered this practice by making the Educational Department nonsectarian to as great a degree as possible, allowing general courses to be taught by non-Jews and attended by non-Jews; and in so doing, he made for a more intimate and symbiotic relation between the Y and the broader community.

When Kolodney was initially asked what his intentions were with regard to the Y, he stated, "New York is the cultural center of the world, and the Jews are a very important part of the cultural tradition. It is fitting, therefore, that the Y, which is the largest Jewish Community Center in the country, be a vital force in the artistic, literary, and educational life of the city."[74] This remark indicates how Kolodney, more than Herman Jacobs or the rest of the Y leadership, was set on transforming the Y from a community-oriented institution into a major cultural force in New York. In the early years of the program he never directly stated his intention of pursuing the non-Jewish community. Instead, the implication was that in order to obtain a sufficient number of qualified teachers and performers it was necessary for the Y to open its doors to the non-Jewish world. This, in fact, was borne out by Kolodney's actions the very first year of the program, when prominent artists, non-Jewish as well as Jewish, were invited to the institution from all fields of study. Similarly, non-Jews were increasingly made to feel welcome as members and audience, as when Kolodney wrote in October 1935 to a Mr. Frederick Blossom, stating that "admission is on a nonsectarian basis."[75]

In later years, Kolodney justified the nonsectarian character of his program in two different ways. According to Carl Urbont, Kolodney believed that most existing Jewish art could not currently match the quality of work being produced by the wider society. Kolodney therefore felt that, in order to encourage the growth of Jewish artistic expression, sensitive Jews had to be immersed in art of excellent quality, regardless of its origins, and then urged to apply their talents to their own creations. Only then would Jewish culture flourish and help in maintaining Jewish civilization as a whole.[76] In his dissertation and elsewhere, Kolodney also made the argument that "human needs are nonsectarian" and that human beings cannot be departmentalized. "Young people come to any institution, including a sectarian institution," he maintained, "primarily as human beings with total human needs."[77] As far as Kolodney was concerned, cultural needs were part of these total human needs: the arts speak to the fundamental nature of the human being and express deeply felt concerns. As such, participation in the arts cuts across people's differences, "providing a language of communication that unites people of various religious and ethnic backgrounds."[78] To this extent, the arts are and should be accessible to everyone.

These statements show Kolodney's long-term interest in building a general educational program at the Y. At the same time, it should be understood that Kolodney continued to embrace more obviously sectarian efforts. If he believed that the Y should be "a home for all mankind," he also felt that the "philosophy of Jewish community center work as formulated by the Jewish Welfare Board is the development of Jewish group life on the highest possible plane."[79] This included the ongoing sponsorship of Jewish artists and a constant desire that the Y be a magnet for young Jews interested in the arts and ideas.

Around the time of the Second World War, overall concern for the so-called Jewish dimension of the program grew particularly acute as Jewish survival came into question in Europe. The Y's leadership became engaged in creating a closer connection between the educational and religious dimensions of the programming because of a belief in the need to reassert Jewish matters as central to all aspects of the institution. Kolodney fully participated in this trend, and he presented a paper in 1940 in which he stressed that the "Jewish Center believes in developing a distinctive Jewish culture in America." For Kolodney this meant, among other things, "giving financial and other support to those Jewish artists, writers, and other creative workers who can produce Jewish cultural material to serve as the basis of Jewish life in America."[80]

For Kolodney, however, as for the Y leaders and membership, it was never a matter of promoting *either* Jewish or general culture; it was the convergence of the two that was important to maintain and that seemed to closely embody the values of affluent and middle-class second- and third-generation New York Jews. Throughout his tenure at the Y, Kolodney continued to uphold the importance of a broad program. Indeed, this was true even during the Second World War, when he still supported the need for what he termed a neutral program alongside the support of specifically Jewish artists.[81] As Urbont observed, Kolodney was committed to both the universal and the Jewish as sources of human enrichment. It was precisely in this dual commitment that Kolodney felt most comfortable and where he managed to create a unique educational department.

• • •

JEWS AND CONTEMPORARY CULTURE

Kolodney expanded the existing program at the Y and increased the number of non-Jews involved in its activities. These changes were defended in various ways throughout his life, in both his early and later writings. Another important aspect of Kolodney's programming philosophy was never as fully articulated, namely, his choice of contemporary art and ideas as the substance of the new program. The word *contemporary* is meant to describe the ideas and art works circulated at the time that were perceived as new and exciting by the intellectual New York community. The term appears frequently in course descriptions at the Y, showing that Kolodney used it himself to describe what was going on. In terms of the arts, Kolodney displayed a particularly strong inclination toward such experimental and modern work as experimental theater, modern literature, modern poetry, and modern dance. At the same time, the notion of contemporary embraced innovations occurring in more traditional genres, such as classical music and ballet. The Budapest String Quartet, for instance, or Lincoln Kirstein's Ballet Caravan found support at the Y alongside the work of someone like Martha Graham. In this sense, the Y embraced many different kinds of new thoughts and practices along with the modern.

Kolodney's early interest in contemporary culture can best be seen by considering the large number of activities centering on contemporary themes during Kolodney's 1935–36 season as educational director. A course in contemporary philosophy, for instance, was offered by Sidney Hook, head of the Department of Philosophy at Washington Square College at New York University. The course was devoted to an analytical consideration of contemporary trends and currents in European and Anglo-American philosophy, including works of Bergson, Husserl, Russell, and John Dewey.

With regard to the arts, Kolodney also chose to concentrate on contemporary trends. "Ideas and Ideals in Modern Literature" was taught by Ralph Gilbert Toss, an instructor in philosophy at City College. This course consisted of a study of the "great historical tendencies in modern literature," starting with a historical glimpse at Christopher Marlowe and ending with Friedrich Nietzsche.[82] A series of lecture-demonstrations on the history of experimental theater also was offered, focusing on the Little Theatre movement from 1916 to 1929 and given by the directors of the Group Theatre (an experimental company, formed in New York in 1931, modeled on the Moscow Art Theatre, and influenced by the methods of Stanislavsky).

In April 1936, Kolodney moved to create a Jewish American theatre, which would be a contemporary community theater exploring a distinct Jewish identity and Jewish values. A policy established that "this theatre will concern itself with plays [in English] reflecting Jewish life as it is affected by its history, its problems of the present, and its aspirations for the future."[83] Dr. Henry Infeld, who had received his Ph.D. degree from the University of Vienna, was hired as artistic director. Infeld had escaped from Nazi Germany and wanted playwrights to use the theater at the Y as a testing ground for original Jewish plays with a social point of view. These were to be directed using the Stanislavsky method.[84]

Despite all this activity, Kolodney's broad support of contemporary culture is nowhere articulated or defended in a cohesive manner in his writings. Instead, it may be explained by considering Kolodney's desire, shared with many other Jews, to participate fully in contemporary American life. Like those who preceded him at the Y, Kolodney recognized the importance of having Jewish participation in the current debates and issues of the time. This seemed particularly true in the mid-1930s, a time when anti-Semitism was on the rise and instilling uneasiness among many Jews.[85] In the United States there was a proliferation of anti-Semitic feeling, and within this context, Kolodney wanted to use the arts as a way of changing people's misconceptions and stereotyping of Jews. This sentiment is well captured in a remark made in a letter to Kolodney recommending Dr. Infeld for the position of artistic director of the new Jewish American Theatre: "In times like these, with the Jew facing misunderstanding of every kind, with the movies presenting only misrepresentations of this people who must be understood if they are to be accepted completely in American life on their own terms, such a theatre, directed at non-Jews as well as Jews, would undoubtedly be a contribution to American life as well as the American Theatre."[86]

Moreover, progressive education theory seemed to specifically advocate concentration on contemporary issues. The New School for Social Research, a primary site of adult education in New York at the time, entered its second decade of existence with a clear statement of purpose that closely resonates with Kolodney's practice. The 1929–30 New School catalog states, "So far as concerns the content of adult education, the way is already clearly marked. The adult mind is essentially contemporary in its interests." This is because, according to the catalog, focusing on contemporary art allows adults to see the arts as a living entity related to modern life. Only through this realization can adults be inspired to look at the achievements of the past.

The New School preoccupation with contemporary art was also closely linked to the interests of New York Jewry, as documented in a history of the New School by Peter M. Rutkoff and William B. Scott. Their study indicates that the artists who taught at the school were young, considered themselves modernists, and were mostly Jewish. These artists "in one way or another, saw themselves as outsiders. To a person, those who were not Jews were either immigrants, refugees, or American provincials. . . . Many of those who did come from metropolitan areas were children of Jewish immigrants."[87]

The example of the New School reinforces the idea that many Jews in New York were actively interested in participating in and shaping contemporary society. At the 92nd Street Y, Kolodney assumed the responsibility of taking this impulse as far as he could within the boundaries of a Jewish community center. When he first met with the board of directors to outline his new program, what seemed most troubling to them was the scale of the proposed changes. As Kolodney had feared, certain members of the board thought he was trying to change the basic character of the Y. Kolodney, however, had the support of president Frank Weil and Nadel and, with their assistance, was able to convince the board to adopt his plans. The result was the newly revised educational program that went into effect in the fall of 1935.

Over the years, Kolodney developed his ideas more fully and added other important dimensions to the Y's program. In 1939, for instance, he inaugurated a poetry center, focusing on contemporary poetry, with readings by William Carlos Williams, Genevieve Taggard, Merrill Moore, W. H. Auden, and Langston Hughes, among others. Through his efforts the 92nd Street Y became a role model for countless other YMHAs and Jewish community centers and succeeded in becoming a substantial new focal point for the cultural life of New York in general. Kolodney's personal presence at the Y played a central role in the way the arts came to flourish there. He was tenacious in his fight to establish new programs, constantly battling with the Y's board of directors to support his work. Although he became extremely bitter at times, Kolodney was not without a sense of humor regarding his job. In November 1951 he spoke to the board and copied his recently completed dissertation for the members to read. As part of his statement he dryly observed, "One of the main purposes of the program is to help people eliminate or reduce tensions which beset them in this uncertain age. However successful it may have been in this regard, it has had the opposite effect on the Educational Director."[88]

From the perspective of dance, the Y's progressive orientation and Kolodney's more expansive implementation of its mandate were of the utmost importance. His belief in the uplifting qualities of art made it possible for people to conceive of serious dancing at the Y, and his idea of hiring non-Jews greatly influenced the Dance Center's choice of teachers. Interest in contemporary trends defined the content of the program and meant that it would encompass up-to-date experiments in various genres, with a particular emphasis on modern dance. These beliefs laid the foundation for Kolodney's early encounters with the dance community. In time they helped to define modern dance practice and broaden its interpretation.

Its Dance Center was formed with real intuition
just at the period in the development of the modern dance when
the things it most needed were stability and an intelligent respect for
what it was trying to do.
John Martin[1]

(2)

FOUNDING THE YM-YWHA
DANCE CENTER, 1934–36

• • •

The formative years of the Y's Dance Center illustrate an initial attempt on Kolodney's part to become primarily aligned with a particular sector of the emerging modern dance community as represented by John Martin, Martha Graham, Doris Humphrey, Charles Weidman, and Hanya Holm and the problems that ensued from this association. Widespread difficulties faced by modern dancers in the 1930s, including poor performance conditions and overall lack of respectability, left room for the Y to play a significant part in the validation of modern dance as an art form. Within this struggle for recognition, Kolodney's choice of advisers reveals his initial decision to affiliate with the powerful and less politically motivated forces of the dance world rather than with the insurgent left-wing dance movement of the time. A shared humanist discourse that placed aesthetics over politics solidified the relationship from an ideological standpoint, although Kolodney's empathy with Jewish and less experienced dancers, many of whom were involved in the more leftist "radical" groups, made for a fluid and complex set of relations with the dance world. Eventually, the Y's location outside the midtown theater district and its perceived status as a sectarian recreational institution eroded the association with Martin, and Kolodney's own broader interests led him to revise his strategy. The resulting diversification of influences led to a more heterogeneous program at the Y that was no longer as synchronous with the more mainstream elements of the dance world.

• • •

ORIGINS OF THE DANCE CENTER

In 1974, while hosting the 92nd Street YM-YWHA's gala evening of dance celebrating the one-hundredth anniversary of the institution, Walter Terry recalled the origins of the Y's Dance Center. He told how William Kolodney had read Isadora Duncan's autobiography, *My Life,* as a college student and had become fascinated with its passion-filled pages. In particular, Kolodney was captivated by Duncan's description of a moonlit trip to a beach in Italy, where she saw a fisherman and said to him, "Give me a child." This seemed pretty racy stuff to the youthful Kolodney, who decided that the art of dance deserved further investigation. "It's because Isadora Duncan took a fancy to an Italian fisherman that the YM-YWHA has a Dance Center," Terry concluded.[2]

While this colorful anecdote may contain an element of truth, it seems more likely that Kolodney's idea for a center originated in the fall of 1934, when he began his tenure as Educational Director of the Y. One of Kolodney's concerns, as he planned his newly expanded cultural program, was how best to use the Kaufmann Auditorium. During the early 1930s, its use had been restricted to "the purposes of the Young Men's Hebrew Association itself and occasionally by such communal, philanthropic and cultural groups as do not operate for profit, and whose purposes are auxiliary to the work of this institution."[3] An auditorium committee would meet several times yearly to assess applications to use the space by a range of mostly community-based Jewish organizations. Yet it was a very attractive, well-equpped theater, with 855 green leather seats (608 in the orchestra, 247 in the balcony) and an elegantly modeled, air-cooled interior free of pillars, with a well-raked floor for clear visibility from all seats and excellent acoustics; circling the room was a walnut frieze engraved with the names of famous men throughout the span of history, including David, Moses, Shakespeare, and Jefferson.[4] Although the stage was on the small side—twenty-two feet deep to the footlights, approximately forty feet wide and forty-four feet high—it was equipped with a modern switchboard and fly gallery to the height of the actual stage. Wing space was limited to one-and-a-half feet stage left and eight feet stage right. As there was room for solo and small group works, Kolodney's wife, Leah (Rothaus), an avid dance supporter, suggested that it be used for dance recitals, and Kolodney started to investigate the possibility of building a more extensive dance program at the Y.[5]

Unlike poetry and chamber music, dance was not one of Kolodney's areas of expertise but was an art form he greatly admired. Following his youthful infatuation with Duncan, he had attended a recital by Martha Graham in Cleveland, where he "felt the same devout, enveloping aura one feels in a church or synagogue."[6] While dance resonated closely with his own humanistic ideals regarding the uplifting role of the arts, his experience was clearly limited. Feeling that he must educate himself with regard to how the Y's dance program might fit into the existing cultural landscape, Kolodney began to seek the advice of prominent members of the general dance community.

The first person Kolodney approached was the celebrated ballet choreographer Michel Fokine, who had settled in New York in 1923 and continued to choreograph new pieces and revive old works both in America and abroad.[7] As Fokine apparently was not enthusiastic about the idea for a new center for dance and was unable to provide Kolodney with the kind of advice he needed in order to proceed with his plan, Kolodney next turned to the dance writer and theorist John Martin, who turned out to be much more accommodating.

• • •

JOHN MARTIN AND THE
FORMATION OF THE DANCE CENTER

Martin wielded immense power as the dance critic of the *New York Times*, for which he had been writing about dance since 1927. His widely read reviews were influential in shaping dancers' careers as well as the public's perception of dance. Kolodney was eager to gain the assistance of so authoritative a person and approached correspondence between them with great seriousness. Here would be a key opportunity to expand the Y's relations with the dance world and make a name for the Y in the broader New York artistic community. Martin's response was immediately positive. He wrote to Kolodney, "I should be very glad indeed to talk with you about your dance project for the Y.M.H.A," and in December the two men met to discuss the matter in more detail.[8] The results were encouraging, for Martin believed that the idea for a center was well worth pursuing and that modern dance, in particular, should form the core of its substance. Kolodney later recalled, "After considerable deliberation we decided that classical ballet did not need a home. It was most adequately represented in the concert halls and stages. However, modern dance was another story, it needed a home, and so we agreed to have classes and recitals at the Y."[9]

Martin's enthusiasm for Kolodney's project was closely connected to the state of modern dance in the mid-1930s. At this time the form was gaining in credibility yet was still in the process of becoming a viable form distinct from other styles of dancing. The lack of wide-scale recognition for modern dance was evident in the shortage of performance spaces open to modern dancers. The spaces that were available for recitals tended to be expensive Broadway theaters or ill-equipped union halls and high school auditoriums. In 1934 the most frequently used theaters included the Guild, Booth, Alvin, and Forrest Theatres; City College Auditorium, Washington Irving High School, Carnegie Hall, and Town Hall were other available halls.

While the Broadway theaters had good, well-equipped stages, they were usually available only on Sundays, the one night when regular Broadway shows were not permitted owing to the so-called Blue Laws, which forbade performance of plays that night of the week.[10] The other possible stages were platforms or barely missed being such. They were shallow and wide, with doors, rather than wings, leading to the stage space. Mostly there were very few lighting possibilities and little room for sets. Town Hall and Carnegie Hall, in particular, were good for singers and musicians but poor for dance, lacking wing space and with little rake in the auditorium. In the educational institutions the stages were sometimes slightly larger, but there was only basic seating for the audience; and in the Washington Irving High School, posts spoiled the sightlines.[11] Moreover, in the mid-1930s the only institution producing a series for young dancers was the New School for Social Research, where, in the spring of 1935, Sophia Delza had begun a subscription series of fortnightly recitals titled Modern Recitals.[12] However, the stage was small and circular and considered one of the worst for dance in the city.

Such limited conditions left room for the establishment of a new home for modern dance that could provide an adequate stage and audience. The 92nd Street Y under Kolodney's advisement was prepared to do just that, as was understood well by Martin, who from the beginning of his tenure at the *Times* was closely involved in watching the efforts of modern dancers and supporting their growth. Martin's role in the modern dance world, however, was far from neutral. Rather, he brought to the Y a particular set of interests that had long been evident in his writing and teaching. This meant that the origins of the Y's Dance Center grew out of Kolodney's association with a particular sector of the modern dance community as represented by Martin and his supporters.

This was evident from the very beginning of the dialogue between Kolodney and Martin. Having agreed on modern dance as the preferred style, the two men discussed who should take part in planning the project. Kolodney, trusting to Martin's superior judgment in this area, allowed him to take the initiative in making this important decision; Martin suggested Graham, Humphrey, and Weidman. In January 1935, Martin contacted each of them, discussing the feasibility of starting a center at the Y. On the basis of these initial exchanges he reported to Kolodney that he thought something could be worked out.

Martin's choice of participants closely reflected the critic's preference for these dancers over others working in the modern idiom. In his 1936 book, *America Dancing*, Martin wrote that Graham and Humphrey "together with Charles Weidman . . . constitute the principal shaping forces of the contemporary dance."[13] To Martin, these choreographers exemplified the highest artistic achievement and were creating work that was innovative in concept and design. They were, in his consideration, formulating the basis of a dance form distinct from earlier experiments made by Isadora Duncan and Ruth St. Denis and also from the work of Mary Wigman and her disciples in Germany. Martin's desire to involve these choreographers in the Y's plans also followed naturally from his ongoing affiliation with them in other enterprises. Since 1931 he had engaged them in his lecture-demonstrations at the New School, and in the summer of 1934 all of them had worked together to establish the Bennington School of Dance at Bennington College.

Martin's association with this particular group of dancers was connected to his concern about the fate of modern dance. Martin wanted to ensure that the ideas and practices of what he considered the best of modern dance practice would be preserved and passed down to future generations. While he respected the work of Helen Tamiris, Esther Junger, and Sophia Delza, they were not among his favorites, any more than the revolutionary, left-wing dancers who were closely associated with trade unions and Communist organizations. These performers enjoyed a large following but by June 1935 were largely disdained by Martin, who found them overly political and largely untalented. He wrote an open letter to the New Dance League, formerly the Workers Dance League, accusing it of "soapbox electioneering in the middle of a performance and compared the whole thing to a medicine show."[14]

Working alongside Graham and Humphrey at the New School and Bennington, Martin realized that he could oversee the activities of several institutions, which could play an important role in legitimizing modern dance and giving it a popular following. Martin's lectures at the New School were largely concerned with educating the general public about modern dance and building an audience. Focusing on "Contemporary Dance: Its Mechanics and Its Art," as the fall 1932 course was aptly called, Martin continued to give lecture-demonstrations there until 1940. Between 1931 and 1937, Humphrey also offered technique lessons at the school. The Bennington summer program addressed a different but equally important population, primarily young women studying and teaching in higher education. Physical education teachers, in particular, flocked to Bennington's classes in technique and appreciation, finding the experience a thrilling indoctrination into a new and vital dance form. Greatly stimulated, they returned to their host institutions, where they taught other groups of enthusiasts. Modern dance was gradually conquering the university establishment, and, significantly, it was doing so in its nonradical form. Ellen Graff has observed that, "the dancers who established themselves more prominently and securely within the new system of educational academic patronage were those who had been least concerned with political activism during the 1930s."[15]

All this activity provided the backdrop for the initial exchanges between Kolodney and Martin. It especially demonstrates that, far from being an unusual situation in which Martin and his favored dancers were to find themselves, they were well prepared to consider Kolodney's proposal of establishing a dance center at the Y. The institution offered yet another opportunity for the group to exercise its influence over the way that modern dance was being disseminated to the broader community. Kolodney, for his part, appeared willing to give preferential treatment to Martin and his associates while remaining open to other factions of the dance world (as demonstrated by his later presenting more left-wing dancers of the time). He was delighted to have the attention of the influential critic and greatly respected his opinions. Moreover, Kolodney was aware that Graham and Humphrey treated their vocation with great seriousness and that they had many devoted followers. As a man who understood what it was to fight for one's vision, he empathized with the people for whom modern dance was a serious cause, for the cultural program at the Y was a cause for him as well. He therefore agreed with Martin that they would be perfect for the Y, and he immediately wrote directly to each, "Mr. John Martin of the New York Times told me that you would be kind enough to advise me in my plans for an organization of a dance center at the Y.M.H.A."[16]

In March 1935 there was an exchange of letters between Kolodney and Martin as they sought a possible meeting time for everyone concerned. Kolodney expressed his eagerness to get things underway, stating that he had spoken about the project to the president of the board of directors and to the executive director and that both were very enthusiastic about it and promised full cooperation. He added that he was planning a series of Sunday evening recitals and "shall have to lean heavily upon your advice about the choice of dancers."[17]

In April, Martin met with the choreographers, along with Graham's musical adviser, the composer Louis Horst, to discuss the kinds of classes that might be offered at the Y. He later reported to Kolodney, who was not present at the meeting, that they had discussed the program's content and structure and would meet again. Martin also indicated that he did not think the dancers would be willing to give recitals exclusively at the Y, saying the stage was too small to accommodate their larger group compositions, and their performances would not be reviewed "since it is out of the district where concerts are covered."[18] In response to Kolodney's request for names of dancers for a performance series, Martin continued, "If you will let me know how many dancers you plan to use in your subscription series and whether you want them to be 'big timers' exclusively, also whether those who do more or less 'radical' dances would be acceptable, I can give you more help on that matter." (Martin seems to have quickly rethought this commitment; on June 13 he writes, "It is against the rules for me to suggest any [dancers]!")

The group decided that, along with their own techniques, elementary modern dance should be taught. For this they recommended the director of the Mary Wigman School, Hanya Holm, reassuring Kolodney that despite her being German-born she was "an excellent teacher and a thoroughly fine person." Martin, clearly sensitive to the growing anti-German sentiment at the time, observed that many of Holm's students were Jewish and concluded by stating, "I can understand that the Y might possibly have some reservations, but we all feel that Miss Holm is extremely valuable and would like very much to have her associated with us here as she is at Bennington College and the New School."[19]

Readily accepting the suggestion about Holm, Kolodney pressed forward with preparations to test the support for a dance center at the Y. He organized

```
              FREE SYMPOSIUM
                    on
    T H E   M O D E R N   D A N C E
                    by
MARTHA GRAHAM, LOUIS HORST, DORIS HUMPHREY
     CHARLES WEIDMAN and HANJA HOLM
John Martin, Dance Critic of New York Times, Chairman

      ILLUSTRATIONS BY THEIR DANCE GROUPS

   Saturday, May 25th, at 8:45 o'clock in the
       THERESA L. KAUFMANN AUDITORIUM
                  of the
        YOUNG MEN'S HEBREW ASSOCIATION
         92nd Street & Lexington Avenue
 Free tickets may be obtained at the Y.M.H.A. or
 by sending a self-addressed and stamped envelope.
```

Announcement for Free Symposium on The Modern Dance, 1935.
92nd Street YM-YWHA Archives.

a free lecture-demonstration for May 25, 1935, at 8:45 P.M., featuring Graham, Humphrey, Weidman, and Holm. In the *YMHA Bulletin*, the event was advertised with great fanfare as the first of its kind: "It was John Martin, dance critic of the New York Times, who said in conversation with leaders at the Y that this festival will mark the first occasion on which these . . . prominent groups will have been together on one stage. It is one of the signal honors in the history of the Y."[20]

The evening was a resounding success, with a packed auditorium. Martin acted as the master of ceremonies, presenting the four choreographers in a discussion and demonstration of their various techniques. The choreographers explained their philosophies of movement and presented their students in short technical and choreographic studies. In his thank-you letter to his advisers, Kolodney enthusiastically wrote:

Dear Miss Graham [Humphrey, Weidman, Holm]

Mr. Frank Weil, the President of the Y.M.H.A., and Mr. [Jack] Nadel, our Executive Director, have asked me to tell you how very much they appreciated your participating in what proved to be one of the most successful, inspiring affairs in the entire history of this Center.

From the point of view of inaugurating a Fine Arts Center in the "Y," you helped us accomplish more in one evening than we could have done over a long period.[21]

At the conclusion of the letter Kolodney went on to observe, "I feel certain now that our dream of establishing a national dance center in the 'Y' can be realized, if you participate in it."

Graham, Humphrey, Weidman, and Holm had shown their willingness to come together on the Y stage; now it was time to draw up a blueprint for classes and a performance series. Here, Martin once again played a central advisory role. Following the symposium he wrote to Kolodney, "I am delighted that the symposium was so successful, and I hope that it may lead to something really fine at the Y."[22] Around the same time, Martin submitted to Kolodney a three-year course of study in modern dance instruction.[23] The plan included a class in fundamental body technique and composition classes by Louis Horst, followed by more challenging technique classes by Graham, Humphrey, Weidman, and their assistants. The suggested progression was from a solid background in the basics of modern dance to rigorous immersion in the individual techniques of the masters. Filling out the curriculum were notation, ballet technique, percussion playing, and costuming, as well as lectures on dance history and aesthetics to be given by Martin.

The final conception was a dance program of significant dimensions; like a college dance major it would be a course of study demanding a commitment of three hours a day, five days a week on the part of the students and requiring a considerable teaching load of its choreographers. Martin projected approximately eleven hours a week for Holm and at least four hours a week for the others. Such a calculation would make the Y a central point of their attention, suggesting that it might eventually share time with the choreographers' private studios, where they did most of their teaching.

The choice of choreographers and structure of the training pointed to Martin's ongoing interest in designing a program of study that avoided the creation of "rival academies" in the modern dance world. His Y plan followed the Bennington model, where Martin supported the attempt to "gather the best styles together and offer the whole spectrum to students at once."[24] The idea was to create a well-rounded curriculum in which students would be exposed to the unique gifts of well-known choreographers while learning the fundamentals of modern technique and choreography in more generalized courses.

The concept of fundamental body technique seems to refer to classes started at Bennington by Martha Hill and Bessie Schönberg. These courses were intended to break down and codify systematically the basic principles of modern dance practice. Marcia B. Siegel has pointed to the way this process

<u>PROPOSED PROGRAM FOR DANCE CENTER</u>

<u>Submitted by</u>

<u>John Martin</u>

Three year course, thirty weeks a year, five days a week, three hours daily.

<u>FIRST YEAR</u>

   Fundamental Body Technique - Hanya Holm - 10 hours per week

   Dalcroze Eurhythmics - Elsa Findlay   - 1 hour per week

   Notation   - 1 hour per week

   History and Esthetics - John Martin   - 1 hour per week

            Monthly attendance at group rehearsals
            conducted by Martha Graham, Doris Humphrey
            and Charles Weidman.

<u>SECOND YEAR</u>

   Dance Technique - Martha Graham and Assistants - 4 hours per week

               Doris Humphrey   "   4 hours per week

               Charles Weidman   "   4 hours per week

   Pre-Classic Forms - Louis Horst   2 hours per week

   Notation   1 hour per week

   Percussion Playing - Hanya Holm   1 hour per week

<u>THIRD YEAR</u>

   Dance Technique - Martha Graham, Doris Humphrey
               <u>or</u> Charles Weidman   10 hours per week

   Composition - Louis Horst   2 hours per week

   Notation   1 hour per week

   Ballet Technique   1 hour per week

   Costuming - Pauline Lawrence   1 hour per week

     Children's classes and lay classes - Hanya Holm - once or
                          twice a week each.

John Martin's Proposed Program for the Dance Center, ca. 1934.
92nd Street YM-YWHA Archives.

was used to maintain order and standards as modern dance was passed to teachers of the next generation. The dance educators who attended Bennington were "avid to learn the latest methods and techniques" and "perhaps for the first time, the need was perceived to teach modern dance technique on a large scale, without the originators of each technique being present."[25] This need was satisfied by basic courses in techniques of dance movement. Martin was very supportive of this attempt to pin down basic principles, deploring what he considered the anarchic state of modern dance, not to mention the idiosyncrasies of even the best modern dancers. He saw these generalized courses as a means to perfect the most effective elements of modern dance and eliminate its mannerisms. This perspective is evident behind the Y plan, in which Martin allots ten hours a week to training in fundamental body technique, taught by Holm.

The choice of Holm as the teacher of this basic class may have arisen out of Martin's association with her at the New School, where she had started teaching a course called "An Approach to the Dance of Mary Wigman" in the spring of 1933. This was "a course in the fundamental principles of movement underlying the dance of Mary Wigman, adapted to the needs of dancers and laymen."[26] Holm continued to offer this course the following year and was teaching it during the fall of 1934, when Martin was first approached by Kolodney. At the same time, placing Holm at the base of the pyramid, with higher levels taught by Graham, Humphrey, and Weidman, suggests that Holm was in some ways regarded as less significant than the others. This corroborates Claudia Gitelman's observation that Holm was mostly regarded as a teacher, not as a choreographer, until 1936. It was only then, with a series of premiere performances by her newly established group at Bennington College on August 7 and 8, that Holm established her independence from Mary Wigman and provided what Martin referred to as "the formal debut of Miss Holm in this country."[27]

Martin's limited regard for Holm in 1934 was also perhaps connected to his gradually changing views of German modern dance. In the early 1930s, Martin had championed Wigman's art, holding her up as a model of modern dance practice. Susan Manning shows, however, that by 1936 and the publication of *America Dancing*, Martin was changing his position to frame modern dance as an American practice. Manning traces this transformation to the Bennington experience, which "showed the possibilities of a national experience shared by dancer and spectator."[28] In the new historiography, Wigman was pushed to the periphery of Martin's awareness, and Holm, although increasingly recognized by Martin as adapting her methods to the American context, was considered slightly less significant than the home-grown artists.

Despite his great interest in Martin's proposal, Kolodney was unable to implement it. No doubt he recognized that, aside from his desire to establish a program of the highest quality, the Y was a recreational facility. Most students would not be able to commit themselves to such an intense schedule, and the choreographers in whom he was interested would be unwilling to devote so much of their time, at least initially, to such a setup. Moreover, Kolodney had many other programming plans for the Y's Educational Department, including a lecture series on art, current events, books, and famous individuals; seminar courses on contemporary philosophy and sociology; and lecture-discussion courses on literature, psychology, music, and drama. These events revolved around distinct fall and spring seasons, which started anew at the beginning of each few months' cycle. He likely needed to preserve this structure and avoid giving the board of directors, to whom he was accountable, a reason to think he was trying to create a long-term degree program in any one area.

However, Kolodney did his best to adapt Martin's basic approach by putting together a course of study involving each of the symposium presenters and a performance series that highlighted their companies. In his Proposed Program for the Educational Department 1935–36, he stated that the "Dance Center was to consist of classes in the Technique, History and Appreciation of the Modern Dance, taught by Martha Graham, Doris Humphrey, Charles Weidman, Louis Horst and John Martin." By early June 1935, Kolodney had hired Graham, Humphrey, Weidman, and Holm to teach individual classes in modern techniques in the fall and was negotiating with Martin for a lecture course, "Theory and Practice in the Modern Dance," although he canceled it in early October because it too closely resembled the New School class already taught by Martin.

In the first year of its existence the Dance Center followed Martin's overall concept of assembling the more significant movements in modern dance on a nonprofit basis. Nine evening classes were offered for adults, one hour each, between the hours of 5:00 and 8:00 P.M., Monday to Thursday. The more advanced classes were taught by Humphrey, Weidman, Graham, and Holm. A letter to Graham from Kolodney, dated June 17, 1935, confirms the fee of $20 per session to Graham (including the fee to the accompanist) if there were at least ten students in the class. Student tuition for ten lessons is listed as $20 for nonmembers and $18 for members.

The schedule shows that Kolodney preserved Martin's idea of bringing together the different schools of dance. Where it differed was in the choice of teachers for the beginners' classes, as Holm was now elevated alongside Humphrey and Graham as a teacher on the higher level. In her place, "classes for Beginners" were taught by young dancers familiar with each of the major styles, including Anna Sokolow and Bonnie Bird for Graham technique, Helen Bach and Joan Levy [Bernstein] for Humphrey-Weidman, and Nancy McKnight [Hauser], a student of Holm. Following Martin's original plan, Dalcroze eurythmics was also offered, by Elsa Findlay. There was no apparent attempt to teach a general, or "fundamentals," class, although the teachers of these classes attempted to break down their exercises so that newcomers could grasp the basics of each style.[29]

The choice of a young Jewish dancer, Anna Sokolow, as the main teacher of basic classes (she taught three of the five in the fall of 1935) suggests that Kolodney was motivated by Jewish community interests as well as Martin's priorities. By supporting Sokolow, he displayed an early interest in assisting Jewish artists, which he was to continue throughout his career. At this time, Sokolow was considered a talented young dancer and choreographer. A member of Graham's company, she had formed her own Dance Unit in 1933, which included primarily Jewish dancers like Marie Marchowsky, Ruth Freedman, Ronya Chernin, and Florence Schneider.

Initially, the dancers were pleased with the new teaching opportunity because it provided them with much-needed income. In her biography of Doris Humphrey, Selma Jeanne Cohen observes, "Losses on the [recent] tour had been considerable," so Doris was pleased when Kolodney "approached her with his plan for creating a Dance Center at the institution. . . . Here was a most welcome offer of a small but steady salary."[30] The income was also cherished by the younger dancers, just starting out on their careers. Larry Warren remarks in his book on Sokolow, "For the many artists who were leading a hand-to-mouth existence, the Y was something of a gift from heaven . . . for Anna because she earned a substantial part of her living by teaching beginning Graham technique classes there."[31]

During this year, Kolodney also designed a series of "30 Outstanding Evenings" of film and live performance (which included a "Major Subscription Series" consisting of a selection of fifteen presentations of dance and drama). The series featured an eclectic sampling of Jewish and non-Jewish performers and events with a particular focus on contemporary culture. *All Quiet on the Western Front* and *Trouble in Paradise* were popular films in general intellectual circles; Celia Adler and Molly Picon were celebrities of the Yiddish theater. In dance, Kolodney presented five recitals that strongly reflected his commitment to both Jewish and non-Jewish artists. Graham performed in a solo recital, and the Humphrey-Weidman group appeared, along with recitals by Jewish choreographers Benjamin Zemach, Helen Tamiris, and Anna Sokolow.[32] Kolodney explained to the board his belief that "this Subscription Series may prove to be the most important addition to the present program of Y activities, and through the very wide contacts the Y will make, may help to establish the Y as an important Fine Arts Center to which thousands of people will gravitate for artistic inspiration just as thousands of people are attracted to the Y now for physical recreation."[33]

The pieces presented on the programs by Tamiris and Sokolow demonstrate an early presence of leftist concerns at the Y, revealing that despite the close association with Martin and his followers, Kolodney was still willing to present more left-wing dance. Tamiris opened her recital on March 8 with *Protest (Cycle of Unrest)* and ended with her now famous dances depicting the struggles of African Americans, *Four Negro Spirituals*. Sokolow's Dance Unit included on its program *Strange American Funeral*, which was "based on Michael Gold's poem of a worker who was caught in a flood of molten ore — whose flesh and blood turned to steel." *Inquisition*, an antivigilante piece, and *Suite of Soviet Songs* were additional works with a political orientation.

Although busy with their numerous other teaching and performing commitments, Graham, Humphrey, and Weidman were pleased with the financial arrangements of the new series — being paid a fee for their services, negotiated individually with each company, which contrasted sharply with the more common practice of having to pay out of one's own pocket to perform. An article from the *Dance Observer* put the cost of self-producing a New York dance recital in 1934 at approximately $860, which included securing a manager, theater rental, advertising, printing, addressing, stagehands, and an accompanist.[34] At the Y, however, Kolodney paid the choreographers a negotiated fee, offered inexpensive rehearsal space, and took care of the bulk of the publicity. Known fees for the 1935–36 season were Tamiris, $100, plus 50 percent of single admissions; Zemach, $300; Humphrey-Weidman, $350.

At the same time that Kolodney was doing his best to accommodate his dancers, he was also striving to please his audiences. In presenting his first subscription series to the board, Kolodney had emphasized that this aspect of his new cultural agenda would be varied enough, of sufficiently high standard and inexpensive enough to attract a large number of Jews who were not accustomed to attending Jewish institutions for enjoyment of the arts. The series was likely subsidized with money from the Educational Department fund, allotted to Kolodney at the beginning of each year by the Federation for the Support of Jewish Philanthropic Societies and the Y's board of directors.[35] To ensure complete equality of access, there would be no scaling of the auditorium, that is, charging higher prices for the better seats. Subscriptions were $5.50 to members and $7.50 to nonmembers for the entire season of "30 Nights" of cultural entertainment. For Martha Graham's performance on January 6, 1936, single admissions were 50 cents for members before ninety minutes to curtain and 75 cents after that, with nonmembers admission $1 at any time.

As Kolodney had prophesied, the Major Subscription Series and the revised educational classes were tremendously successful in drawing new patrons to the Y. In January 1936, Kolodney reported that his innovative programming as a whole had "attracted over five hundred members and several thousand nonmembers who come specifically for educational activities."[36] Some of these were non-Jews, who had previously stayed away from the Y, thinking they were unwelcome. With Kolodney's policy of appealing to a wider, nonsectarian audience, non-Jews were increasingly drawn to the quality programming. However, the majority of those attending were Jews inspired by the arts and humanities, as Kolodney had predicted. Jack Nadel later observed that he had never seen as many board members at activities at the Y "until Kolodney." They were seeing "the best that there is, if not better than some places and it was home to them."[37]

Dance performances and classes were particularly successful in attracting the attention of Jewish New Yorkers. Registration records for the first year show a total enrollment of approximately 150 students, predominantly Jewish, traveling from Manhattan, Queens, the Bronx, and Brooklyn to take dance classes. Audience attendance at the Y dance performances in the first year also was large, varying from five hundred to full capacity per performance—the highest being for Martha Graham's concert. This audience, "with a generous sprinkling of hardy perennials, was essentially a new dance audience."[38] The low admission fees attracted the poorer members of the Jewish community, and many wealthier Jews, like the members of the Y's board, came to see what was happening in contemporary dance.

While the Y's new dance program was finding enthusiastic supporters in the Jewish sphere, its standing in the broader dance community was less clear. There were some indications that it was making its mark, and others that it remained relatively ineffectual. Only *Dance Observer*, a publication focusing on modern dance activity, begun by Louis Horst in 1934, offered its outright support. In October 1935 an announcement in *Dance Observer* for the new Y program stated that it should be "encouraged, supported and publicized for the instrument it should prove, with direction, for the good of the dance in its urgent development."[39] By the spring of 1936, a review by Marjorie Church of the Humphrey-Weidman recital held on April 26 referred to the "now celebrated Lexington Avenue . . . Y.M.H.A.," stating, "The Y.M.H.A. has established itself as a center where the best in dance, music, and drama, among other things of a cultural nature are seen at moderate prices, and at frequent intervals. The building fairly buzzes with activity most of the time."[40]

Another important indicator of the Y's growing status was its role as host of the First National Dance Congress and Festival, May 18 to 25, 1936. This event came at the culmination of the Y's first season and showed how far the Y had come in establishing itself as an important dance center. The National Dance Congress was the first meeting of its kind and, according to the press release, was "expected to mark the initiation of a movement to unite and coordinate the activities of all dancers in the country." The congress consisted of panels, lectures, and performances by a wide variety of dancers, including those with more left-wing leanings, which represented the diverse dance activity of the period. Along with modern dancers, there were ballet, folk, and Broadway-style revue dancers, all meeting together for the first time to discuss the state of dance in America.

The use of the Y's facilities for the congress was arranged between Kolodney and members of the Joint Committee of the first National Dance Congress, an eclectic group of twenty people from different parts of the dance world that included Sophia Delza, Doris Humphrey, Edna Ocko, Senia Gluck Sandor, Mura Dehn, and Benjamin Zemach. A contract was drawn up that allowed the congress free use of designated facilities over a period of eight days. All the lectures, panels, and performances were held in the Kaufmann Auditorium, and two additional rooms were devoted to a "pictorial exhibit of dance subjects" under the direction of Lily Mehlman.[41] Performances began with a ballet program on Monday, May 18, featuring the work of Nora Koreff (later known as an internationally celebrated ballerina under the stage name Nora Kaye), Lisa Parnova, Vladimir Valentinoff, Arthur Mahoney, and Thalia Mara, followed by a folk dance program (featuring American, Polish, English, Ukrainian, Bahamian, and Swedish groups). Two modern dance programs presented a range of dancers: on May 20, José Limón and Letitia Ide,

Jane Dudley, Sophia Delza, Hanya Holm, Lillian Shapero, Benjamin Zemach, and Anna Sokolow's Dance Unit; on May 23, Fe Alf, Anna Sokolow, Miriam Blecher, Gluck Sandor, Felicia Sorel, Helen Tamiris, Sophie Maslow, and Charles Weidman. In addition, there was a demonstration program (with Graham, Paul Boepple, Humphrey, the Rebel Arts Dance Group, Franziska Boas, Polly Korchien, Anita Zahn, and their groups), and a Variety and Theatre program, with pieces by Roger Pryor Dodge, Edna Guy, Mura Dehn, Belle Didjah, John Bovingdon, Anita Avila, and Jack Nile. Friday night, during the Sabbath, was the only evening when the theater was quiet.

As a whole, the congress marked an important moment in American dance history. Writing of the event in the left-wing publication *New Theatre*, the dance critic Edna Ocko reflected that it "was one of the most notable achievements in the field, and one of which the dance world can be duly proud . . . For the first time in the United States there was not only dancing for audiences, but sessions for dancers; there were not only discussions on esthetic credos, but on economic and organizational problems as well. For the first time the profession was viewed in its entirety, rather than in segregated, self-centered groupings."[42]

The Y's support in the National Dance Congress brought a considerable degree of visibility to the institution. It introduced many new dancers to its stage and to Kolodney's hospitality, and in later years many were to return to teach and perform at the institution. But the National Dance Congress was only one event in a year that was filled city-wide with dance performances, classes, and lecture-demonstrations, activities that in certain ways overshadowed what was occurring at the Y. Despite the expense and poor conditions, many dancers continued to perform at established downtown spaces. During the 1935–36 season in New York, individual performances were held at the Guild, Venice, Adelphi, and Majestic Theatres, Town Hall, and Carnegie Hall's Studio 61, among others. At the Guild alone there were at least eight dance performances: Humphrey performed there in October; Esther Junger, Graham, and Berta Ochsner in November; Yvonne Georgi in December; Tina Flade and Harald Kreutzberg in the spring. The previous season at the Guild had included Graham, Humphrey-Weidman, Agnes de Mille, and the Duncan dancer Anita Zahn.

Along with these performances, the long-established Students Dance Recitals series was held on Saturday evenings at Washington Irving High School, located at 40 Irving Place, a few blocks north of Fourteenth Street. The series had been started by Joseph Mann in 1925 to introduce new audiences to the best of a variety of dance styles. As modern dance grew in popularity, Mann altered his aim "to bring the best modern dancing to students and workers, teachers and artists, at minimum prices."[43] Starting in the early 1930s, Mann presented between six and twelve dance performances a year. During the 1935–36 season, eight recitals were offered: Charles Weidman, Ted Shawn, Miriam Winslow, Helen Tamiris, Carola Goya, Martha Graham, Jacques Cartier, and Agnes de Mille.

These dance events demonstrated that, from a broader perspective, there was a considerable amount of activity to compete with what was going on at the Y, even though what the institution had to offer seemed to be much needed. Advertisements for Kolodney's Major Subscription Series were prominently displayed in *Dance Observer,* but they were beside announcements for performances at the Guild and Washington Irving High School.

More significantly, the Dance Center and performance series received scant newspaper coverage. Even though the Y had a beautiful theater, it was outside the theater district, which was centered in midtown, around Broadway, so its performances were rarely reviewed. Even Martin, who had helped to inaugurate the dance program, kept to an established rule regarding his column at the *Times* not to stray outside the theater area. On June 29, 1935, after Kolodney asked if Martin could announce the opening of the Dance Center, Martin refused, saying that school matters were religiously excluded from his column; and during the year, despite Kolodney's requests for more extensive coverage, Martin announced upcoming recitals but wrote no reviews.[44]

Martin's refusal to review performances at the Y suggests that what was occurring there was not unusual enough to warrant his bending the "rules." This is borne out by looking more closely at the first Major Subscription Series in relation to the other performances around New York. Graham and Humphrey, for example, who were featured on the series, performed similar programs in the theater district before appearing at the Y, choosing the midtown theaters as the place to premiere new work. Graham gave her major concerts of the season at the Guild Theatre on November 10 and 17, 1935, and February 23, 1936. Martin covered these performances, offering a rave review of *Frontier* in his November 11 column, and a highly critical response to the use of mobiles created by Alexander Calder in the premiere of a new cycle, *Horizons,* on February 24. Humphrey, for her part, presented *New Dance* and the premiere of *Theatre Piece* at the Guild on January 19, 1936, and then performed both again at the Adelphi Theatre on April 5, 1936. Consequently,

Martin likely saw no pressing need to review the Y recitals of Graham on January 5 or the Humphrey-Weidman Group on April 26, respectively, since they included no new work.

The situation reflected the subsidiary role the Y assumed in the lives of the major dance figures who had helped to establish the Dance Center. Although Martin, Graham, Humphrey, Weidman, and Holm no doubt appreciated the respect and institutional support initially offered by Kolodney, in other ways the Y increasingly became a distraction. Martin was busy at the *Times* and the New School, while the choreographers had their own studios and performing careers and were engaged in developing ideas, training techniques, and new work. In the end the masters had little time for the Y and had trouble meeting their commitments. Students started to complain that the teachers were hiring substitutes and canceling classes, leading to growing frustration for Kolodney. Some years later he referred to such problems in a letter to Weidman, in which he strove to explain the early difficulties he had had with Weidman and the other choreographers: "You see, students will not accept a substitute for a person as prominent as you in the Dance World, no more than they were willing to accept a substitute for Martha Graham, [or] Doris Humphrey . . . all of whom had problems similar to your [sic] in trying to meet their obligations to the Y as well as to their careers as dancers."[45]

The problems Kolodney experienced show that the initial convergence of interests between the modern dance world and the 92nd Street Y was not completely successful in achieving Kolodney's long-term goals. The first year of the Dance Center's existence, Kolodney had sought ways to expand the Y's cultural program and gain prestige in the broader New York community. The needs and interests of modern dancers in the mid-1930s made a meeting of interests possible. Conditions drove dancers to look for new opportunities to teach and perform. In particular, the Y fit neatly into Martin's agenda to use educational institutions to disseminate the ideas and practices of Graham, Humphrey, Weidman, and Holm.

However, while the dance program created a vital new cultural center within the Jewish community, it remained relatively inconspicuous within the broader dance world. Consequently, Kolodney needed to find new ways of developing the Y's programming. This, in fact, is exactly what he proceeded to do. From 1936 onward he drew on his entrepreneurial ingenuity to transform the Y into a more distinctive place that continued to involve Martin and his associates but also reached beyond them to embrace younger performers, European-trained dancers, dancers of different ethnic origins—Hispanic, African American, and most particularly, Jewish—and dancers who largely operated outside New York City. In this way, Kolodney broadened the Y's palette of dance offerings, and in so doing he actively began to reshape people's conceptions of contemporary dance.

Democracy is [Humphrey-Weidman's] fall and recovery. . . . Standing up
straight becomes a philosophy. . . . If you're going to move, then you have to shift the
center of weight . . . this concept of the fall, you go out [into space] . . . and therefore you
have to be willing to meet other people on their terms . . . that's a very democratic thing.
You're not going to be turned in on yourself.
Nona Schurman[1]

(3)

DEMOCRACY IN ACTION

Educating the Human Being through Dance

· · ·

The educational component of the Y's dance program developed during the next few decades as a clear expression of Kolodney's ideals, as refracted through the lens of the increasingly varied members of the dance community who taught there. Reaching mostly a Jewish lay population, the classes and lectures aimed at uniting people through the love of dance as an art form and instilling in them principles of moving that would lead to self-discovery and improvement. The teachers provided students with methods to control their bodies, express their emotions through movement and represent their experiences in dance, rather than stressing the need to learn and perfect particular styles or pieces of choreography. Such an approach to teaching, as well as exposure to various types of modern and Jewish dance and to lectures on dance of all varieties, freed people to pursue their individual interests and value different kinds of dance, thereby supporting Kolodney's democratic vision for the Y.

The teaching of modern dance also brought its own set of concerns to the Y. It meant that specific movement techniques involving strong, full body actions moving through space were literally shaping the bodies of Jewish women and men, while a discourse of freedom of self-expression was influencing their ideas about themselves. Modern dance was helping to mold, in particular, a powerful, artistic, individualistic, contemporary identity that challenged traditional notions of femininity within Judaism. Women from religious backgrounds (of which there were a few) who attended classes at the Y learned how to move large, fast, and on the floor; while those from less observant households embraced a movement style that seemed to embody their modern, urban experience as educated working women and philanthropists.

At the same time, dancers who taught at the Y were as much shaped by Kolodney and the Y's broader values as helping to effect them. Numerous people who taught at the Y were active elsewhere in New York, either in private studios or later on at the New Dance Group or Juilliard, where the focus was on producing professional dancers. At the Y the emphasis was different, as the teachers necessarily participated in presenting dance as an activity of personal and social as well as aesthetic value. The most successful of the Y's instructors were consequently those who recognized and valued this aspect of their work. In the area of modern dance, initially, these were European-trained dancers and, from the mid-1940s on, followers of the Humphrey-Weidman philosophy like Nona Schurman, who taught at the Y for more than twenty years. Both groups of dancers were intent on improving contemporary life along the humanist, egalitarian lines envisioned by Kolodney. The hiring of Fred Berk and other Jewish dancers simultaneously satisfied the Y's aim to provide leadership in the creation of a consciously defined Jewish culture. All these teachers demonstrated to Kolodney that there was a larger number of people devoted to contemporary dance than initially exemplified by Martin and his associates. Kolodney welcomed them in his creation of a program that gave expression to human creativity, intellect, and spirit, within the physical and cultural framework of Jewish values.

• • •

EXPANSION AND DIVERSIFICATION, 1936–39

Between 1936 and 1939 the Y's program of dance classes for adults grew steadily. Over the next few seasons Kolodney displayed his commitment to hiring new faculty, expanding classes, and building an enthusiastic student body. By the end of the decade the Dance Center had grown until it was "probably the largest single group of teachers and students on the modern dance in the country."[2] In the fall of 1939 there were as many as two hundred students attending sixteen classes in some form of modern dance. The expansion of the educational dimension of the dance program was the result of a successful meeting between Kolodney and a growing cross-section of the dance community. European-trained dancers, in particular, shared Kolodney's ideas about the place of arts in education and were compatible with the Y's progressive setting. Kolodney also engaged more dancers who were exploring Jewish subject matter in their work.

Changes to the program began when Kolodney relied less heavily on the direct presence of the the the "Big Four." During the next few years these choreographers faded from view; by 1939 none of the original cast of "master" teachers was left on the Y's faculty. In this period Holm and Weidman became less visible, except for teaching a couple of classes in the fall of 1938.[3] Graham offered a class in the fall of 1936 and then made guest appearances once a month at the beginning of the 1938–39 season. Doris Humphrey returned to the Y in the spring and fall of 1937 to teach advanced technique but otherwise was busy with her own studio and touring commitments. In their place, Kolodney drew on members of these choreographers' companies. Among them were individuals who had taught at the Y the previous year, but others were new to the program. Between 1936 and 1939, representatives of the Graham style included Anna Sokolow, Anita Alvarez, and Dorothy Bird. For Humphrey-Weidman there were Joan Levy and Frances Kinsky, and for Hanya Holm: Nancy McKnight [Hauser], Henrietta Greenhood (Eve Gentry), Ruth Ledoux and Carolyn Brooks. In addition, William Bales, a young dancer who had performed with Weidman, was advertised in the fall of 1936 as teaching a course at the Y in musical comedy.

These young dancers filled two related and important roles: making the notions and motions of modern dance more accessible to everyday people and assuring the longevity of the new dance form by codifying and disseminating it within an institutional context. Many of these dancers had, in fact, assisted their teachers at other institutions, where they had performed a similar function. Bonnie Bird, an early Graham dancer who taught at the Y briefly in the spring of 1936, notes that these assistants saw their job as extremely significant. They were expected to explain the exercises from the same philosophical stance as their teachers had, yet make them clearer by breaking them down into more manageable parts. The responsibility involved "modeling yourself from the way Graham shifted or changed the class ... we didn't try to influence what she was doing or why she was doing it. We tried to understand it."[4] Dancers like Bird analyzed the work of their mentors so that the various styles were more easily understood and appreciated by lay persons and beginning dancers.

In modern dance, the use of assistants increasingly separated the teaching of technique from the training of dancers for specific choreographic projects. At the Y, many students were learning modern dance practice and philosophy, with little aim to perform professionally. Such codification played a central role in the development of modern dance as a whole and was connected to the idea of the fundamentals classes at Bennington. Modern technique was becoming divorced from the original creators and gaining a life of its own as it became an entity, like ballet, that could exist, proliferate, and crystallize into a long-lasting genre. Within the context of the Y, however, this did not mean that modern dance or indeed any other technique was seen as an end in itself or as a simple means of exercise. Rather, with its emphasis on the arts as a means of aiding individual growth within contemporary society, dance classes were seen as providing principal tools for personal and, by extension, social transformation.

The drive to understand and explain the benefits of modern dance to a largely lay membership was increasingly exhibited in the course listings in the Y's catalog. If few detailed class descriptions appeared in the first couple of years, they were soon an important part of the Y's listings. These accounts spoke of systematically analyzing movement in order to gain control over the body as an instrument of expression. Phrases employed included "mechanics of body movement" and "control of every part of the body." The approach was perhaps best summed up in this description: "By isolating various parts of the body the function of each is discovered. From this beginning is achieved a disciplined, coordinated instrument."[5]

Other aspects of the descriptions emphasized how understanding the emotional and ideological dimensions of movement could help in coping with contemporary life. A 1937 course description in intermediate modern technique offered by Nancy McKnight (replaced in the actual course by Henrietta Greenhood) stated that "technique is not solely the functional preparation and moving of the body, but an actual knowledge and experience of the laws of movement as applied to the dancer and the space and time in which he moves, it is the intention to make the student more fully conscious of the problems which confront him today, both technically and ideologically, and to help him toward an objectification of his views into dance form." In the fall of 1938, Agnes de Mille, recently returned from Europe, offered a class specifically titled "Techniques of Expression," in which students learned to analyze feelings "for the determination of basic physiological characteristics, and for their modification in regard to dancing, acting, the producing of

SCHOOL OF THE DANCE

Note: A semester consists of 15 weeks.

Advanced Technique Classes

TECHNIQUE OF THE MODERN DANCE   Charles Weidman

Thursday, 7 to 8 P.M. Fee: $13 per semester, or $4 per month.

Leading American dancer and choreographer. Has conducted a school of the dance with Doris Humphrey. Teacher in Bennington School of the Dance and Academy of Allied Arts. Has appeared as soloist and with Doris Humphrey and company in performances of the Cleveland Civic Opera Company, the Philadelphia Symphony Orchestra, the Theatre Guild, and in recitals throughout the country

Open only to students who have had at least two years' instruction with qualified Humphrey or Weidman teachers, and to advanced students who pass the audition.

TECHNIQUE OF EXPRESSION   Agnes deMille

Monday and Thursday, 6:30 to 7:30 P.M. Fee: $25 per semester, or $7 per month.

Graduate, University of California; trained thoroughly in music and the piano; studied ballet technique under Theodore Kosloff, Tamara Karsavina Egorova, Marie Rambert, Sokolowa, and at the School of American Ballet; studied pre-classic dances with the Dolmetsches in Haslemere, Surrey. Lectured at the University of California and the New School for Social Research. Taught at the Perry-Mansfield Camp and the Neighborhood Playhouse. Conducted extensive classes in Los Angeles and London. Coached Norma Shearer, Kitty Carlisle, Gertrude Lawrence, Paul Haakon, Idzikowsky, Erin O'Brien Moore, Merle Oberon, Greta Nisson, Leslie Howard. Choreographer for "Romeo and Juliet" (M.G.M.—Thalberg), "Nymph Errant" (C. B. Cochran), "I, Claudius" (London Films—Von Sternberg), "Hooray for What" (Minelli-Shubert), Ballets in the Hollywood Bowl, "The Black Crook" (Christopher Morley). Danced in concert seasons in New York, Los Angeles, London, Paris, Brussels, Oxford, Copenhagen.

This course begins October 31.

I. Exercises for bodily control, strength and range of gestures. Exercises at the bar for the turning out of the hips, the stretching and strengthening of the feet, ankles, thighs and back, the control of impulses in positions of balance and tension. Exercises in center floor for balance. Exercises on the ground for strengthening spine and abdomen. Exercises for speed and change of direction with emphasis on rapid footwork. Jumps. Falls. Walking and Running with emphasis on style and deportment. All these exercises for bodily technique are taken in close coordination with exercises for emotional expression.

II. Exercises for Dynamics. The variation of touch on the floor. The variation of stress in torso and arms. Methods of "attack" in gesture.

III. Exercises of imitative expression of emotion. Expressions of intense physical experience. Expressions of simple emotion. Mixed emotions. Interplay of emotional reaction—in sequence with one actor; between two or more actors. (This code of expression exercises is studied for the determination of basic physiological characteristics, and for their modification in regard to dancing, acting, the producing of tragic, comic, and ironic effects, and for the representation of personal and folk character in both dancing and acting.)

IV. Exercises for Style in Dancing. Pre-Classic Ballet Forms. Folk Dances. Simple Ballet Patterns. Experimentation in American folk expressions.

TECHNIQUE OF THE MODERN DANCE   Anna Sokolow

Tuesday and Thursday, 6 to 7 P.M. Fee: $16 per semester, or $5 per month.

Former member of Martha Graham's concert group for the past eight years; assistant to Louis Horst at the Neighborhood Playhouse for six years; received a fellowship in the Bennington School of the Dance; soloist and group recitals with the Dance Unit of which she is director; directed dances and movement in the following Broadway productions: "Noah" and "Valley Forge". Taught at the Group Theatre Studios. Choreographer and dancer of Federal Theatre Project's coming production of "Sing For Your Supper".

21

Class descriptions for the 1938–39 season from the *Bulletin of Educational Activities.*
92nd Street YM-YWHA Archives.

tragic, comic, and ironic effects." The students studied "exercises of imitative expression of emotion," which examined "expressions of intense physical experience. Expressions of simple emotion. Mixed emotions."[6]

The inclusion of Agnes de Mille's class indicates how Kolodney was beginning to broaden the modern dance palette at the Y. While he continued to be interested in offering the techniques of Graham, Humphrey-Weidman, and Holm, Kolodney moved beyond them to include a greater variety of dancers and approaches. In the spring of 1937 he hired Esther Junger and Irma Otte-Betz. Junger was American-born; Otte-Betz had received a Laban diploma in Berlin in 1925 and had run her own studio in Germany. Along with Irmgard Bartenieff, she introduced Laban's notation system to the United States.

Following Hanya Holm, Otte-Betz was the first of a series of teachers hired by Kolodney to bring a solid European training in modern dance to the Y. In his proposal to the board in 1938, Kolodney wrote of his plan "to increase the number of evening teachers of the dance from eleven to fifteen, adding schools of the dance not taught here previously, among them the Kurt-Joos[s] School and the Hellerau-Laxenburg School." Representing the former was Erica Stolzberg; the latter, Gertrude Ulmann, both dancers who had recently arrived in New York. Kolodney further expanded the European presence in the fall of 1939 when he hired Juana de Laban, Rudolf von Laban's daughter, to teach elementary modern technique and Hungarian folk dance.

The European-trained dancers brought a set of interests to the Y that made their classes particularly suitable for the institution's recreational and progressive emphases. They were interested in helping ordinary people to become physically fit and to learn how to move expressively so that they could enjoy a healthier, more "harmonious" lifestyle in the modern world. In the fall of 1937, Otte-Betz offered a class in body movement in which "expressive body movement" was developed through "a system of vigorous exercise." The description continued: "Emphasis will be placed on correct breathing, which is the essence of balance, endurance and harmony in the dance and in every sport." In particular, courses taught by Stolzberg and Ulmann focused on the use of everyday movement, as opposed to highly developed technique. Ulmann was a product of the body culture trend in Germany, which stressed the holistic aspects of exercise. The description for her classes in 1939 explained: "Body culture is the development of a sound and well-integrated body, actively expressed through body movement, by relaxation and constructive body building. Relaxation frees the body for complete naturalness of movement, accomplished without conscious effort." The following year Ulmann further elaborated how this kind of training offered the mover "physical and mental relaxation to offset the nervousness and tension of modern ur[b]an life." Ulmann's perspective clearly followed Kolodney's view of art as a means of relaxation in modern society. At the time he was hired by the Y, Kolodney was carrying out research for a paper, "A Philosophy of Adult Education in an Industrial Civilization."[7] Although this particular project was not completed, Kolodney stressed in his final 1950 dissertation, on the history of the Y, that industrialization is fatiguing and a recreational program aims to provide freedom from tension through the arts.[8]

If Kolodney's view of the arts made for a comfortable connection between European-trained dancers and the Y, his more sectarian interests led to the diversification of the dance program. As early as the fall of 1936, Kolodney began to explore ways of expanding the center to include dance based on Jewish themes. In his annual proposal to the board of directors he announced that, in addition to the classes in modern dance, "an attempt will be made to develop a Jewish dance group, using Jewish content as the ideational basis for the choreography." The ensuing Jewish Dance Laboratory was led by Benjamin Zemach, who had recently returned to New York from Los Angeles to choreograph the dances for Max Reinhardt's biblical drama, *The Eternal Road*.[9]

At the Y, Zemach continued the dramatic work on Jewish subjects that he had been pursuing in Los Angeles (and earlier in New York). According to the historian Naima Prevots, Zemach's choreography was a personal synthesis of Dalcroze eurythmics, ballet, and modern dance, with a special emphasis on inner characterization, emotional gesture, and dramatic rhythm, all of which were part of his theatrical training in Russia.[10] Frieda Maddow, a dancer who accompanied Zemach to New York in 1936, described his process of working, explaining how much it was geared toward self-discovery: "Benjamin made you participate in the creative process, he made you feel you had something in you, that you had ideas. . . . He opened up a whole world of expression and possibilities to me. . . . Each class was based on a theme, and you learned to improvise and look into yourself."[11] The emphasis on creativity and individual growth was clearly something Zemach shared with many modern dance teachers of the time. At the Y, however, it took on special significance, as Zemach's methods were taught within a space trying to promote new forms of Jewish expression as part of a broader attempt to reconstruct Jewish life in America. Within this context, his work acted as a catalyst in shaping a new, modern way of conceiving of Jewish identity that valued individuality and self-expression along with custom and religion.

Zemach's laboratory was offered without a fee to members of the Y. The group consisted of about ten people who met throughout the 1936–37 season, from two- to three-and-a-half hours a week. When Zemach left the Y at the end of the year to pursue other projects, the idea of a permanent dance group at the institution was picked up by another Jewish dancer, Lillian Shapero, who had danced with Graham and staged dances for Maurice Schwartz's Yiddish Art Theatre, one of the most prominent Yiddish theaters of the time.[12] Her Jewish Dance Theatre, "designed to create a concert dance group consisting of trained dancers who will compose ballets based on traditional and contemporary Jewish themes," was planned for the fall of 1937 but was ultimately postponed and never readvertised.[13] In 1939, Rose Blumkin, a dancer with an eclectic education who had studied with Holm, Harald Kreutzberg, Gertrud Kraus, and Zemach, taught a Hebrew Dance course also designed to explore dance movement based on Jewish themes.[14]

Kolodney's intention to include a more sectarian component in his educational programming began as a localized desire to assist individual Jewish artists, but increasingly became part of a broader institutional appeal. Prior to Kolodney's tenure at the Y, classes with particular Jewish content had fallen under the jurisdiction of the Religious Department. Kolodney's mandate, like that of Herman Jacobs before him, was general educational programming. In the fall of 1939 this situation shifted when Kolodney reported that "an attempt is to be made to undertake a greater volume of Jewish content, not as isolated departmentalized adjuncts but in integral relation with the rest of the program."[15] The change was motivated by the escalation of anti-Semitic activity by the Nazis in Germany, the growing awareness of the extreme threat to the survival of Jews and Jewish culture, and an intensifying belief in the need to support the settlement of Jews in Palestine. In 1940, Kolodney's paper at the National Association of Jewish Center Workers illustrated the new commitment by Y staff to specifically Jewish content in their program. Kolodney declared, "The Jews of the world are now at war, by virtue of the fact that Germany has declared a war of physical extermination against the Jews and political Communism in Russia has declared a war of cultural extermination against the Jews." He continued:

> The Jewish Center believes in developing a distinctive Jewish culture in America. Acceptance of this principle implies the following: (a) Giving financial and other support to those Jewish artists, writers, and other creative workers who can produce Jewish cultural material to serve as the basis of Jewish life in America. (b) Setting aside a substantial portion of the money collected for building a Jewish Center, to be devoted exclusively to the creation of Jewish materials and the promotion of a Jewish educational

program . . . (c) Developing a neutral cultural program of so high a caliber that the artistically sensitive Jews, specifically those interested as creators, participants, or spectators in art, music, drama, literature, philosophy, would be attracted to the Jewish Center. An attempt would then be made to interest them in taking an active part in the Jewish life of the Center.[16]

Growing concern over the Jewish content of the cultural program coincided with increasing financial problems at the Y. At the end of 1939 the board of directors found that they faced a large deficit. Believing that the high cost of the cultural program was partly responsible, they asked for a review of the Educational Department and its activities. In February 1940, the reporting committee informed the board that "the Cultural Activities deficit is considerably less than anticipated . . . [and] cultural activities . . . create only a minor part of our deficit." A breakdown of expenses was presented as proof. It indicates that educational and cultural programming received $24,795 from the Federation for the Support of Jewish Philanthropic Societies and $16,256 from recital and class fees. The net deficit, after calculating all the expenses, was recorded at $1,790.

Despite this detailed examination, a few months later an officially established Budget Deficiency Committee recommended that changes be made in the Educational Department owing to a high deficit of $4,200 projected for the department for the following year. The June 1940 "Minutes of the Executive Committee" stated that "a sacrifice should be made in this [Educational] department. We do not recommend the suspension of the full program but rather, a curtailment." In this way, the Y leadership exerted pressure on Kolodney following a particularly successful season for the entire Dance Center (including modern dance, Dalcroze, notation, Hebrew dance, ballroom, tap, and body building). Figures for the 1939–40 season suggest that there were approximately 240 students enrolled in twenty classes taught by fifteen instructors. Nevertheless, Kolodney proceeded to reduce the scope of the program for the following season.

The result of Kolodney's efforts during 1940–41 was a mixture of modern dance and folk dance taught by two newcomers, Saida Gerrard and Noami Aleh-Leaf, alongside continuing classes taught by Junger and Ulmann. Gerrard had studied with Zemach, Holm, and Graham, and Aleh-Leaf was a newly arrived dancer from Palestine who had studied there as well as in Europe and the United States. Both taught modern technique, and Aleh-Leaf also offered a folk dancing class on Tuesday evenings.

This season was the culmination of Kolodney's programming direction over four years. In direct contrast to the first year of the Dance Center, which showcased Graham, Holm, Humphrey, Weidman, and their students, the new roster of teachers highlighted Gerrard, Aleh-Leaf, Junger, and Ulmann, working in a variety of styles. These dancers were able to commit to the Y several hours a week, and they brought to the institution approaches to dancing particularly suited for an educational context devoted to individual growth within an egalitarian context. In direct contrast to the first year of the program, which more or less tried to imitate the early efforts of the Bennington School of Dance, the combination of Jewish and modern dance traditions, along with other dance forms, reflected Kolodney's desire to create a program that would use the arts to unify people from varying backgrounds, especially young Jews, while allowing them the freedom and providing them the tools with which to pursue their own particular paths of personal and social development.

The distinctiveness of the Y's program is recognized by looking at other dance schools in New York in the late 1930s. Other than the private studios, which featured the work of one choreographer, there were no dance centers where such a broad mixture of modern dance styles was available to the general public. The Neighborhood Playhouse School of the Theatre, established in 1928, held movement classes that were well attended. These largely revolved around the work of Martha Graham and Louis Horst, even though Irene Lewisohn created pieces for the students and orchestral dramas, including those on Jewish themes, such as her staging for Ernest Bloch's *Israel: A Symphony for Orchestra* in 1928. The New Dance Group, a leftist organization formed in 1932 by a group of students from Hanya Holm's Wigman studio, was another important source of early modern dance teaching. However, although they still performed, the group was not particularly active as a school during the late 1930s.[17]

The programs most similar to the Y's could be found at local colleges, where the Big Four reigned supreme. At the New School for Social Research, for instance, lessons continued with Martin, Humphrey, Holm, and Boepple (Dalcroze eurythmics). Otte-Betz briefly offered dance notation there in the springs of 1937 and 1938. In 1938, however, modern dance classes at the school more or less came to an end. A survey of modern dance courses was started in 1937 at Columbia's Teachers College. Graham, Holm, Humphrey, and Weidman presented their approaches, along with lectures by Horst, Martin, and others. This course continued until 1941, by which time it was largely devoted to the work of Doris Humphrey and Charles Weidman.

The larger context left the Y's Dance Center as an important means for shaping public perception of modern dance as a serious art form in the late 1930s. Kolodney recognized this, making it clear in his proposals that the purpose of the Y's classes "will be to teach appreciation of the dance as an art through the practice of the technique of the modern dance."[18] To help further the educational process, teachers encouraged students to attend the dance recitals concurrently given at the Y. Kolodney explained in his "Proposed Educational Program 1940–41" that "classes are coordinated with the work of the Dance Theatre in that most of the students become subscribers or attend individual dance recitals. Discussions based on observation of the dance recitals will be included in the technique courses next year."[19]

• • •

THE WAR YEARS: REDUCTION AND REASSESSMENT

As the Dance Center became more defined in terms of structure and purpose, American involvement in the Second World War placed the Y under increasing duress. With the implementation of the draft, the Y began to lose its staff, along with a large part of its male fee-paying membership.[20] In the Dance Center, Kolodney further reduced the staff and the number of classes. Gertrude Ulmann continued on, but the other teachers were replaced by the modern dancer Felicia Sorel and by Marva Spelman, a recent member of the Hanya Holm Concert Group who had attended the University of Wisconsin, danced in Europe, and studied at the Hellerau-Laxenburg school near Vienna. In accord with the Y's educational philosophy, Spelman's classes included the "analysis of dance technique for those who wish to learn to dance, and for those who want to increase their enjoyment of dance concerts through greater understanding of the logic of movement."

By the end of the 1941–42 season, prospects for the Educational Department were extremely bleak. Another large deficit expected for the coming year, along with full-fledged American participation in the Second World War, created difficulties for Kolodney. In July 1942 the board approached him with regard to a future saving of $500 with the suggestion that the reduction might well be made in the Dance Division. In response, Kolodney argued that he would "change the fees to be charged for dance recitals and some of the other recitals so that instead of reducing his budget by $500 he hoped to increase his income by that amount, thus obtaining the same result."[21]

Meanwhile, Kolodney attempted to reassess the dance program by circulating a questionnaire requesting information on changes that should be made in the Dance Center. Among other things, students were asked if they were interested in other kinds of classes along with modern dance. Specifically, Kolodney made reference to classes in music analysis for dancers, dance composition, percussion, acting, ballet, and lectures on dance appreciation and history. The responses must have shown that students were interested in some of these options, because the 1942–43 season advertised courses in dance composition, taught by Horst, and ballet (no teacher listed). In addition, a series of lectures was offered, "Dance in Today's Culture," with subjects such as vaudeville and musical comedy covered by the writer George Beiswanger, religious dance by choreographer Ruth St. Denis, ballet by critic and author Anatole Chujoy, photography and dance by Barbara Morgan, dance in time of war by writer Don Oscar Becque, and composing music for dance by Henry Cowell.

The 1942–43 season proved to Kolodney that it was possible to continue his program despite the war. As early as October 20, 1942, he observed that the loss in the number of young men "was made up, to a large extent, by the increased number of girls, and a larger number of older men and women." In the Dance Center, where the majority of students had always been women, the effect was minimal. As of November 13, 1942, there were around 160 students enrolled in the various dance classes. Moreover, after a shaky start in the fall of 1942, when it seemed that it might not run, the yearly series of dance recitals had made a surplus of $289 by March.

Nonetheless, in the summer of 1943, the Y was hit by the greatest institution-wide financial crisis it was yet to face. The overall budget drastically diminished because of reduced income, owing to a "large loss in membership through [military] induction."[22] The Y leadership considered the elimination of almost all of the cultural courses in view of the fact that the subsidy for educational programming had to be reduced from approximately $4,000 to $500. While Kolodney agreed to eliminate many free lectures and reduce the number of classes, he increased tuition fees in order to preserve the majority of his offerings, thereby proving his extreme strength of character and loyalty to his cultural program.

With regard to the Dance Center, the financial crisis again affected programming but did not completely disable it. Modern dance and composition continued to be taught, and the rest of the classes were dropped. Kolodney turned to Martha Graham and her associates to provide the main focus of the next season.[23] Graham had offered one class at the Y the previous year, and in the fall of 1943, according to the Y course listings, she taught two classes on Wednesday evenings in intermediate technique. One of Graham's dancers, Nina Fonaroff, taught additional classes on Mondays and Thursdays and assisted Horst in teaching dance composition. This included Horst's now familiar "Pre-Classic Forms," which was "an analysis of the historical and musical aspects of dance composition," and "Modern Forms," "an analysis of the backgrounds and immediate materials in everyday life which present the substance of Modern Art. The accent in this course, in distinction from the Pre-Classic, is upon the texture and qualities, rather than upon the form."[24]

In the ten years since its inception the dance school had expanded to embrace a richly diverse program of instruction. The problems caused by the Second World War, however, and the difficulty in administering such a large program, conspired against this variety, and by 1943, Kolodney had streamlined the school into a much simpler entity, focusing on the Graham technique. His high regard for Graham had not diminished over the years, and as of 1941, he increasingly relied on Horst for advice on his performance subscription series. At the same time, Kolodney's broader agenda continued to drive the program as more changes hovered on the horizon.

Kolodney's attempt to save the Dance Center, as well as the rest of the arts programming during the 1943 – 44 season, succeeded. As of November 1943 there were approximately 140 students enrolled in ten classes. If this was a far cry from the height of the program in 1939, it signaled that the Y had overcome the worst. In the annual report of 1943, Kolodney observed that "it was expected that most classes would be eliminated, but the contrary was true in that several more classes had to be offered. Persons who had not paid for courses before or had paid a nominal fee were now willing to pay a more substantial fee." And in May 1944, Kolodney delightedly reported to the board, "The experiment [in charging higher fees] indicated that when a firm foundation of interest is laid on the basis of authenticity of subject matter and instruction, the educational department can weather a financial crisis such as occurred at the end of the last season, when the usual subsidy was necessarily denied."

· · ·

THE HUMPHREY YEARS: PHILOSOPHY IN ACTION, 1944–58

The year 1944 witnessed the birth of a revised dance program designed to, once and for all, fulfill Kolodney's long-time desire to create an outstanding program of instruction that combined his interest in maintaining high artistic standards with his hopes for the Y as a place that promoted democratic values and Jewish culture. The major impetus in achieving his goals came in the guise of two outstanding individuals whose visions regarding the nature of dance resonated closely with his own. Kolodney first hired Doris Humphrey as a teacher and adviser to the center and later supported Fred Berk in establishing the Y as a focal point for Jewish folk dancing. These pivotal teaching choices coincided with the Y's gradual recovery from the effects of the war and growing financial security for all its departments. By the mid-1950s the Dance Center had reached a stable, more or less unchanging form that successfully reflected Kolodney's manifold hopes for the cultural program.

Kolodney invited Humphrey, who had last taught at the Y in 1937, to return to the institution in the summer of 1944. The offer came at a timely moment as she sought new opportunities following the dissolution of the Humphrey-Weidman company and studio. Humphrey was pleased to accept the opportunity to teach; the Y would provide her with a small income and a place to disseminate her ideas on choreography. That fall, Humphrey offered a course called "Dance-Making for Choreographers." The rest of the dance program consisted of beginning classes in Humphrey-Weidman technique, given by Marion Scott, and intermediate and advanced classes taught by Weidman, who was also striving to make ends meet during this transitional time in his career.

The 1944 course bulletin announced the arrival of Humphrey and Weidman with unprecedented excitement. Kolodney was clearly pleased to gain the support of two people who seemed so sympathetic to his views and who were also such prominent members of the dance world. For the first time there was an extensive foreword proclaiming the philosophy of the center as dictated by the main teachers: "Miss Humphrey and Mr. Weidman believe that the modern dance is one of the greatest integrators of the human personality and that it can and does change individuals into more complete and better people as well as better dancers. . . . The Humphrey-Weidman system of training aims at recreating the individual in both meanings of the word: that is, in remaking him, also in giving him pleasure, during the process."[25] The statement firmly declared a close affinity between Humphrey and Weidman and Kolodney's views of the arts as a means of enjoyable recreation and self-improvement by engaging the entire human being. It would soon become evident that Humphrey herself and the Humphrey-Weidman philosophy were extremely well suited to the Y.

In 1945, Kolodney officially hired Humphrey as director of the Y's Dance

Center, although no official duties seem to have been attached to this title; Kolodney retained administrative control and oversaw the day-to-day functioning of the center. Rather, the title attested to Humphrey's role as the principal adviser to Kolodney concerning courses and faculty, although this did not mean that Humphrey was solely committed to the Y. Throughout this period she was extremely busy with many other choreographic and teaching endeavors, the most important being her role as artistic director of the José Limón company and, after 1954, director of the Juilliard Dance Theatre. Nonetheless, for the following decade, until her death, Humphrey's influence was to be felt in many aspects of the Y's dance program—as adviser, teacher, and audience member.[26]

In 1945 – 46, Humphrey gave two courses, fundamentals of choreography, for dancers with no fewer than two years of training, and advanced choreography, for professionals. From then, until 1955, she taught a class at the Y in advanced choreography, usually in the spring semester.[27] This class focused on the teaching of repertory as a starting point for analyzing the components of choreography. The course description, which remained fundamentally the same over the years, noted: "Miss Humphrey believes that knowledge of choreography comes best with an analysis of actual dances; hence, the problems are dealt with visually and not theoretically. In her course, Miss Humphrey will teach whole dances or parts of long ballets from her repertory, and will analyze them as to music, content, gesture movement, space design, speech, etc., both for solo and group. Miss Humphrey will also advise as to problems presented by members of the class." Dancers flocked to the Y to take these classes and learn from the master. In October 1947, Humphrey reported to her friend Helen Robinson, "The enrollment is very good, nearly double last year. I have fifteen aspiring students in my class."[28] As the dance scholar Marcia B. Siegel has noted, "This course, together with the teaching of her own repertory, became the vehicle by which she imparted sound, clear principles of dance-making to hundreds of students through the years."[29]

At the end of each year, students from the choreography class were encouraged to present their original compositions as well as sections from Humphrey's own repertory. The May 1949 student recital included "Variations and Conclusion" from *New Dance*, and in May 1950, as part of their program, the repertory class performed her *Partita in G Major* to the music of Bach. Such recitals as these gave Humphrey an opportunity to present her work as well as encourage the development of a new generation of young choreographers.

Doris Humphrey teaching, 1949.
92nd Street YM-YWHA Archives. Photographer: Erich Kastan.

At the Y, in particular, Humphrey's approach to composition converged with the aspirations of Jewish dancers intent on formalizing their choreographic process. For instance, in the early 1950s the Jewish dancer Felix Fibich arrived at the Y to take Humphrey's choreography class. Fibich had grown up in Poland, where he had studied Wigman technique at a school run by Judith Berg, his future wife, best known for her choreography for the 1937 Polish film *The Dybbuk*.[30] During the war, Berg and Fibich escaped the Nazis by performing in Russia with a Jewish revue theater that performed dances based on Jewish themes. When the war ended, the couple returned to a desolate Poland, where they were engaged to teach dance to surviving Jewish children. In 1949, Berg and Fibich traveled to Paris to perform for UNESCO and the International Archive of Dance, among other organizations. The couple moved to New York in 1950.[31]

Fibich possessed a great desire to develop his work as a performer and choreographer and found in the Y's dance recitals and choreography classes tools for improving his craft. Fibich later recalled of Humphrey's course, "We learned the principles of choreography. You learned to analyze the ingredients of dance . . . she gave us assignments every week . . . variety of rhythms, or variety of designs . . . or different dynamics."[32] As a result of these exercises, Fibich began to be aware of how particular movement elements, such as time and space, might be consciously shaped in order to make a well-crafted work. Humphrey's classes made him reexamine dances that he had previously performed intuitively. He stated, "She could pinpoint with a name every ingredient of the dance. So later on when I choreographed, I was able to analyze if what I did is correct, if it is not too repetitious, if it has enough variety in rhythm, if it's interesting enough in designs, etc. . . . so she taught me a lot, and she made an order in my head because intuitively I did certain things . . . but I didn't know why." As a result of this and of later workshops and classes with modern dancers, Fibich developed dances and a lecture-demonstration based on Jewish movement, in which gestures drawn from Jewish ritual or everyday life in Eastern Europe were extended with technical ·ʒg lifts and turns and combined according to the principles imparted by ł ımphrey.

Fibich toured the lecture-demonstration circuit for many years, drawing on Humphrey's vocabulary and analytic methods to help to explain, for instance, the tendency of Jewish movement to have opposing tensions in the body (as when the arms reach upward while the lower body lowers into the ground or the head and torso strain to one side, while arms and hands reach to the other). For Fibich, these movements were expressive of joy mixed with sorrow, a typically Jewish experience owing to their long history of persecution. In this instance, Humphrey's observations regarding the value of asymmetrical body design as a powerful ingredient in choreography helped to give physical and verbal expression to conceptions of Jewish identity that were emerging in America.[33]

While Humphrey was taking care of choreographic instruction, Humhrey-Weidman technique was taught by a variety of teachers. Between 1945 aı.ʲ 1948, Weidman taught at the Y, along with José Limón, Marion Scott, Doris Goodwin, Nona Schurman, and Dorothea Buchholz.[34] Approximately six classes in technique, one hour each, were offered each semester. By the commencement of the 1948 – 49 season, Weidman and Limón had left the Y, and the teaching passed to Schurman, Buchholz, and Miriam Pandor. Between 1949 and 1956, the style was offered by an ever-shifting combination of dancers who had trained with Humphrey, Weidman, or Limón. These included Buchholz, Pandor, Katherine Litz, Lucy Venable, Dorothy Bird, Virginia Copeland, and Schurman. From a few classes in the first 1944 – 45 season, the program blossomed so that by the spring of 1951–52 there were about fifteen classes in modern dance technique and composition and about two hundred students.

By 1956 the teaching of Humphrey-Weidman technique to adults became fully regulated and institutionalized at the Y. Approximately six classes in elementary, intermediate, or advanced intermediate were offered each week. All of the classes were overseen by Schurman, the sole remaining teacher of those who had come before. From the fall of 1955 until 1958, during which Humphrey stopped offering her choreography class, Schurman taught beginning choreography. (Schurman had offered an Elements of Composition class during 1946–47, and beginning choreography in 1953–54.) Thereafter, Schurman continued to teach technique classes at the Y (as well as at the New Dance Group) until she left New York in 1968. Her extensive years of teaching present an excellent opportunity to analyze how modern dance both reflected many of Kolodney's ideals and aided in shaping a new female Jewish subjectivity.

Schurman had danced in the Humphrey-Weidman company between 1940 and 1943 and had joined the faculty at the Y in 1946. Her classes were highly structured and consisted of initial standing exercises, floor stretches, different falls, and rhythmically challenging combinations across the floor, all based on the Humphrey-Weidman approach. Characteristic exercises from her classes are recorded in Labanotation in her book, coauthored with Sharon Leigh Clark, *Modern Dance Fundamentals* (1972).[35] They are vigorous and require extremely stretched and strong thighs as well as a flexible back. While movements usually involve swinging, they require a strong attack and a clear sense of rhythm.[36] The rigorous technical demands of the class drew many supporters, and over the years, Schurman developed a devoted following at the Y. Her students were mostly young and middle-aged Jewish women; morning classes consisted of the highly educated wives of doctors and lawyers, and in the evening, working women from different professions arrived for an inspiring workout. These women came to appreciate deeply the underlying philosophy of Humphrey-Weidman and the intricacies of the exercises. One of Schurman's students raved on her 1947 registration form: "The finest class in Modern Dancing, or any other kind of dancing, it has been my privilege to attend."[37]

Schurman was especially valued by Kolodney because of her ability to recognize the affinity between the Humphrey-Weidman approach and the Y's progressive educational aims. Schurman later observed that the Y was "an

Nona Schurman, *Running Laughter*, ca. 1943.
Courtesy of Nona Schurman

educational department and whatever was there was to educate . . . the
Humphrey-Weidman particular style of dance, plus the whole philosophy . . .
worked very well for the Y."[38] To Schurman the brilliance of the style was that
it was "philosophy in action." Instead of dictating prescribed movements tied
to particular choreography, Humphrey identified basic principles that could
then be used to generate many different kinds of exercises or compositions.

This kind of creativity flourished at the Y, with its long history of progressive art education as a means of allowing individuals to fulfill their own artistic potential by better grasping basic principles.

A prime example of such a principle, according to Schurman, was Humphrey's "fall and recovery." Rather than dictating a particular kind of movement, it could act as a generator of widely different sorts of sequences. For instance, it could be the basis of an exercise standing in place, in which the body hinged backward until it slid onto the floor, then returned to a vertical standing position. Or it could generate a traveling sequence across the floor in which a student had to walk purposefully through the space, thrusting her weight forward with each step. Moreover, fall and recovery embodied a dramatic potential for expressing something about the human condition. The Humphrey-Weidman style embraced the "democratic way of life," in which man meets man on equal terms by falling off-center, into and across space. Schurman argued that this aspect of fall and recovery was an especially strong indicator that Humphrey's overall ideology was well suited to the Y as an institution open to all kinds of people, both Jewish and non-Jewish, and a place where everyone could feel welcome.

· · ·

WALTER TERRY'S DANCE LABORATORY:
UNDERSTANDING THE VARIETY OF DANCE

As the Second World War receded from immediate view and the overt threat to Jewish survival lessened, Kolodney again turned his focus to transforming the Y into a nonsectarian institution open to everyone. During the 1950s, Kolodney was frequently heard to declare that the arts provide a medium of communication that connects people of different religious and ethnic backgrounds. And by the end of the decade, Kolodney was claiming that "the Y should be a home for all mankind," bringing people together in a positive atmosphere to share knowledge and creativity.[39]

This openness was evident in other aspects of the Y's dance programming in the late 1940s and through the 1950s. Throughout the decade the dance critic Walter Terry offered yearly lecture-demonstrations at the Y, known as dance laboratories. Terry, who wrote for the *New York Herald Tribune*, was first invited by Kolodney to organize two Sunday afternoon events at the Y for the 1946 – 47 season. These were a panel, "The Function of Dance Criticism," on November 24, 1946, and a lecture-demonstration, "Contemporary Music for the Dance," on December 15. The Y's *Bulletin of*

Educational Activities for the year listed the participants for the music panel as Jess Meeker, Ted Shawn, Morton Gould, Jerome Robbins, Bernardo Segall, and Valerie Bettis; the dance criticism panel consisted of Minna Lederman, Martha Graham, La Meri, Talley Beatty, Sol Hurok, Vincenzo Celli, and Robert Posey. The success of the afternoons was so great that the following year Terry gave the first of his dance laboratories, with eight events presented on Monday evenings. From 1947 to 1963, Terry offered the laboratory as part of the Y's Dance Center, and it grew in size to become a major event in the Kaufmann Auditorium.[40]

Terry's idea for the laboratories was to develop appreciation for dance by explaining its history and cultural context, and introducing people to choreographers and dancers from all sectors of the dance world. He once stated at the beginning of an event that "our purpose has been to share with you the behind the scenes motivations of dancing in many different phases."[41] Terry would introduce the topic or person of the day and proceed to a lecture or discussion. Often, dancers would then perform excerpts of work to demonstrate a particular point. Since the public was allowed to ask questions, they were, according to Terry, "part of our laboratory experience."[42]

Kolodney invited Terry to speak on the diversity of styles that characterized dance in America. The year the series began, Terry gave an overview of the powers, functions, and purposes of dance with lectures called "Why Man Dances," "Dance as Ritual for Religio-Magic Purposes," "Dance as a Social Force," "Dance as Theater" (with separate lectures on ballet and modern dance), "Folk and Ethnologic Forms," "Use of Dance in Contemporary Theater," and "Dance Education."[43] The following season, 1948 – 49, Terry's laboratory was titled "Dance in the American Theatre." This series of lecture-demonstrations devoted evenings to "Aims of Theatre Dance," "Revue Dancing," "Ballet," "Modern Dance," "Primitive and Ethnological Dance," and "The Meanings of Movement." The series reflected Terry's broad interest in explaining the central characteristics of many different dance styles of the time. Demonstrators included Pearl Primus, La Meri, and Martha Graham, along with dancers from American Ballet Theatre and popular Broadway musicals.

Other topics over the years included "Dance Immortals" (1949 – 50), with presentations scheduled on Ruth St. Denis, King David-Muni Bharata, Noverre-Vestris-Taglioni, Petipa-Fokine, Isadora Duncan, and The Heritage. From then on, most of Terry's series revolved around interviews with leading personalities of the dance world. "Open Interviews" (1950 – 51) consisted of lively one-on-one discussions with Jerome Robbins, George Balanchine, St. Denis, Humphrey, Tamiris, Graham, Florence Rogge, and Agnes de Mille, "The Art of Performing" (1952–53) featured interview-demonstrations with Alicia Markova, Martha Graham, Janet Collins, Bill Callahan, Pearl Primus, Bambi Linn and Rod Alexander, Igor Youskevitch, and the internationally celebrated ballerina, Nora Kaye (who originally danced under the name of Nora Koreff).

These interviews provided audiences with in-depth understanding of the artists involved. Rogge, for instance, who was the director and choreographer for the Radio City Music Hall corps de ballet, outlined the problems and conditions she faced in her work, including the audience, the size of the theater, the production-spectacle format, and the mechanical equipment. The discussion then focused on the ballets *La Valse, Rhapsody in Blue, Les Sylphides, Swan Lake, The Sleeping Beauty, Chopin Concerto,* and *Victoriana Suite.* She introduced ten dancers who performed *Victoriana Suite.* Collins, for her part, shared how she prepared for a performance, the differences between the techniques of ballet and modern dance, and her philosophy of performing. She then performed phrases from her dance *Spirituals,* explaining the movement, ideas, and feelings on which the dance was based.

One of the more unusual of Terry's labs was titled "Sex Dances of Mankind" (1951–52). This series was meant to treat the "sex factor in dance as it pertains to the theatrical, ethnologic, folk and popular dance fields."[44] According to the announcement in the *Bulletin,* "Primitive fertility dances, romantic pas de deux from the ballet, ethnic rituals, contemporary theatrical dances deriving from this source and other dance actions stemming from the ancient sex impulse" were to be covered. The series presented Maria Tallchief with Nicholas Magallanes and Ted Shawn, Jean-Léon Destiné and Myra Kinch, Janet Collins and La Meri, John Butler and his company, and Valerie Bettis in a fascinating series of discussions and demonstrations that touched on the sexual element in a wide variety of dance forms.[45]

• • •

FRED BERK AND THE JEWISH DANCE DIVISION

While the Y welcomed everyone, it remained a focal point for Jewish dancers in the early 1950s. At the institution, Jews could study modern dance practice and choreographic methods at an affordable rate and in supportive surroundings. In keeping with his philosophy, Kolodney's desire to open the Y's doors to all mankind did not hinder him from continuing to

Fred Berk, ca. 1972.
92nd Street YM-YWHA Archives.

develop a specifically Jewish dimension of the educational department. The events surrounding the Second World War acted as a tremendous catalyst to Kolodney in this process, since they rallied the Jewish community around consciously defined Jewish interests in an unprecedented way and provided Kolodney with the kind of support he needed for more sectarian programming.

While Humphrey and Terry were developing a dedicated following, Kolodney was busy working with the modern dancer Fred Berk on the construction of a Jewish dance division at the Y.[46] Berk was an Austrian-born Jew who fled to the United States via England and Cuba to escape the Nazis.[47] He and his wife at the time, Katya Delakova, began teaching at the Y in 1947; they conducted a Jewish Dance Repertory Group and a class for Palestinian and Jewish folk dance. Berk had trained in Europe under Gertrud Kraus and was familiar with a dramatic style of modern dance that focused on individual characters and their emotions. At the same time, he was increasingly inspired by wide-scale experiments in Palestine from the mid-1940s onward to produce a uniquely Jewish folk dance. The originators of this new folk form drew on various Jewish and Arabic cultures, including the Yemenite and Eastern European (Hungarian, Romanian, Polish) in creating their dances.[48] After traveling to Israel in 1949, when the new country was barely twelve months old, Berk prepared to teach the new dances to Americans.

In 1952 the classes in Jewish folk dancing became a solid part of the Y's curriculum. At that point, Kolodney and Berk discussed the need to build a really exciting and dynamic context for teaching the dance form. The result was a Wednesday evening class called an open session, for which students could pay each time they attended rather than registering for a whole term. Berk began the class with a warmup, a few basic steps complicated with variations in rhythmic accents and spatial direction, then proceeded to teach "some Arabic, Yemenite and Eastern European dances; Jewish folk dances created in this country; and the newest Israeli dances."[49] The classes were a huge success, with enrollment climbing to well over a hundred. Between 1953 and 1956 the class was held to great acclaim, and in the fall of 1957, Berk added a training course for Jewish folk dance instructors, which was partly sponsored by the American Zionist Youth Foundation.

The Israeli folk dance classes of the late 1950s saw the culmination of an active period at the Y. Before 1945 the YMHA had been a place to learn the ideas and methods of Graham, Humphrey, and Holm as well as various forms of European modern dance. After 1944 the diversity remained but in a different form. Instead of arising from a wide variety of modern dance styles, it emerged from the coexistence of the Humphrey-Weidman approach, Walter Terry's Dance Laboratory, and the Israeli folk dance movement.

Two other important dance programs established in New York during the time shared the Y's broad approach to programming but did not have a similar commitment to Jewish concerns. Beginning around 1940 the New Dance

Teen-age Dance, 1955.
92nd Street YM-YWHA Archives. Photographer: Herbert Sonnenfeld.

Group announced that it would offer classes in modern dance, ballet, composition, folk, and ballroom. Jane Dudley, a Graham-trained dancer, was the director, with additional classes taught by Sophie Maslow (Graham technique), Nona Schurman (Humphrey-Weidman), Henrietta Greenhood (Holm), and Ann Wiener (ballet). Sarah Bartell and Gertrude Wexell taught general beginners' classes. Within a few years the group was offering a course in ethnic dance studies, with classes in Hawaiian and Spanish dance by Jean Erdman, and African and West Indian dance by Pearl Primus.

After 1944, when the New Dance Group became a nonprofit organization maintaining studios and a school with low tuition rates, the organization became a magnet for many aspiring dancers throughout the next decade. The same was true of the Juilliard School, which opened its doors to dance in the fall of 1951. The new program offered training in modern dance and ballet, with additional courses in composition, notation and music for dance. The initial faculty consisted of the most influential figures in the dance world and many of the same group that had been involved in Bennington, the New School and the 92nd Street Y: Martha Hill, Graham, Humphrey, Limón, de Mille, Robbins, Antony Tudor, Ann Hutchinson, Horst, and Helen Lanfer.

There were a few important differences between the Y, on the one hand, and the New Dance Group and Juilliard School on the other. One was that the latter two institutions did not connect as intimately with the Jewish community. They did not have a consistent policy to support Jewish dancers and art through workshops and classes. Second, they were not geared toward the lay person. Instead, those two institutions attracted young people primarily interested in becoming professional dancers. The students who attended the New Dance Group and Juilliard took classes with the clear aim of improving their dancing. The stress was on technique as a tool for performance, as opposed to a means of educating the entire human being for personal and social betterment. The Y's educational programming in dance consequently retained a distinctive place in the dance world throughout the 1950s. The shared humanist concerns of Kolodney, Humphrey, and Berk led to a successful merging of modern dancers with the Y's agenda as a Jewish community center. Ultimately, this made for a broad program of classes and the unique opportunity for students to experience a diverse range of movement practices, with Jewish dancers playing a significant role. This special combination of features was reflected in other aspects of the Y's dance program, including its performance groups and subscription series.

On our magic merry-go-round
Our magic merry-go-round
We'll make believe we're taking a trip
To countries sunny and green.
We'll even see some people
That nobody's ever seen.
Merry-Go-Rounders script[1]

(4)

AUDIENCE BUILDING, JEWS,

& GLOBAL CULTURE

The First Season of the Merry-Go-Rounders

• • •

The central role played by the Y in audience building in New York was nowhere as visible as in the Merry-Go-Rounders, a company founded in 1952 by Doris Humphrey, Bonnie Bird, and Fred Berk to educate children about dance and to create a future public for the performing arts. As with the rest of the Y's educational programming, observation of performances by the company at the institution and on tour deepened many people's appreciation and understanding of dance as an art. With its carefully designed scenarios, which involved active participation by those watching, youngsters learned about different movement components in an entertaining and joyful way as they rocked, gestured, and shouted in their auditorium seats.

The Merry-Go-Rounders also provided a unique opportunity to disseminate the complex ways in which Jewishness was defined in relation to general culture at the Y. During its initial season the company introduced children to dance styles from a variety of countries while placing special emphasis on dance in Israel. Near the end of the production an imaginary plane ride transported the children to the different countries, including Mexico and

India, where they learned simple songs and movements emblematic of those cultures. Three conceptions of Jewish identity were implicit in this imaginary journey. Reference to world culture conveyed the idea that expressing one's Jewishness through a richly differentiated general culture was an acceptable and preferred way of being Jewish in America: being aware of Indian mudras (symbolic hand gestures) was part of one's Jewish identity as much as knowledge of the hora. In addition, by presenting Jews as simply one among many different ethnic groups, the Merry-Go-Rounders' creators suggested that people are different but equal and that all groups should respect and appreciate each other. Here, as in all the educational programming, Jews were presented as distinct yet closely linked with other cultures in a multicultural world. Finally, Jewishness was celebrated in a highly stylized form in the dance *Holiday in Israel*, where Jewish identity was located in Israel and a life of rustic simplicity, harmony, and joy. Again, the notion of unity in spite of diversity was the central theme, for *Holiday in Israel* represented Jewish settlers from different places coming together to celebrate their common commitment to life in the new state.

The Merry-Go-Rounders' presentation of dance forms from different countries involved subtly fusing together modern dance structures and choreographic conventions with movements, costumes, and music referring to other cultures. Folk dance steps were performed in clear formations, with a beginning, middle, and end, and were arranged to best highlight the dynamic and expressive character of each. For the young modern dancers who made up the company, the approach helped to reframe modern dance as open to foreign influence. As dancer Jeff Duncan observed, "I did not want to do anything but a narrow range of movements. I thought I knew what modern dance was made of and I certainly did not want to do any folk dance. I was arrogant, but during the rehearsals I began to like the movements very much."[2] As with other aspects of the Y's programming, The Merry-Go-Rounders' staging of Jewish life in the context of a global, general culture helped to expand the definition of modern dance.

· · ·

ORIGINS OF THE MERRY-GO-ROUNDERS

The Merry-Go-Rounders grew out of the work being done in the children's dance department in the early 1950s.[3] William Kolodney hired Bonnie Bird in 1951, and by the following year she became the head of the children's department. Under Bird the program was organized and streamlined so that only

Bonnie Bird teaching dance class, 1955.
92nd Street YM-YWHA Archives. Photographer: Herbert Sonnenfeld.

people committed to developing a point of view about teaching dance to children were retained. These instructors included Bunny Mendelsohn, Lucy Venable, Flo Peters, and Fred Berk. Together, through newly established faculty meetings, they developed an approach to teaching dance that encouraged children to use their imagination as well as their emerging technical abilities. As Bird later observed, these people were not really "big-shot names," but this was not a concern since they "were really devoted to the questions that we had to answer about the creative teaching of dance to children."[4]

The faculty established a syllabus and developed a perspective as a department. They spoke of the progress of the children, instituted individual reports on each student, and related to parents in a direct way in order to "educate them as to what we were doing with the children." They established open classes for parents and before beginning, the teacher would explain the point of view that she was taking and how to look at what the children were doing and accomplishing, "to get the parents to be part of the observational and supporting process of the children." In this way the children's department was committed to educating adults as well as children about the nature of dance—what was involved in doing and watching it.

Like Humphrey in her composition classes at the Y or Terry and his dance laboratories, Bird and her teachers challenged the prevailing conception of dance as an unthinking, frivolous activity; instead, they promoted it as a highly skillful, educational form of human expression, "so that the parents gave up saying things like, 'What did you learn in dance today' and the child goes blank and doesn't want to talk about it, or 'Show my friends what you learned in dance today,' so you'd become a little donkey." This approach was crucial to the success of the program, since the adults were the ones who brought the children to the classes. As Bird observed, "One of the things that was clear was that the biggest motivation for the people coming to class was from the parent and not from the child." The children liked to move, but the parents had to "learn how to look for what was important about the child studying dance." To further aid this process the teachers developed an end-of-year concert, overseen by Bird and Humphrey, that provided the students a chance to enjoy the performance experience and the parents an opportunity to see their children's improvement.

Over the years the Y continued to be a major innovator in the field of children's dance instruction. In 1954, Lucile Brahms Nathanson (who later assumed the directorship of the Dance Center following Humphrey's death in 1958) formed the Division of Teacher Training in Children's Dance, which was designed to prepare the trained dancer and others for teaching dance to children. That season, in January 1955, the Y also sponsored the National Conference on the Creative Teaching of Dance to Children, the first such conference in America, with 259 teachers in attendance.

It was out of this dynamic educational setting that the idea for a performing company for children emerged. Faculty members at the Y were highly motivated in their teaching but searching for a creative outlet in order to feel that they were evolving as artists as well as educators. At the same time, the teachers felt that children were seeing a very limited view of what dance could be and that more ways were needed to introduce them to the diversity of dance expression. As Bird recalled: "You realized that because . . . they'd been to a ballet, they'd seen tutus and toe shoes, that was their idea of dance. Well if their parents . . . took them to see the New York City Ballet, I can remember that [Jerome Robbins's] *The Cage* was new. Well it was about predatory females and so on, and I thought 'what a thing to send the children to see.' There was no *Nutcracker*, and nothing designed for a family." Although Alwin Nikolais held excellent performances for children in the early 1950s at the Henry Street Play-house, these productions did not travel. Edwin Strawbridge also had a small group that toured extensively but, according to Bird, was poor in quality. Room, therefore, existed for another company to be formed.

At a series of faculty meetings the teachers decided to found the Merry-Go-Rounders as a group of adult professional dancers devoted to building a repertory for young audiences from six to twelve years old. Bird was named administrative director, with Berk as assistant administrative director. Humphrey, the director for the entire Dance Center at the Y, became the artistic director of the enterprise. Each of these individuals was excited by the project because of their interest in using performance to educate the younger generation. Since the Y was already a focal point for their combined energies, it was easy for them to converge around this new venture. The rest of the staff consisted entirely of members of the Y's dance faculty. Bunny Mendelsohn was the production coordinator; Lucy Venable, the company notator; Eva Desca, company director; and Beatrice Rainer, the music director. Publicity was handled by Vivian Siegal who later became a Y board member. Kolodney provided free use of the Y's studios for rehearsals on weekday mornings and access to the institution's charge accounts at various stores as a way of offsetting expenses for costumes and props.

Although many of the teachers themselves wanted to perform, it was decided, after looking at the poor track record of other small companies, that it would be best to hire professional dancers and focus their own energies on administration and choreography. As a result, an open audition was called for Friday, November 7, 1952. From this session, a group of ten dancers was chosen: Patricia Cooper, Sally Fitzpatrick, Flo Peters, Elizabeth Ray, Barbara Shivitz, Roberta Singer, Rima Sokoloff, Manon Souriau, Gloria Spivak, and Jeff Duncan. These dancers were trained in modern dance, many fresh from the dance programs at Juilliard, Sarah Lawrence College, and New York University. Rehearsals commenced November 17, and the company began to function as an official entity.

· · ·

THE PRODUCTION: TRAVELING ON
THE MAGICAL MERRY-GO-ROUND

Bird, Humphrey, and Berk chose three pieces for the first performances of the Merry-Go-Rounders. These were *The Donkey*, *The Goops*, and *Holiday in Israel*, by Alwin Nikolais, Eva Desca, and Fred Berk, respectively. The pieces,

Bernice Mendelsohn, the Magic Mechanic, 1950s.
92nd Street YM-YWHA Archives. Photographer: Lionel Freedman.

selected for their ability to capture the imagination of children, were woven together with the help of two speaking parts, a Ringmaster and Magic Mechanic. The artistic directors conceived of these characters as a means of communicating more directly with the youngsters. The Ringmaster was an enthusiastic character who explained to the children what was going on, with the Magic Mechanic assisting when things went awry.[5] The two appeared in an introductory and a closing section, as well as between the dances. As a whole the performance was designed to "evoke audience participation through new techniques evolved for this kind of interplay between performer and audience [and] provide entertainment geared for the young child."[6]

Bunny Mendelsohn wrote the scripts for the Merry-Go-Rounders' performances. Although she had no prior experience, she was encouraged by Bird to work out a dramatic text for the connecting sections of the show, and the results were a tremendous success. The dialogue immediately captured the mood sought by the artistic directors. From the moment the performance began there was a feeling of excitement and mystery. The Ringmaster burst through the center curtain and exclaimed:

> Ladies and gentlemen! Boys and girls!
> I have the surprise of the year
> It's a merry-go-round, right here.
> The horses prance, and the animals dance
> And you can all ride it and cheer.

The Ringmaster then encouraged the children to clap and sing to make the merry-go-round appear. The song immediately established the performance as a participatory educational adventure, in which the children would be introduced to different people and places. The Ringmaster concluded:

> On our magic merry-go-round
> Our magic merry-go-round
> On our animals off we'll go
> All together let's shout hi-ho
> On our merry-go-round
> Our magical merry-go-round.

At the end of the song the curtain opened to reveal a merry-go-round of dancers dressed in striped clown costumes riding hobbyhorses with different animal heads (deer, rooster, etc.). The dancers were attached to a central pole and moved in a circle, as in a maypole dance, performing slow triplets with a periodic rocking motion back and forth. This image of the merry-go-round

Merry-Go-Rounders, ca. 1966 – 67.
92nd Street YM-YWHA Archives.

acted as the leitmotif of the entire performance and symbolized the imaginary trip that the children would take to unknown lands, both imaginary and real.

Before this trip could happen, however, the merry-go-round "broke down." As the dancers stumbled and came to a standstill, the Ringmaster called on the Magic Mechanic (waiting backstage) to fix it. The Mechanic, dressed in colorful overalls, entered and examined the merry-go-round, determining that more magic was needed to get it up and running again. So the two characters momentarily exited to get their "magic chairs." Once the Ringmaster and Mechanic were seated, the children were enlisted in a participatory learning experience to aid in the making of the magic. The audience was given the formula for magic: "First, if your feet reach the floor plant them there. And place your hands very firmly on the arms of your chair. And rock. Then, look up, and pick little pieces of magic right out of the air. And put them into an invisible magic cup. And stir. Then rock again, and pick, and put. And rock again. And you will see. The merry-go-round will work once more." Here the children were introduced to the creation of a dance phrase with three contrasting kinds of movement: a forceful, full-bodied, forward and backward rocking; a delicate, detailed hand movement of "picking";

and a round, stirring motion of the arm. The repetition of the phrase created a little dance that had a particular rhythm and inner variation of dynamics.

The success of the children in getting the merry-go-round up and running allowed the first piece of the afternoon to be introduced. In the premiere on Sunday, February 1, 1953, this was Nikolais's *The Donkey,* based on one of Aesop's fables.[7] The dance concerned a farmer and son who are traveling to the market to sell their donkey. On the way they encounter different groups of people who criticize them whatever they do, whether they let the animal walk free or whether the father or the son mounts him. Murray Louis, appearing as a guest artist, played the Donkey, Jeff Duncan the Farmer and the rest of the dancers were Silly Girls, Clowns, and Brats, all of whom used rhymed dialogue along with pantomimic gesture to make clear the meaning of the story.

The Ringmaster and Mechanic then introduced the children to the Goops. The idea for *The Goops* came from Humphrey, who as a child had loved Gelett Burgess's book *Goops and How to Be Them.* In this text all the characters are misbehaving children who cause havoc for their mother, each possessing a punning name that captures their particular foible (such as Verivaine, Verislow, Teeza). Humphrey recommended Eva Desca, one of her former dancers, to choreograph the work, since she had experience in working with children and was already acting as Humphrey's assistant in her choreography classes at the Y. The result was a charming dance which, like *The Donkey,* combined movement and introductory dialogue to tell the story. In this case, the piece recorded the pranks of a group of children who drive their mother out of her wits by their bad behavior.

The section began with the Ringmaster saying that the merry-go-round was so special that she did not think she would let anyone ride on it. The Mechanic responded that the Ringmaster sounded just like the Goop Nevershair, who "has many, many toys, but will never share them." The two then engaged the audience so that everyone acted like a Nevershair by saying, "YOU can't have it, you CAN'T have it," until all the children knew the lines by heart. The phrases with stresses on different words were used to introduce all the Goop characters so that the children understood the personality of each one before it appeared.

The dance proper began when the mother woke her children, who lay sleeping on different parts of the stage. They jumped up and down, played horsey and brushed their teeth (using mime), then skipped offstage, kissing their mother good-bye. The rest of the piece consisted of little vignettes in which the dancers were engaged in various activities: reading, kite flying, playing with a bat, and carrying presents to a party. The different Goop characters eventually displayed their inherent nature as they became increasingly naughty. Krysoe had a solo tantrum of flailing limbs, and Quarrlin picked an argument with the other kids during a game. At the end of the piece, the mother rounded up the performers, scolding them and asking if each of them had been a Goop. They turned away, ashamed of what they'd done. She then turned to the audience and asked, "Are you a Goop?" The audience, by that time totally caught up in the work, screamed out "No!"[8]

Walter Terry, in his announcement of the premiere of the new company, wrote, "Through this system of participation the directors hope that the children, while having a good time, will learn the ingredients of dance."[9] *The Donkey* and *The Goops* both achieved this through their use of clear characterization and narrative format. In these pieces there was a straightforward attribution of distinctive movements to particular characters. For instance, thrashing, writhing movements were attributed to Krysoe in *The Goops*, showing that the character was having a tantrum. This made the story easy for the children to understand while also teaching them about different kinds of movement qualities.

The narrative format of these pieces was, in fact, closely connected to Bird's philosophy of how children learn to dance. Experimentation within the Y's program had shown that students could not remember sequences if they were taught from a strictly functional or anatomical point of view. Rather, the teacher needed to draw on images and create vivid stories as a way of achieving desired movements. Bird recalled that "unless we had a very rich kind of imagery for them, they tended not to remember. If an exercise was taught totally mechanically, and I experimented with this . . . the children *never* remembered those exercises, but do something about the cat that's going to spit, their little bodies would immediately go into the kind of positioning you wanted."[10]

These pieces were consequently designed to be instructional in their combination of movement with imagery to express a particular point of view. Indeed, the very humor of the pieces was important because it gave the children an exhilarating experience of dance performance. Bunny Mendelsohn remembered that "the Merry-Go-Rounders expressed the joy of dance."[11] Humphrey, Berk, and Bird believed in the dignity of the human being and in leaving children with a positive feeling through their training.

• • •

DANCE AS PART OF CULTURE

One of the central goals of the Merry-Go-Rounders was to "produce *lively* but *culturally valuable* dance works." [12] For the presenters, this meant the inclusion of works on the program that would link dance to the lives of everyday people and show how it operates as a joyful expression of communal identity. In line with this philosophy, the last section of the performance was a clear tribute to dance as a part of culture (the first two pieces of the original repertory were narrative and not tied to any particular time and place). The specific dance chosen to illustrate the close connection was *Holiday in Israel*, by Berk, who was concurrently teaching folk dance and an occasional modern dance class at the Y. Berk was interested in the Merry-Go-Rounders as an outlet for his choreography; he had recently given up performing owing to an arthritic hip. His *Holiday in Israel* was based on the ancient festival of the first fruits, Shavuot, as celebrated in Israel.

Holiday in Israel was the last dance on the original program. As an introduction to the piece, the Ringmaster and Mechanic decided to go on an airplane trip. The Mechanic was the pilot and the Ringmaster the copilot. They announced to the audience, "We're taking an airplane trip around the world. . . .We're going to make stops in several countries along the way, to pick up new passengers." In order to take off, they suggested, "We'll need a great deal of help running the motor, like this: Mmmmmm Mmmmmmm Mmmmmmm." With the aid of the children in the audience, the imaginary plane took off.

Before arriving in Israel, the plane traveled to a number of countries where the children were introduced to different cultures' characteristic movements and songs. The idea behind this, as Mendelsohn later explained, was that "spectators could learn to recognize thematic dance movements by acting out simplified versions of them." [13] The children first flew to (imaginary) Mexico, where they learned the handclap and castanet clicks from a dance called the Chiapanecas. The next stop was the Swiss Alps, where they learned a song, and then on to India, where they were taught a story using the Indian hand gestures known as mudras: "Mechanic: In India they do a dance which is a sort of sign language of the hands and head. These signs are called mudras, and mudras can tell a whole story. For instance, this is a bird: Try it. And this bird lives in a tree. Make the tree. Then there is another bird, a

woodpecker. Face your hands out and put the heels of your hands together."
After India, the plane arrived in Israel:

> Mechanic: Pilot to co-pilot, pilot to co-pilot, we're over Israel.
> Ringmaster: Israel, and just in time for the festival of the first fruits.
>   Land the plane in Israel.

With this brief interlude, Berk's piece began.

Holiday in Israel focused on the joy and celebration expressed during
Shavuot, as displayed by different groups of Israeli settlers. The piece was
choreographed for ten dancers and consisted of a suite of five dances introduced by an offstage narrator. The first was "Salenu," a welcoming dance, in
which the dancers greeted one another while carrying baskets of fruit, bread,
and wheat. Different groups of settlers were then represented by individual
dances. According to the descriptions written in the Labanotation score,
"The Broiges Dance" represented the Polish settlers; the "Debka," the Yemen-
ites; and the "Dundai," the American immigrants. The piece ended with a
glorious hora, the newly established national dance of Israel.[14]

Each of these sections was inspired by a different folk dance and displayed
a markedly unique movement style.[15] The "Broiges Dance," for instance, was
loosely based on the *Broyges tants* traditionally performed at Eastern European weddings, in which two women dance with a handkerchief.[16] In Berk's
slow and stately version six young women took measured steps, pivoted, and
gracefully raised and lowered their arms. One of the special arm movements
involved a stylized clap over the head in which the palms met without making any sound. The main feature of the dance, however, was the use of
scarves as a way of creating designs in space. The high point of the piece
came as the group of dancers formed a circle, each with her inside hand
holding onto the end of the scarf of the person opposite. A star form was
created this way, and as the outside arm floated upward, the dancers slowly
circled clockwise. To end the piece, the star form split apart into two groups
of three, and the women performed variations on the opening walk and the
stylized clapping, making their way off at the downstage right corner.

The next dance, the "Debka," provided a strong contrast to the "Broiges
Dance." The narrator told the children, "Watch them closely. How strong are
their backs and how quick and intricate the movements of their feet."[17] The
"Debka" was much more forceful and vigorous than the first dance. In general, the dance used strong, direct movement that was performed with a tremendous sense of pride. Each step was clearly on the beat, the feet moving

precisely in continuous, complicated footwork. The body was held erect, and the dancers moved in unison, usually facing the audience. The dancers entered from the upstage left corner performing tiny hops, leaps, and heel clicks. They traveled in various linear formations around the stage, maintaining the pulse of the music with their small stamps and jumps. The highlights of the dance were the deep knee bends intermittently sprinkled throughout and then performed repeatedly in a flourish near the end. These final phrases had a feeling of contained energy, leading to large bursts. Like the first group, they exited by the downstage right corner.

If the first dance was slow and stately; the second, strong and solid; the third was lighthearted and joyous. The "Dundai," representing the American settlers, was a "gay and vibrant dance, full of turns and spins," as described by the narrator.[18] This dance involved two couples who used the whole stage space as they lightly hopped and spun alone and with their partners. The spins were freewheeling and fun as the dancers pulled away from each other and their dresses flew into the air. At various points the dancers changed partners and then performed a bouncy polka, once again whirling around the stage space. The section ended as it began, with small hops and turns, as the dancers exited stage right.

The grand finale of *Holiday in Israel* was the hora. The narrator set the mood: "It is evening now. Our tired but happy procession is arriving at a huge vineyard to place its offering. Then, one by one, all join hands in the big circle for the Hora, the national dance of Israel. In the circle, no one is first, and no one is last. All are together as one. This dance of joy and happiness moves faster and faster, wilder and wilder, far into the night."[19] As he finished speaking, the entire cast of dancers appeared carrying lighted torches and formed a large circle in the center of the stage. Each dancer grasped the torch of the person to the left until all were connected. The dance began quietly, with a feeling of containment as the dancers stepped firmly in place. Then, gradually, the group circled clockwise, with lilting crossover steps and a low syncopated leap as the legs kicked forward. As the dancers built momentum, the circle broke into two, then three smaller circles. At this point the music stopped as the dance came to its peak. Then the single large circle was once again formed as the dancers began moving again, circling as much as possible, with enthusiastic shouts of "*Hey!*" The lights had faded by this time; all that remained were the silhouettes of the torchlit dancers as their shadows loomed large in the background, creating a magical effect that was thrilling to see.[20]

Fred Berk's *Hora* from *Holiday in Israel.*
Dance Division, The New York Public Library for the Performing Arts, Astor, Lenox and
Tilden Foundations.

• • •

JEWS, ISRAEL, AND WORLD CULTURE

The inclusion of dances of other countries in Merry-Go-Rounders' productions reflected a general trend of the period. The company was created at a
time when interest in non-Western cultures was at an all-time high in America. The Second World War had exposed people to foreign locations and peoples, and during the early 1950s there was an explosion of information on
other countries. In the dance world, fascination soared with what were
termed "ethnic" dances, seen as the traditional dances tied to religious and
social customs of a people.[21] Dancers who specialized in such ethnic dances
performed all over New York during the period, and the Y's own performance and educational programming followed the trend. Children were
taught to understand and value dance forms of different cultures. In the
1950–51 season, for instance, a class on American Indian dancing was offered
at the Y by Tom Two Arrows.

How world culture was staged at the Y, however, was distinctly influenced
by its nature as a modernist, Jewish-run institution. The Y's particular enthu-

siasm for other cultures took shape in line with its long-standing practice of embracing general culture even while it asserted Jewish uniqueness. Through the narrative of the plane ride and the eventual trip to Israel, the Merry-Go-Rounders presented Jews at once as one ethnicity among many as well as unique in their cultural expressions. In particular, the specific choice of *Holiday in Israel* as the culminating dance was far from arbitrary, but it linked Jews with land and statehood, making them equals on the new postwar geopolitical world map. Indeed, the dance celebrated Israel as a haven of the democratic spirit, where Jewish people from different backgrounds—Poland, Yemen, and America—were welcome. For non-Jews, the imagery of acceptance and unity could be appreciated on a general level as a potential model for a pluralistic America. Here was a place where people were united despite differences in where they came from.

For American Jews, the narrative of celebration at the arrival of different settlers supported making aliyah at an imaginary, if not real, level. Here was the Jewish spirit at its most exalted acting as a magnet for young modern Jews eager to affiliate with their heritage. In recalling *Holiday in Israel*, Bonnie Bird reflected that it came at a very important time because Israel had recently achieved statehood. For her, Berk's piece provided the Merry-Go-Rounders with the means to introduce American children and their parents to Israel and to celebrate its creation. Clearly, the piece promoted the cause of Jewish nationalism by presenting such a positive and uplifting view of Israeli culture.[22] In Berk's dance, Jewish nationalist sentiment manifested itself in his choice to focus on the ancient festival of Shavuot and themes of "the land," a certain rustic simplicity, the joy of existence, and unification in spite of diversity. The appeal of such themes to Jewish Americans was immense. The folk dances symbolized Israel and a unified Jewish people and did so in a manner that seemed to bridge all differences. Whether you were religious or secular, rich or poor, young or old, you would be included in the circle of dancers in the hora.

• • •

RECEPTION AND INFLUENCE

The premiere of the Merry-Go-Rounders at the Kaufmann Auditorium enjoyed an enthusiastic reception. The *Dance Observer* review stated that "the Merry-Go-Rounders charmed their audience with an afternoon of chatter, singing, and dancing . . . a frequent adult problem was which to watch—the dancers or the audience."[23] The success of the performance launched the company, and for the next twenty years the Merry-Go-Rounders brought

Audience member, Merry-Go-Rounders, 1953.
92nd Street YM-YWHA Archives. Photographer: Albert Fenn/Time Pix.

pleasure and insight to hundreds of children and parents. While they often performed at the Y on Sunday afternoons, catering mostly to Upper East Side families, eventually schoolchildren were bused in from other areas around New York. The company also began touring the local school system, driving in a van to the various sites, with everyone pitching in to make the performances possible.

By 1964 most of the original people who had made the company successful had either left the Y or were no longer interested in the company's continuation. Joan Aboushar, the business manager of the group at the time, believed that it should be preserved and bought the rights to the music, along with the scripts, props, and costumes. She then transferred the Merry-Go-Rounders from under the Y's auspices and ran it as an independent commercial entity. Unfortunately, Aboushar's attempt to make the company a for-profit enterprise was unsuccessful, and in a few short years she was happy to pass it on to someone else. In 1968 the modern dancer Shirley Ubell purchased the group's properties and moved them to her Center for Modern Dance Education in New Jersey. There Ubell ran the Merry-Go-Rounders until 1973, when the enterprise became too expensive and she was forced to fold the company.[24]

Nonetheless, as long as the Merry-Go-Rounders was under the Y's protective custody, it was extremely successful in meeting the expectations of the Y's teachers regarding creative opportunities. *The Enchanted Balloons*, by Bonnie Bird (April 5, 1953), *Forest Adventure*, by Bunny Mendelsohn (March 14, 1954), and *Tyrolean Wedding*, by Fred Berk (March 14, 1954) were just a few of the pieces choreographed by the Y's staff. These individuals subsequently went on to work with other major institutions. Bird, for instance, joined the Laban Center faculty in England in 1974, where she remained an influential force to the end of her life.

The Merry-Go-Rounders dancers also gained invaluable experience that helped them in pursuing professional careers. In 1953, Bird hired the young Robert Joffrey to give the dancers ballet class as a warmup for the rehearsals. She stated, "We were giving them plenty of contemporary work. What we needed was something that got at detail, verticality, use of the arms, the articulation of the legs, particularly use of feet." Joffrey left the following year and was replaced by the well-known ballet teacher Alfredo Corvino, who concurrently taught at the Juilliard School. Corvino offered advanced technique for adults for two years at the Y. During the 1955 – 56 season his classes were held Monday through Thursday between 1:00 and 2:30 P.M. Along with the actual performance experience, this drew talented young performers to the company. The dancers "saw it as a marvelous preparation" for a professional career in dance, "and so the word of mouth was that it was a good thing to be in the Merry-Go-Rounders."

In particular, the company exposed the young dancers to folk dance and non-Western dance forms, helping them to see these as important elements for modern dance. With *Holiday in Israel*, for instance, Berk clearly stated, "This dance is based on folk material, but it should be performed by dancers trained in both modern and folk dance."[25] While some of the dancers were resistant to the work, finding it less serious than conventional modern dance of the time, they grew to appreciate it. The experience was best expressed by Jeff Duncan, who later cofounded Dance Theater Workshop as a major New York performance venue, a presenting organization, and a service for artists. Duncan believed he was a typical modern dancer until he met Berk and worked with the Merry-Go-Rounders, and then things radically changed as he began to learn folk dance steps and see them as an important part of his repertory: "I became very involved. Berk encouraged me and taught me many performance tools. He was one of those very few who cared about their art. He and Doris Humphrey were both like that and it made for a very sympathetic and strong directorship."[26]

The Merry-Go-Rounders was an unusual phenomenon, born from the special atmosphere of the 92nd Street Y. The institution made it possible for the interests of non-Jewish and Jewish modern dancers to coexist through the combined leadership of Humphrey, Bird, and Berk. Their efforts enriched the lives of children and adults, disseminated various contemporary conceptions of Jewishness, and provided a multicultural view of society that celebrated the variety of world culture. The staging of Jewish life in the context of global general culture and the opening up of modern dance resulting from this process, however, went far beyond the specific case of the Merry-Go-Rounders to the yearly programming of dance performances on the Kaufmann stage. There, Kolodney's ideals for the Y were played out in the most extended manner and had the greatest influence on the artistic and intellectual life of New York.

*I am very anxious to appear in New York this year with my group, and
your offer of the use of your lovely theatre is like manna to one who has seen no hopes
of ever making a debut in New York under the present conditions.*
Merle Hirsh[1]

(5)

PRODUCING ON THE EDGE

The Y as Debut Dance Hall and Alternative

Performance Space

• • •

Throughout the years the 92nd Street Y maintained an active educational program for children and adults. It is as a producing venue, however, that the Y is best known. Between 1935, when Kolodney first began presenting dance, to changes in the 1960s that reduced the number of recitals, more than 450 dance performances were held there, and this figure excludes the many lectures, demonstrations, and film showings with dance as their main focus.[2] Everybody, it seems, performed on the Y's stage at one time or another. This is especially true of those in the modern dance field, although dance mimes, ballet, and tap companies and dancers specializing in non-Western forms also appeared there. Some of the most celebrated performers include Angna Enters, Ruth St. Denis, Ted Shawn, Martha Graham, Erick Hawkins, Anna Sokolow, Agnes de Mille, José Limón, Pearl Lang, and Merce Cunningham. All could be seen at the Kaufmann Auditorium in memorable performances. Agnes de Mille once observed that "it is the veritable cradle of the modern-dance movement. It cannot be praised too highly for the enormous sponsoring work it provided."[3]

The sheer volume of dance presented at the Y is noteworthy in comparison to other theaters of the time. What particularly distinguished the Y within the New York dance landscape, however, was that it functioned as *the* place where many choreographers, dancers and their companies appeared in their first or near first New York appearances. The Y was not only a space for the already celebrated; it helped to make many people famous by launching their career in debut performances and providing them with support at a vulnerable time in their career. The spectrum is wide, encompassing many choreographers who have since become revered in the annals of dance history, from Pearl Primus, Katherine Litz, and Alvin Ailey to Ballet Caravan, the Joffrey Ballet, and Lester Horton's Choreo '53.

Also setting the Y apart was its ongoing support of dancers who, for whatever reason, were unable to find many performing opportunities elsewhere. Such dancers might be those unable to afford a Broadway theater, who were insufficiently popular, or who worked primarily in other cities, or they might be from an ethnic or religious minority, such as African American or Jewish. The Y's support of potentially marginalized artists also went beyond debut opportunities for the young to long-term relationships with lesser-known and minority choreographers, which sometimes extended over several decades. The African American dancer Pearl Primus returned frequently to the Y after it had launched her career, and Jewish dancers like Anna Sokolow, Sophie Maslow, and Pearl Lang maintained lifelong connections to the institution even as they found performing opportunities elsewhere. Throughout the 1950s the Y continued to support many female modern dancers, like Valerie Bettis, May O'Donnell, Betty Lind, Marie Marchowsky, Mary Anthony, Ruth Currier, and Natanya Neumann, who otherwise had limited outlets for their choreographic efforts.

As a frequent debut performance space for New York and world premieres, the Y acted, in the 1930s and 1940s especially, as an incubator of new dance. It provided a space for dancers to experiment with elements of the modern style as it took hold and matured within America. The support of diverse artists, for its part, meant that the kind of new dance being developed often involved research into the integration of so-called ethnic elements, as minority artists made reference to African, Spanish, or Jewish elements in their works. At other times it was the presentation of diverse kinds of performers in one space, from tap-ballet dancer Paul Draper to the Spanish-ballet blends of Carmelita Maracci, that challenged a single, purist notion of the nature of contemporary dance.

From the position of the dance world, Jewish support of contemporary dance through the productions and audiences at the Y was very important. The ongoing support of second- and third-generation modern dancers provided steady institutionalized support of the style of modern dance, helping to reenforce its status as a serious dance form. Perhaps more significantly, although not always evident, was the importance of the Y in providing a steady alternative to the increasingly commercialized downtown performance spaces and to the lionized "Big Four," who gained in reputation as the century progressed. In 1953, when the Y briefly stopped offering its support to less-established artists, many cried out that this meant the complete eradication of a place that supported dancers in trying out new ideas, either to succeed or to fail. The point made clear how important the Y had become in supplying the kind of generous patronage so crucial to the evolution of the art form.

For the Jews whose values the Y most closely reflected, the productions fulfilled their desire to participate in contemporary, general culture within a Jewish framework. These Jews had largely (though not exclusively) exchanged religious observance for the contemplation of art, and there was great satisfaction in seeing the celebrated names of the period as a means of personal and collective inspiration. The presence of dancers like Graham also brought status to the Jewish community, signaling their acceptance by the culture producers of America. As for the support of unknowns and minority artists, that was another, although more public and influential way, along with the educational classes and lectures, to promote Jewish causes within a carefully constructed democratic and multicultural context that reflected the long-standing ideals of the institution.

• • •

SERIES AND POLICIES

The Y produced various dance series over the years, the terms and circumstances of which were constantly changing and overlapping. Beginning in 1935, the Y had presented recitals as part of the Major Subscription Series, which offered the public a mixture of entertainment for a single low price.[4] In 1937, however, the majority of dance recitals were separated out and combined on their own subscription series, known as the Dance Theatre Subscription Series.[5] This subscription series remained more or less intact until 1952, when it was discontinued. Throughout this period individual dance recitals also were presented by the Y's Dance Center. In the late 1950s, a subscription series was reinstituted, this time as the Dance Center Subscription Series.[6]

The performance aspect of the Y's dance programming reveals the complexity of the convergence between the Y and the dance world. Policies regarding the use of the Kaufmann Auditorium were not decided on the basis of any one set of criteria. Instead, they resulted from a constant exchange between Kolodney and various advisers from the dance community, including Martin, Horst, Humphrey, and members of Kolodney's specially established Dance Teachers Advisory Committee. Kolodney relied heavily on these individuals in trying to relieve himself of the strain of decision making and administering the programming. He valued their informed opinions and clearly wanted to harness influential forces in the dance community to help to make the Y a major cultural center in the city.

At the same time, Kolodney remained in charge of the recitals and initiated a number of key policies in line with the needs of the Y and his own deeply held ideals. As previously noted, the Y's location outside the heart of the theater district, and its sectarian, recreational basis situated the institution in a liminal space on the edge of the dance community. From this unstable yet potentially innovative threshold, Kolodney balanced both the established and fringe forces of the dance world, supporting the celebrated dancers as well as less well-known performers. Guiding his programming decisions was his vision for the Y as a site of refuge for all artists and lovers of the arts, including those who found little support elsewhere. His deep belief in providing performance opportunities to artists of all backgrounds guided him toward dancers with limited New York performance experience, whether they were out-of-towners, young, or from minorities—especially Jewish and African American. Through these efforts, Kolodney helped to broaden modern dance to embrace diversity in terms of ethnicity, race, age, experience, and stylistic experimentation.

• • •

PRESENTING LESSER-KNOWN DANCERS
ON THE Y'S STAGE, 1936–39

During his first two seasons at the Y, Kolodney designed the Major Subscription Series as a showcase for the best in contemporary drama and dance. As outlined earlier, in the first year of the series, 1935–36, recitals were given mostly by well-known dancers: Graham, Tamiris, and Humphrey-Weidman, along with Zemach and Sokolow. The following year Graham and Humphrey-Weidman returned, but Kolodney expanded the number of dance recitals to incorporate performers and companies less familiar to New

York audiences. Ballet Caravan, for instance, was a touring company newly formed by Lincoln Kirstein to promote American ballet. The company gave its first New York performances at the Y on October 31 and November 1, 1936. Carmelita Maracci, who lived and performed primarily in Los Angeles, gave her initial East Coast performance at the Y on April 11, 1937. Edna Guy and Alison Burroughs directed the Negro Dance Evening held on March 7, 1937. This historic recital was one of the first in America to present the work of African American choreographers as serious artistic dance rather than entertainment. The evening included performances by Asadata Dafora Horton and his African dancers, Edna Guy, and Clarence Yates and marked Katherine Dunham's New York debut.

The early transformation of the Y into a debut dance hall was easily made. The mixed success of the 1935–36 season had demonstrated that Kolodney would need to seriously address the fact that the Kaufmann stage existed outside the daily newspaper review circuit. Focusing on lesser-known dancers allowed him to begin to fulfill a personal interest in supporting relative unknowns and to simultaneously distinguish the Y from other venues in the city, thereby making up for its awkward location.

Kolodney's early enthusiasm for and sensitivity to little-known artists is well demonstrated by his treatment of Carmelita Maracci, the fiery and brilliantly talented West Coast dancer, who combined ballet with Spanish dance. According to Lee Freeson, Maracci's husband, Carmelita arrived in New York in the late 1930s through the encouragement of Erin O'Brien Moore.[7] Moore was an actress in New York who had studied with Maracci in California and become enthusiastic about her work. Freeson explains that Moore engaged the assistance of her lover at the time, the producer Sam Grisman, to present Maracci in New York. The details of the arrangement are unclear, for it seems that Moore lent Maracci some money to help to pay for her transportation, but no formal contract was signed.[8] During Maracci's trip to New York, Moore and Grisman ended their relationship; and out of anger toward Moore, Grisman refused to help Maracci when she arrived in the city. Agnes de Mille, in her colorful description of the event in *Portrait Gallery*, stresses that Carmelita "was abandoned."[9]

It seems that while the problems were occurring with Grisman, Maracci was invited by Kolodney to perform on the Major Subscription Series.[10] Benjamin Zemach was unable to make his advertised April date and had recommended Maracci, whom he knew and greatly admired from his years in California. Kolodney agreed to present her and, in extreme contrast to the

Carmelita Maracci.
92nd Street YM-YWHA Archives.

ex-manager, treated her with the utmost care and compassion. In accordance with detailed directions received from Freeson in a lengthy letter of March 28, 1937, Kolodney made sure all the props were in order for Maracci's performance and directed the backstage help to attend to her needs respectfully and efficiently.

Maracci's appearance at the Y proved an unprecedented success, exploding onto the New York scene with great effect. *Dance Observer* called her "one of the most exciting dancers to visit New York this season. . . . The Y.M.H.A. is to be complimented upon its initiative in securing her for a performance."[11] Maracci mesmerized New Yorkers with her smoldering passion and unique movement style. Here were wonderfully spiraling hands, a spine that arched proudly, and dazzling technical footwork. It was the beginning of a close relationship between the Y and Maracci. On April 26, following the performance, Freeson wrote to Kolodney, "She has particularly asked me to tell you that at no time in her career has she been more pleased with anyone than with her association with you and of the kindness and understanding of the men back stage."[12] Shortly afterward, Carmelita personally wrote that she "would prefer to appear for the Y.M.H.A. than for any other organization or sponsor."[13] The following year Kolodney wrote requesting a repeat appearance. Maracci, unable to accept, nevertheless made it clear that she planned to return sometime in the future and that she would never forget Kolodney's kindness in the face of her earlier mistreatment: "What occurred previous to my dancing at the Y.M.H.A. is a horrible memory and you will never know the state of mind I was in the night of my appearance. I shall truly dance as I am supposed to when I make my next appearance. Until then please accept my heartest [*sic*] thanks."[14]

The success of the dance recitals on the 1936–37 Major Subscription Series, especially of little-known artists like Maracci, was such that Kolodney decided to expand the dance recitals even farther the following season. In his proposal for 1937, Kolodney suggested separating the dance recitals from the rest of the Major Subscription Series. He would establish what he called a Dance Theatre, which would be run as a distinct subscription series focusing exclusively on dance. In establishing this series, Kolodney made it clear that he wanted to focus on talented young dancers and their groups, as opposed to the more established choreographers: "We have had to turn several hundred away at each major dance recital. It is therefore planned to start a dance theatre on a subscription basis, which will present dance recitals particularly by talented young dancers and their groups, on alternate Sunday afternoons. Like the Major Subscription Series and the Cinema Guild, this is to be conducted on a self-supporting basis."[15]

The decision to concentrate on younger dancers was fueled by the success of the debut recitals and the large number of requests Kolodney was currently fielding from young dancers who wanted to use the auditorium. The inclusion of dance in the Major Subscription Series had demonstrated that there was an attractive new venue in the city overseen by a man sympathetic to dancers' concerns. In the mid-1930s the only institution producing a series for young dancers was the New School for Social Research, where, in the spring of 1935, Sophia Delza had begun her fortnightly subscription series, "Modern Recitals," held on the small circular stage that was more of a platform than a real theater. Dancers who were struggling to find a genuine theater in which to perform turned to Kolodney to ask if they could use the Kaufmann hall. Kolodney, eager to help them, believed that a change in policy would allow him to meet their demands while satisfying his own desire to carve a special place for the Y.

The Y's Dance Theatre was subsequently conceived as an annual subscription series of recitals offered on Sunday afternoons. This series was to run more or less in place from 1937 to 1952, attracting hundreds of dancers and thousands of audience members to the Y.[16] While Kolodney remained committed to the more youthful and less familiar members of the dance community, he also continued to present more-seasoned choreographers. Over the years the Dance Theatre presented myriad performers at all levels of experience and celebrity, making it difficult to discern any single direction to the programming, although Kolodney's choices perfectly reflected his varied interests in contemporary art, Jewish culture, and social justice.

The adaptable and decidedly flexible nature of Kolodney's approach to presenting was rooted, in part, in his stance regarding the use of the Kaufmann Auditorium. The Y's auditorium policy, as initially set down in the early 1930s, suggests that the Kaufmann hall could not be rented and could be used only by groups in some way associated with the institution. Following this policy, an Auditorium Committee was established that considered requests and granted or denied permission to use the hall. Clearly, this procedure worked well as long as the Y served the immediate Jewish community and requests to use the space were limited in scope and nature (such as renting the hall for a meeting of a local Jewish agency). Once the Kaufmann Auditorium became a substantial cultural locus under his jurisdiction, however, Kolodney had to decide how to control its use—would he rent the hall or personally decide who would perform there?

With the Major Subscription Series, Kolodney chose the latter option. He determined who would appear on the series and paid them a negotiated fee. However, with the decision to start the Dance Theatre he had to resolve the issue of the Y's accessibility. Was he going to let the hall be rented to anyone and everyone or control its use in some way? In the end, Kolodney walked a fine line between these possibilities by making it appear as if anyone could use the auditorium while he carefully controlled its handling. On the one hand, he clearly established that no outside rentals were allowed—people would not be able to simply rent the theater for a set price. At the same time, he made it known that any dancer or company could *apply* for use of the Kaufmann theater (most commonly by writing him a letter asking to perform there). If Kolodney was interested in their work, there was then a variety of options open to them, the most common being some kind of equitable cost-sharing policy, in which the expense of producing the concert was split between the Y and the artist.[17] Taking this flexible position allowed Kolodney to maintain control over who performed at the Y while making it potentially accessible to anyone. This strategy gave the Y an air of openness yet permitted Kolodney to act as producer. Most significantly, it allowed him to work in affiliation with the central, influential forces of the dance world while retaining his own varied agendas.

Kolodney's desire to oversee the Y's stage can be seen in the way he went about publicizing the Dance Theatre idea. Rather than accepting random requests, he actively sought advice on who should perform from numerous members of the dance community. Letters, which explained his concept and requested the names of dancers and groups who were "competent to present a program for at least an hour and a half,"[18] went out to a dozen or so people, including Frances Hawkins, Edna Ocko, Mikhail Mordkin, Martha Hill, Mary Wood Hinman, John Martin, Louis Horst, Stephen Karnot, Lincoln Kirstein, Gluck Sandor, Felicia Sorel, and May O'Donnell. In one such letter, Kolodney stated that he would like to "offer talented young dancers and dance groups, who can not afford to hire the Theatre Guild or Town Hall, an opportunity to present recitals on a professional stage." He continued: "I feel particularly keenly about this problem because throughout my brief stay at the 'Y', I have had numerous calls, letters and visits from both unknown and fairly well known dancers who wish to rent the auditorium, which, of course is not permitted under the 'Y' regulations. My plan amounts practically to an offer of the free use of the auditorium to some of the very persons who wish to pay rent for it."[19]

During the first two years of the Dance Theatre's existence, many of the dancers who performed on the series were on the lists returned to Kolodney from these individuals. An example is the Hampton Institute Creative Dance Group, whose name was submitted (among others) by May O'Donnell.

O'Donnell was a soloist with Graham's company and also a dance teacher. The Hampton group, featuring black dancers, was very interested in taking advantage of the new policy. In May 1937 one of the directors, Charles Williams, wrote to Kolodney of the group's hope to perform there the next season. On November 14, 1937, the company appeared at the Y in an evening of choreography by Williams and Charlotte Moton Kennedy. They performed *Juba, Cake-Walk, Negro Spirituals, Labor Rhythms,* and *African Dances,* which displayed a richly conceived range of styles, including social, modern, and African dance.

Kolodney's reliance on others in choosing the performers for his series shows the extent to which he was willing to depend on outside advice. Far from opening the Y to anyone, or any company, Kolodney carefully chose who would be presented based on his inquiries. His aim was to discourage mediocrity by choosing people with established credentials, though clearly this limited the possibilities for the Y as a performance venue. However, by writing to a number of people, Kolodney received a cross-section of opinions from the dance community that allowed for a certain degree of diversity. John Martin, who clearly represented the more mainstream perspective, provided a list of five people, all of whom were fairly well known: Esther Junger, Benjamin Zemach, Anna Sokolow, the Catherine Littlefield Ballet, and Hanya Holm. At the other end of the spectrum, Edna Ocko, a Jewish writer mostly active in left-wing circles, brought the more radical dancers to Kolodney's attention. Her list of ten names included Miriam Blecher, Lily Mehlman, Sophie Maslow, Jane Dudley, Lillian Shapero, Lil Liandre, and Fe Alf. Ocko wrote during the 1930s for the leftist publication *New Theatre* as well as for *New Masses* and *Daily Worker,* where she promoted the efforts of the revolutionary dance movement. Her inclusion in Kolodney's mailing demonstrates his willingness to familiarize himself with the more political wing of the dance movement, then an important expression of Jewish working-class values.

The first year of its existence (1937–38) the Dance Theatre consisted of eighteen performances. Out of these, Hanya Holm and Ted Shawn were the only prominent names on the series. Most of the other performers were presented as the result of the new policy. Along with the Hampton Institute Creative Dance Group, dancers in this category consisted of Lil Liandre, Eleanor King, and Lillian Shapero, all of whom had been recommended to Kolodney by either Edna Ocko or May O'Donnell.

Other young choreographers were presented at the Y under the sponsorship of the American Dance Association (ADA) on three separate afternoons in November 1937 and January and February 1938. The ADA was an umbrella organization formed in 1937 from the amalgamation of the New Dance League, the Dancers Association (helping dancers survive economically and artistically), and the Dance Guild (organizing forums on dance-related subjects). Kolodney had contacted Louis Horst, who was currently in charge of the Artistic Committee of the organization, to assist in cases where dancers were not well known to him. He wrote to Horst in October 1937: "In accordance with the conversation we had in my office, I have referred these persons [no names given] to you . . . I should appreciate getting a report from your committee which would guide me in my decision to these applications." Horst and Kolodney occasionally corresponded regarding the possibilities of various dancers. If the dancer was unknown to Horst as well, he or she was invited to audition before the ADA Artistic Committee. Horst either recommended dancers for their own performance at the Y or arranged with Kolodney to present them with others on a recital sponsored by the ADA. The first of the ADA performances was held at the Kaufmann on November 21, 1937, featuring José Limón, Sophie Maslow, Jane Dudley, and Lily Mehlman, all young dancers who were growing in popularity at the time. Their performance consisted of thirteen different dances, mostly solos, which were either character studies, such as Mehlman's *Girl*, or dances with a left-wing bias, like Maslow's *Two Songs about Lenin*.

Horst's central role at the Y in supporting young dancers demonstrates his openness to fresh talent despite his strong affiliations with Graham as her musical director.[20] Horst was involved in many aspects of the modern dance world, as pianist, composer, teacher of choreography, and editor of *Dance Observer*, which he had founded in 1934. During the 1930s, Horst taught at numerous institutions, including the Neighborhood Playhouse, Bennington College, Sarah Lawrence College, and Teachers College and Barnard College of Columbia University, where he influenced and encouraged many of the young dancers to perform and choreograph. At the same time, it is necessary to point out that Horst's conception of choreography was highly defined and to a great extent inflexible, meaning that he was certainly not enthusiastic about everyone's experiments. Horst supported attention to formal concerns through the careful use of musical structures as a guide to choreography, and he demanded precise aesthetic reasoning for every movement. At the same time, Horst's insistence on adhering to formal concepts of structure and to the abstraction of dance materials at the outset of the creative process gave form and intelligence to a practice that had until that time largely been intuitively (and frequently, poorly) conceived. In so doing he prescribed a set of boundaries that established the norm of the time regarding choreographic method.

From 1938 to 1939 the Dance Theatre was repeated, with a larger number of prominent dancers included on the series. Kolodney soon discovered that, in order to protect the Y from losing money, it was necessary to maintain even greater control over who performed there. People who were not celebrities simply did not draw an audience, despite his fairly aggressive advertising attempts. The result was that he combined better-known with lesser-known dancers in more equal proportions. The series presented Agnes de Mille, Humphrey-Weidman, and Angna Enters, along with the newly formed Theatre Dance Company, in Eleanor King's *Icaro* and also a debut performance by Juana de Laban, Gertrude Ulmann, and Erica Stolzberg, all currently teaching at the Y.

At this time, in the late 1930s, Kolodney was one of two presenters of contemporary dance. Joseph Mann continued to offer his Students Dance Recitals Series, which also consisted of a subscription series of dance performances at a single low price. Mann presented about ten dancers a year, similar to the Y. And every year a few of the same dancers would perform on both series, appearing for Mann on Saturday night and for Kolodney, on Sunday afternoon. This was the case with Graham in 1938, who danced at Washington Irving High School on November 26 and at the Y on November 27. What now differentiated the Y, in contrast to the 1935–36 inaugural season, was Kolodney's interest in helping young dancers. According to the historian Margaret Lloyd, Mann was more interested in introducing "proven" dancers to new audiences than in helping to develop talent.[21] Mann's idea was to bring the best in dance to people whom otherwise could not afford it. This is borne out by looking at the dancers appearing on his series. For the 1938–39 Students Dance Recital Series performers included Carola Goya, Ted Shawn, Martha Graham, Humphrey-Weidman, Helen Tamiris, Hanya Holm, Angna Enters, and the well-known German dancer Harald Kreutzberg, all well-established performers at the time.

● ● ●

UNIVERSITY AFFILIATIONS AND THE
DANCE TEACHERS ADVISORY COMMITTEE

In the summer of 1939, Kolodney decided to further develop his idea for including young artists by more fully engaging the educational community in his efforts. In his presentation to the board for the 1939–40 season, Kolodney proposed that the dance series be "sponsored by representatives of the universities, colleges and high schools, who are interested in promoting the Dance Theatre at the 'Y.'"[22] As part of his new plan, Kolodney established an adivisory committee chaired by Mary O'Donnell, head of the Dance Department at Teachers College, with additional participants from New York University, Barnard, and Hunter Colleges.

Little seems to have been accomplished in the first year of the committee's existence. The group rarely met, and Kolodney acted on his own in presenting dancers whom he was by now familiar with, including Maracci, Sokolow, and Humphrey-Weidman. The following year, however, the committee—now called the Dance Teachers Advisory Committee—became more active. The 1940–41 season saw the initiation of recitals by the dance clubs of Hunter College, New York University, Bennington, and Sarah Lawrence. These groups gave demonstrations of modern dance technique at the Y, followed by dances created by the students and directors of the troupes. In the first such recital, on April 6, 1941, for instance, Hunter College presented *Techniques of Movement* followed by a series of dances entitled *Creation, People of the Land, The Last Flower,* and *Folk Themes.*

These university concerts appear to have been the direct outcome of an early discussion between Kolodney and Martha Hill, who was in charge of the dance program at Bennington College and very involved in dance education. She had written to Kolodney in May 1937, stating that "it might be interesting to give an afternoon or a series of two afternoons to college and school dance groups." Kolodney's response at the time was enthusiastic: "I was particularly interested in your suggestion that we invite college and university dance groups to perform at the 'Y.'" In 1940, with the help of Mary O'Donnell, Hunter College's Eugenie Schein, and Hermine Sauthoff of NYU, Kolodney was able to follow through with this idea.

The fruitful relationship between the Y and the college dance system lasted well into the 1960s.[23] The presentation of dance clubs proved to be a successful way of introducing university and college students to a professional setting and high school audience members to modern dance as an art form. The president of the Vassar College dance group, participating in a concert in 1942, enthusiastically wrote: "This is just to tell you how very much our Dance Group enjoyed dancing for you, and how invaluable we feel the experience was. Also it was very exciting to see just what other colleges are doing, as we have had almost no opportunity to do so in the past."[24] The value of this program was also remarked by leaders in the modern dance world who recognized the important role played by the universities in legitimizing modern dance. *Dance Observer* was an especially enthusiastic supporter of the new recitals. A reviewer of the 7th Annual Demonstration of College Dance Groups, held in 1945, for instance, exclaimed: "The Dance Center of the Y.M.H.A. should be given a round of solid applause for sponsoring these annual college demonstrations. That we can see what is happening with dance in the colleges, that these college groups are given the opportunity to perform for a sizable audience in the metropolitan area—is more than highly commendable. . . . Performances like these weld the modern dance in the colleges into a more well-defined path of activity for the future."[25]

In 1941, Horst agreed to become the new chair of the Dance Teachers Advisory Committee. There were now a total of eleven members, including Mary O'Donnell, Schein, and Sauthoff, as well as Muriel Stuart and Bessie Schönberg. The last two were important new additions, since Stuart taught at the School of American Ballet, and Schönberg was chair of the Dance Department at Sarah Lawrence, among other places. While the committee rarely met as a whole and the members were not active in all Kolodney's decisions, the Dance Teachers Advisory Committee fine-tuned Kolodney's more informal method of advisement and was given a significant degree of responsibility.[26] In particular, the committee helped to oversee the initiation of an annual concert specially devoted to young talented dancers. This concert was open to all dancers, whether student or professional (for in the early 1940s distinctions were often fuzzy between the two).

The first of the recitals of young dancers was held on January 18, 1942. This performance featured six people: Nelle Fisher, Nina Fonaroff, Eleanor King, Welland Lathrop, Noami Aleh-Leaf, and Elizabeth Waters. Each of the dancers presented two or three solos that ranged from character studies and mood pieces to theatrical folk dances. While Fonaroff danced in a Graham style, for instance, Aleh-Leaf presented colorful folk dances from different countries, including Palestine. The response was so positive that Kolodney immediately proceeded with plans to institutionalize the recital as a yearly occurrence.

In May 1942, auditions were held for dancers interested in appearing on the next annual Audition Winners' Concert. The auditions were held on Sunday afternoons and consisted of twenty-minute slots during which the young performer was asked to show two to three pieces to the Dance Teachers Advisory Committee. It was assumed that the best of these dancers would be presented on the following Audition Winners' Concert, though in cases where the dancers were viewed as outstanding, it was possible for them to be considered for a future recital with only one or two others or even by themselves. In a 1942 letter to the youthful Sybil Shearer, Kolodney explained the procedure: "If you pass the audition, the following are the possibilities. . . . You may be invited to appear as one of five or six dancers. . . . If the committee considers you an unusual dancer, you may be invited to take half of a program. . . . If the Committee should feel that you are a "discovery," and on the same level of ability as some of America's great dancers, you would be invited to give a complete program."[27]

The uniqueness of the Audition Winners' Concerts was such that John Martin decided to break his rule regarding covering recitals outside the theater district. On February 21, 1943, he published a rave account of the second Audition Winners' Concert, focusing on Primus as the star of the afternoon: "If Miss Primus walked away with the lion's share of the honors, it was partly because her material was more theatrically effective, but also partly because she is a remarkably gifted artist . . . if ever a young dancer was entitled to a company of her own and the freedom to do what she chooses with it, she is it. Last week's audience literally yelled for more of her, and more there will assuredly be.[28]

The Audition Winners Concert was held annually until the folding of the Dance Teachers Advisory Committee in 1953. Audition winners through the years included Robin Gregory, Matti Haim, Gertrude Lippincott, Carolyn Wilson (February 1944); Jessica Fleming, Eva Desca Garnet, Rheba Koren, Joan Miller, Shirley Wimmer (April 1945); Helaine Blok, Ann Halprin, Miriam Pandor, Ethel Winter, Yuriko (December 1945); and Ronne Aul, Rena Gluck, Nachum and Dina, Nina Caiserman, Lucas Hoving (November 1949) (see Appendix B for a complete list). In 1949, *Dance Observer* hailed the concerts as a way for young dancers to get their start as professional performers: "Graduation from these concerts has meant the beginning of most of today's young leaders in the dance. . . . The Dance Teachers Advisory Committee and William Kolodney of the YM-YWHA deserve credit for this [well-organized program], as well as their part in choosing the performers from among the scores who usually audition."[29]

· · ·

PRODUCING OUTSIDERS AND MINORITIES, 1941–47

While Kolodney was remaking the Y as a stage for young dancers, he continued to promote it as a place for emerging artists from outside New York. In the fall of 1941 he initiated, with the support of the Dance Teachers Advisory

Committee, a policy to "present one new dancer from out of town."[30] The first of these was Virginia Johnson, a modern dancer who traveled from California to make her New York debut at the Y on March 1, 1942. The performance of her dance-drama *The Eternal Heroine,* which "tells six episodes of Woman . . . as pioneer, saint, lady, jitterbug, gay, sad, cruel and sublime," was well received.[31] The review in the *YMHA Bulletin* claimed that "Virginia Johnson and her three accompanying dancers swept into New York City Sunday, March 1, like a refreshing breeze from the West Coast."[32] Lucille Ricker, a member of the Johnson group, was enchanted with the experience, writing, "Mrs. Johnson was very much pleased with the lovely write up given her by your Y.M.H.A. paper . . . I would like very much to have one of the papers as a keepsake and a memory of a thrilling time . . . thank you all for making our stay in the theater so enjoyable."[33]

At this time, Kolodney continued to book a number of young African American dancers. He engaged Katherine Dunham to open the fall season at the Y on November 10, 1940, just a few months after her successful off-Broadway debut at the Windsor Theatre. For this concert, Dunham presented nine pulsating numbers, including *Primitive Rhythms* and *Le Jazz 'Hot.'* On May 16, 1943, La Belle Rosette (Beryl McBurnie) presented *Antilliana,* a full program of dancing from the Caribbean, with a company that included Pearl Primus and Al Bledger.

Dancers specializing in dance based on Spanish, flamenco, and Jewish sources also appeared sporadically at the Y through the 1940s. In addition to Carmelita Maracci, other celebrated performers included Argentinita, Carmen Amaya, and Rosario and Antonio. Many of these dancers already enjoyed an established following but were nevertheless seeking respectable and affordable stages to appear in New York. Jewish dancers included Zemach (familiar to Y audiences by this time), who performed at the Y in 1941, and Hadassah, who first performed her highly expressive solo *Shuvi Nafshi* there on February 12, 1947. Hadassah (Spira Epstein), was a celebrated, deeply spiritual dancer from Israel who had immigrated to the United States with her family in 1924 and made a name for herself as a performer of Jewish, Hindu, and other so-called ethnic dance forms. Along with being a celebrated soloist, she created her own company that debuted at the Y in 1950.

The period between 1940 and 1947 witnessed the crystallization of modern dance as an established, valid art form. Kolodney's policies at the Y contributed to the growth of this style while distinguishing the Y as a prestigious venue open to young dancers. At the same time, the 1940s brought competition in the form of the Humphrey-Weidman Studio Theatre, located at 108 West Sixteenth Street. This studio performance space opened in the fall of 1940 with classes and performances by Humphrey and Weidman. In February 1942, the Dudley-Maslow-Bales trio made their New York debut there, before performing at the Y in May. Between 1942 and 1944 the Studio Theatre was a hotbed of activity. Many of the young modern dancers who performed at the Y also danced there, such as Jean Erdman, Nina Fonaroff, Valerie Bettis, Erick Hawkins, and Virginia Johnson.

However, the Studio Theatre was relatively short-lived. In 1944, with the dissolution of the Humphrey-Weidman partnership, the space, although available for rental, was no longer as lively; it grew less busy through the decade, and by 1948 few recitals occurred there. Moreover, the Studio Theatre did not display the same breadth of programming as did the Y, which also constantly presented the big names from all forms of dance—Martha Graham, Angna Enters, and Paul Draper. Such celebrities did not appear at the Studio Theatre, nor did the likes of Paul Robeson, the Budapest String Quartet, or Jascha Heifetz, all of whom appeared at the Y, for example, during the 1942–43 season. In this case, the broad sweep and excellence of the Y's overall cultural program continued to distinguish the institution within the city and provided an important larger context in which the dance recitals took place.

· · ·

TRANSITIONS AND SUPPORT
OF "ETHNIC" DANCE, 1947–53

Between 1947 and 1953, America's dance landscape changed and with it the nature of the Y's performance series. The postwar years witnessed a dramatic transformation in the dance world as ballet became increasingly popular. The artistic success of Ballet Society at City Center in April 1948 led to its joining the prestigious complex of the New York City Center later that year. The first season of the newly named New York City Ballet occurred between October 11, 1948, and January 23, 1949, when the company danced twenty-four performances to enthusiastic reviews.[34]

At the same time, the post-Second World War exposure to other cultures was leading to the explosion of interest in ethnic dance. This enthusiasm was well reflected in the Ethnologic Theatre of La Meri (Russell Meriwether Hughes). Opened in the fall of 1943, the theater was small, with seating for about 250 people. Throughout the late 1940s and up to 1956 it featured the work of La Meri and her Natya (Hindu) Dancers as well as visiting artists. At the same time, a program called "Around the World with Dance and Song" was supervised by Hazel Muller at the Museum of Natural History. Muller's subscription series ran with great popularity from 1949 to 1952 and featured a wide range of dancers who specialized in African, Indian, Spanish, Irish, English, Hawaiian, and Chinese dance styles.[35]

During this period, changes also occurred at the Y that suggested modern dance was experiencing troubled times. From 1948 to 1951 many single recitals were presented as individual events by the Dance Center along with the Dance Theatre Subscription Series. For the most part, the events that were part of the series did well, drawing more than five hundred people to each performance (the house held around 855). José Limón, for instance, gave the first New York performance of the tragic *Moor's Pavane* at the Y on November 6, 1949, to a large crowd. Portraying the love, jealousy, and intrigue arising in the handkerchief episode from Shakespeare's *Othello*, this is considered one of Limón's greatest masterpieces. The many single recitals of less prominent dancers, however, did much worse. Audience statistics for individual performances for 1949 – 50 and 1951 – 52, for instance, show that about seventeen recitals had fewer than five hundred people in the audience.

Meanwhile, in a 1951 *Dance Magazine* article on various New York booking agents, Doris Hering wrote, "Mr. Kolodney is finding that his audiences are asking for more and more ethnic dance."[36] Indeed, by the 1952 – 53 season, dancers working in a wide variety of dance styles abounded at the Y, such as the Afro-Haitian dancer Jean-Léon Destiné, Spanish dancers Sinda Iberia and Vela Montoya, and classical Indian dancers Dilip Kumar Roy and Indira Devi. Most of the same dancers also appeared on the Museum of Natural History's "Around the World with Dance and Song." In fact, Hazel Muller was listed on the Y's Dance Teachers Advisory Committee for the 1952 – 53 season, demonstrating just how central "ethnic" dance had become.

An East-West Series was also established at the Y in cooperation with the East-West Association, a local New York organization promoting cross-cultural awareness. Kolodney started this series in the fall of 1947 so that "more attention [would] be paid to inter-national relations, inter-cultural understanding and the contemporary scene." A series of ten programs was proposed, "dramatizing the peoples of the world through their music, art and cultural patterns."[37] The 1947 – 48 series presented programs on Palestine, India, the Philippines, Mexico, Latin America, the Caribbean (presented by the Experimental Group of the Katherine Dunham school), and Slavic peoples. These programs involved large casts in theatrical folk dances from the various countries. They satisfied the postwar fascination with other cultures and spawned new interest in dance forms other than ballet and modern dance. They also provided an opportunity for the Y to promote Jewish culture within the framework of world culture; as with the Merry-Go-Rounders, the representation involved conveying implicit messages regarding Jews as equals in a multicultural world.

If Kolodney's main programming efforts during the early 1950s displayed a sensitivity to the general conditions of the dance world, there were still times when he took a chance on unknown performers. The most dramatic of these was his presentation of Lester Horton's company on March 28–29, 1953. Horton was an extremely innovative and influential choreographer, who had spent his life on the West Coast. There he had founded a racially mixed school and performing group that included such dancers as Carmen de Lavallade, Joyce Trisler, James Truitte, and Alvin Ailey. Kolodney had invited Horton to appear at the Y on March 27, 1938, but at the last minute Horton telegraphed to say he was unable to come and wished Kolodney success. Fifteen years later, with the encouragement of Carmelita Maracci, Horton finally appeared at the Y. This was Horton's second New York performance but the first and only serious recital he was ever to give there in a legitimate theater. (In 1943, Horton's group had performed for the opening of a lavish nightclub, the Folies Bergère.) In his biography of Horton, Larry Warren observes: "The 'Y' was the logical place for the debut. For years, under the direction of Dr. William Kolodney, it had provided a showcase for dancers, poets, and musicians who needed a medium-sized New York theater that was nominal in cost. Maracci herself had performed there, and Janet Collins, whom both she and Horton had trained, had been acclaimed four years earlier at the East Coast debut on that stage."[38]

On the Y program were Horton's *Dedications in Our Time*, *The Beloved*, *Scenes with Ballabilli or: The Ways of Love*, *Prado de Pena*, and *The Face of Violence*. These works demonstrated the wide range of choreographic approaches Horton was capable of. *The Beloved* was an electrifying, spare duet inspired by a newspaper article about a man who had beaten his wife to death with a Bible for suspected infidelity. In the work, Horton clearly and succinctly presented a series of images centering on this elemental plot, particularly focusing on the woman's experience. *Scenes with Ballabilli* used elaborate props and costumes in a playful dance that imitated the commedia dell'arte. According to attendance records, only 309 people attended Saturday night and 223 on Sunday afternoon, but the performance left its mark on the people who were there. The *Dance Observer* review stated that the performance showed audiences "theatre dance at its very professional best." And Walter Terry raved that "the Lester Horton Dancers gave cause for pride in the modern dance efforts of Californians and brought freshness of idea, new faces, fine dancing, theatrical verve and even, perhaps, a healthy dash of envy to New Yorkers who attended."[39]

· · ·

CONTROVERSY AND CHANGE IN POLICY, 1953

Despite the artistic success of Horton's performance, the low attendance at this as well as other recitals by little-known modern dancers made Kolodney increasingly concerned. During the 1952–53 season at the Y, twenty or so performances had fewer than five hundred audience members. Kolodney believed that, in general, the quality of recitals put on by modern dancers was on the decline and that this was part of the reason for the lower attendance. Kolodney presented the problem to the Y's board of directors in the following way: "For many years the 'Y' introduced new dancers to the public in our Kaufman [*sic*] Auditorium. At the end of last season this program was evaluated and it was decided that a change in policy was desirable because dancers who auditioned presented [only] one or two numbers, on the basis of which they were permitted a full program. Too often, the total program was unsatisfactory and the dance public was disappointed."[40] At the end of the 1952–53 season, Kolodney decided to end the Dance Theater series as well as dissolve the Dance Teachers Advisory Committee and its accompanying policies. He found the advisory committee increasingly unwieldy and difficult to bring together to make decisions. In an attempt to reach the members, he had even resorted to sending out self-addressed cards, asking them to circle their answers to his queries. In the end, this was doubtlessly time-consuming and counterproductive.

Kolodney resolved to replace the committee with Doris Humphrey. Having closely worked with Humphrey since appointing her director of the Dance Center in 1945, Kolodney felt that it would be easier to consolidate the "School of the Dance and the Dance Theatre under a single Director and artistic head."[41] Most important, he believed that Humphrey might be able to halt the seeming decline in the quality of modern dance presented at the Y. Kolodney explained to the board: "The new policy requires dancers who wish to use the auditorium to audition their entire program for Doris Humphrey."

Performers who were accepted would then be presented in individual recitals sponsored by the Dance Center. There was no limit to how many of these could occur a year. Some flexibility was built into the new approach. For instance, Humphrey was authorized to exempt well-known dancers from the process and "some compositions by other dancers."[42]

The new policy created a tremendous stir in the dance world. Far from being a small, isolated event concerning the Y alone, the change fueled personal vendettas among some of the prominent members of the dance community and pointed to a large shift that was continuing to reconfigure the dance world. Modern dance was going through a major transition in the early 1950s, and the Y's actions raised questions regarding who was controlling its destiny and the right of individual people and institutions to shape its future. With Balanchine and the New York City Ballet securely housed at City Center and Graham with her school and company comfortably located on East Sixty-third Street, there was a real question of how independent dancers were going to survive. Modern dance was still highly individual and tied to particular techniques and aesthetics, but with its growing maturity as an art form, it was striving to gain popular recognition. With outlets such as Juilliard and the American Dance Festival more or less focused on the work of Graham and Limón, the majority of so-called second- and third-generation modernists were increasingly marginalized and at a loss as to where to turn.

The Y's decision to curtail its series and have people audition before Humphrey consequently touched a raw nerve. Suddenly, the Y was highly visible as one of the few remaining reputable places supportive of the work of these second- and third-generation modern dancers. The idea that it should change its policy was extremely disturbing. While some people supported the change, others were angered by the effrontery of an organization playing moralist to such a conspicuous degree. The response from the press demonstrated how the various critics positioned themselves on the question of modern dance's precarious status. Martin, a new convert to the ballet and a strong believer in the decline of modern dance at the time, gave high praise to the change. He enthusiastically wrote in a lengthy *New York Times* article on the Y's decision: "The Dance Center . . . has taken a drastic, courageous and forward-looking step this season in the curtailment of its customary schedule of performances." Martin continued to argue that the Y's program had arisen in response to a particular early need of the modern dance community but that individual performances "continued to decline in quality" and that few dancers of any qualification were participating. He added, "To have continued doggedly on the same line . . . would have been for the Dance Center in effect to condone the decline of the modern dance and even to contribute to it."[43]

Walter Terry, characteristically more equable and optimistic than Martin on the subject of modern dance at this time, was only slightly more circumspect. In his *New York Herald Tribune* article on the policy shift, he cautiously criticized the change and called the new policy "a form of benevolent despotism" by placing Humphrey in charge.[44] Nonetheless, he agreed with Martin that the quality of work had been on the decline in recent years: "In recent seasons these levels had commenced to sink to that point where too many dance beginners, experimentalists, obscurants and, frankly, untalented (or, at least, unprepared) dance strivers" had been giving concerts at the Y.

One person who captured a widely shared opposing view and vehemently attacked the Y's actions was the writer and editor Anatole Chujoy, an ardent balletomane, who also was interested in the fate of modern dance. In his eyes the new policy virtually destroyed the future growth of the form. Writing in his publication *Dance News* in December 1953, he observed, "The immediate result of Dr. Kolodney's new policy is that modern dancers have no place where they can perform for a public, where they can test out new ideas, where they can show their growth and development, or regression, as the case may be. . . . The modern dancer is literally left without the possibilities of a New York performance."[45] Chujoy specifically attacked Martin for his support of the Y's decision. He challenged: "But it is obvious that it is not actually the decline of the modern dance that worries Mr. Martin, but the performances of those dancers who are not yet on Olympus together with the two or three famous personalities whom Mr. Martin considers worthy to represent the modern dance."[46]

Chujoy's observations act as a reminder of the extreme influence wielded by Martin and to a lesser degree by Terry in directing the perception and visibility of modern dance. This influence was indeed very real, since Kolodney had, in fact, consulted with Martin before deciding to eliminate the advisory committee and was undoubtedly pleased when Martin publicly came out in defense of the decision. In justifying the change to the board, Kolodney referred to Martin's words: "John Martin, Dance Critic of the New York Times, wrote an article defending this policy because he felt that young dancers should wait until their technique and choreographic ability show professional competence before presenting a program in a large auditorium to persons who pay regular admission prices. As for mature dancers who have performed for several years, he believes they should not be encouraged to repeat compositions that have proven both artistic and audience failures."[47]

Such a statement suggests the extent to which Kolodney was swayed by Martin's rather self-serving opinion that modern dance was in serious trouble. The extent to which the critic's views lacked objectivity can be judged by the fact that, during the late 1940s and early 1950s, there were numerous signs that modern dance was alive and well. In 1948, for instance, the Music School of the Henry Street Settlement announced the addition to its curriculum of a full course in modern dance under Alwin Nikolais, along with public performances in its Playhouse. In addition, Fred Berk began the Stage for Dancers at the Brooklyn Museum as a new venture to encourage young dancers. For the next few years both Nikolais and Berk continued to work separately and together to produce dance. During the 1951–52 season, for example, the Henry Street Playhouse advertised four dance series: Dance U.S.A. (four concerts introducing dancers from outside New York); the Stage for Dancers, arranged with Berk; Dance Previews (informal concerts introducing new dancers and new compositions); and College Dance (two concerts presenting college dance groups).[48]

Other venues also began to be used for modern dance performances. Hunter College Playhouse was increasingly a hub of dance activity. During January 1952, Jean Erdman, Donald McKayle and Normand Maxon, Merce Cunningham, and Erick Hawkins performed there. In April 1952 the Juilliard School presented Martha Graham's company in the first of a projected series of dance events to be presented by the school. This was the first season of the Juilliard Dance Division, and Martha Graham was on the initial faculty. Although no series actually materialized, the school did begin to present more dance companies, and later that year José Limón performed at the Juilliard Concert Hall.

The sudden flowering of dance programs at Henry Street and Juilliard may have worried Kolodney and been a component in the 1953 change in policy. It seems more likely, however, that Kolodney did not see the work in either of these venues as a serious threat. At the time, these programs were very new and functioned on a small scale compared with the Y. During the 1951–52 season alone, for instance, there were as many as thirty dance events at the 92nd Street Y. José Limón performed there, along with Pearl Primus, Katherine Litz, Angna Enters, the Dudley-Maslow-Bales trio, Pearl Lang, and Ronne Aul. Instead, Kolodney's decision to end the Dance Theatre and the Dance Teachers Advisory Committee was likely motivated by a sincere desire to serve the dance community and to do what was necessary to once again make modern dance successful and popular. In his 1954 report to the board, Kolodney ended by remarking that it was "not a permanent policy and modifications will most likely be made on the basis of our experience this season."

The change, as it turned out, almost immediately proved unsuccessful. Despite Humphrey's reputation for fairness, many young dancers were reluctant to audition before her. They felt that it was impossible to present their entire concert so far in advance and that, despite her openness, she had strong opinions about what constituted good choreography. Such sentiments may have overlooked the Y's admirable intentions and Humphrey's long commitment to nurturing the work of other artists. Nonetheless, these views were widely held by those who had been used to performing on the Y's stage with relative ease. One such dancer later stated, "You know, [Humphrey] was really so set on her own way. . . . She would be critical of the dances people did in terms of her own ideas."[49] The result of the policy change, consequently, was that young modern dancers stayed away from the Y.

Artists who did appear there during the next season included Pearl Primus and Anna Sokolow, both seasoned performers who were likely exempt from auditioning before Humphrey, due to their long association with the Y. Sokolow, in particular, continued to use the institution as the preferred place to present her latest compositions. The world premiere of *Lyric Suite* occurred as part of the New Dance Group Festival held at the Y on March 30-April 4, 1954, and February 24, 1955, saw the world premier of *Rooms*. These dances distilled the range of human emotions into highly visceral movements, *Rooms* focusing in particular on the fear and loneliness that arise from living as isolated individuals in a big city. Both works were signs that modern dance was alive and well, despite the negative opinions of Martin and Terry. Nonetheless, between 1953 and 1955 there was a drastic reduction in the number of modern dance performances at the Y. In 1954–55, for instance, there were a total of four recitals by modern dancers.

In a determined attempt to keep dance active at the Y, Kolodney continued to present individual recitals of dancers falling under the "ethnic" category as well as contemporary ballet companies. The 1953–54 season, for instance, included Inesita, Asadata Dafora, the Japanese dancer Sahomi Tachibana, and the Ballet Theatre Workshop arranged by William Dollar and Robert Joffrey. Joffrey, who was currently teaching for the Merry-Go-Rounders, formed his own company, the Robert Joffrey Ballet, especially for his engagement on May 29, 1954. On this program, Joffrey's *Le Bal Masqué* and his now celebrated *Pas des Déesses* enjoyed their world premieres. *Pas des Déesses* is a dance in the Romantic style for three ballerinas and a male dancer, who represent Marie Taglioni, Lucile Grahn, Fanny Cerrito, and Arthur Saint-Léon. The following year, on March 24, 1955, the company appeared again; this time *Harpsichord Concerto* and *Pierrot Lunaire* received world premieres.

During this time, Kolodney also sought ways to expand the Y's influence and promote quality modern dance. In the summer of 1953, plans proceeded to develop the Y as a performance outlet for Humphrey. Kolodney contacted the Baron de Rothschild Foundation for the Arts and Sciences and asked for support to help Humphrey establish a company to showcase her work. On June 11, 1953, he wrote: "I have discussed with Doris Humphrey the possibility of directing a repertory company at the Y, beginning in January, 1954. The group would consist of the best of modern dancers and choreographers. Doris Humphrey would do some new works, and some of the choreographers in the group would do works of their own under her direction." The project went forward, and the Y received $4,000 from de Rothschild in the fall of 1953. By the following year, however, it became clear that Humphrey preferred to establish a company at the Juilliard School. The Juilliard dance program was specially geared toward gifted young dancers, and a resident company there would be able to provide them as well as other young dancers the training and experience to prepare them for professional careers.

The Y returned the $4,000 to the foundation in January 1954, and it was redirected to the Juilliard School, where it was used to establish the Juilliard Dance Theatre under Humphrey's artistic direction. On January 11, 1954, Craig Barton of the Rothschild Foundation thanked Kolodney for the money, stating, "We, too, regret that you were unable to use the money for the purpose for which it was given. However, we are happy that your original plan for its use can be carried out, and by Doris Humphrey, even though it cannot be done at the YMHA." The creation of the Juilliard Dance Theatre drew much of Humphrey's attention away from the Y and meant that she had less time for its affairs. At the same time, the failure of the Y's new policy and dancers' refusal to audition before one person marked a temporary end to Humphrey's central advisory position. In 1955, Kolodney resumed control of the administration and direction of the recital itinerary, and Humphrey seems to have been relieved of her responsibilities.[50]

· · ·

THE 1950S: A HOME FOR AFRICAN AMERICAN AND
SECOND-GENERATION MODERN DANCERS

A more liberal policy was clearly needed if the Y was going to succeed once more in being an active performance space for dance. Kolodney's response to the dance community was more or less to turn the Y into a booking house. Under the new policy any performer could apply to Kolodney to present a concert at the Y. No audition process existed; a deposit of $100 was required to hold the day of a performance. Kolodney reported to the Y board that "we expect to have more new groups as a result of [this] change in policy. Doris Humphreys [*sic*] will not audition groups. This is an attempt to encourage young dancers."[51] Details of the new policy are laid out in a contract from the 1956–57 season. The artist would receive 70 percent of the income after the following deductions were made: (a) a service charge of $325 to cover the Y's expenses and (b) payment to the artist of $325 for his or her expenses. The Y's service charge covered box office, backstage employees, ushers, cleaning, lights, air conditioning, and printing of tickets and programs. The contract also stipulated that all publicity done by the artist had to be approved by the Y and that no advertising was allowed in the program. The total amount of time for any use of the stage was twelve hours, after which there would be a charge of $10 per hour.[52]

As one might imagine, the new policy was an immediate success in generating performances. The Y was once again available, and there was an unprecedented freedom regarding who could perform there. Kolodney fielded the requests and, in a desire to reanimate the Y, appears to have accepted all those who were able to pay the deposit. The result was that the Y became a haven once more for independent modern dancers who sought exposure within a prestigious theater. Dancers who took advantage of the new policy were primarily young African Americans like Geoffrey Holder and Louis Johnson, along with more seasoned women like Sophie Maslow and Marie Marchowsky, who had performed at the Y throughout the 1940s. Other dancers included young choreographers from a range of backgrounds who worked in the modern idiom.

While individual recitals continued, the success of the season encouraged Kolodney to reinstate a subscription series in 1957, after a hiatus of seven years. In contrast to the past series, however, this would be by invitation only, and the dancers would be offered a straight fee. To guarantee further the high quality of the performances, each recital on the series would be tightly designed to consist of two dance companies and one soloist. Kolodney once again turned to his friend Humphrey to assist with the programming, and she agreed to help decide on the performers. Kolodney, now extremely wary of losing money on any of his experiments, seems to have asked Humphrey to assume some financial responsibility for a possible deficit in running the series. She accepted this suggestion and wrote a contract to Kolodney on June 16, stating, "The undersigned will be responsible for any losses on this series up to $2,700.00 on a proper accounting being submitted at the conclusion of the series, and in case no other underwriting is forthcoming."[53] It is likely, considering that Humphrey did not have extensive financial resources, that neither Kolodney nor Humphrey actually expected her to pay this money. Instead, Kolodney may have been looking for a way to satisfy the Y's leadership that his new program would not place them in a dangerous financial position.

Under Humphrey's direction a broad cross-section of modern dancers were presented on the new series. The first recital consisted of works by Geoffrey Holder, Daniel Nagrin, and William Hug. The audience reaction was tremendous. The *Dance Observer* reviewer stated: "When after a black out of several years, the 'Y' resumed its subscription series policy with a program on October 27, it could not have had a more auspicious opening. The house was sold out, with many standees, the program was excellent and everybody went home happy full of bright hopes for the success of the series. The occasion might easily be termed a bit 'historic.'"[54] Other concerts that year included Merce Cunningham, May O'Donnell, and Iva Kitchell on January 5 and John Butler, Pauline Koner, and Donald McKayle on March 23, 1958.

The series was such a success that Kolodney decided to repeat it the following year. Once again, Humphrey agreed to supervise and underwrite the series, this time up to $2,000. However, financial precautions were unnecessary this time around. Through the efforts of both Humphrey and Kolodney, the Y received support of $1,000 each from the Capezio Foundation and the Lena Robbins Foundation.[55] In his response to Humphrey's inquiries for assistance, Jerome Robbins stated, "Thank you so much for your letter to the Foundation. Naturally we are immensely sympathetic to the whole 'Y' series and the Dance activities there."[56] Many of the performers contacted for the second year were the same as those who had appeared before. When Talley Beatty was invited to perform again for the 1958–59 series, he responded, "I look forward to participating with great pleasure. I should like to thank you

The Dance Center of the YM-YWHA presents

ALVIN AILEY   ERNEST PARHAM

and companies

DELORES BROWN
GEORGIA COLLINS
DON EMMONS   **TALLEY BEATTY, guest artist**
JAIN FAIRFAX
JULIUS FIELDS
RONNIE FRAZIER
LAVINIA HAMILTON
NATHANIEL HORNE
SCOTT HUNTER
JOHN JONES
TOMMY JOHNSON
CRISTYNE LAWSON
JAMES McMILLAN
AUDREY MASON
CHARLES MOORE
CHARLES NEAL
NANCY PERKINS
HAROLD PIERSON
MONA PIVAR
RONALD PLATTS
DORENE RICHARDSON
MABEL ROBINSON
CLAUDE THOMPSON
ELLA THOMPSON
JACQUELINE WALCOTT
LIZ WILLIAMS
NANCY REDDY, SINGER
CLARENCE COOPER, SINGER

Admission: $2.00
KAUFMANN CONCERT HALL
YM-YWHA 92nd St. & Lexington Ave.
New York 28, N. Y.   TR 6-2366

SUNDAY, MARCH 30, 1958   2:40 p.m.

Announcement for Alvin Ailey and Ernest Parham recital, 1958.
92nd Street YM-YWHA Archives.

for the invitation, it is an honor." Indeed, Beatty was one of a number of young African American dancers to benefit from the exposure of the subscription series. During the two years from 1957 to 1959, others were Holder, Johnson, and McKayle.

The Y's support of black artists blossomed during the 1950s. The institution had already established itself as a place where young African American dancers could get their start. However, between 1954 and 1960, Kolodney presented a large number of such choreographers in either their first or near first New York concerts. While some of these were subscription series performances, others were single recitals in which the choreographer reserved the hall for $100, in accordance with the current policy. May 10, 1959, saw the world premiere of Donald McKayle's *Rainbow 'Round My Shoulder*, a powerful work about black chain gangs in the South. Ailey's *Blues Suite* received its world premiere on another such recital on March 30, 1958. The success of this and other performances by Ailey led Kolodney to invite the dancer to appear at the Y again on January 31, 1960, for an impressive flat fee of $600. On that program, *Revelations* was performed for the first time. This uplifting suite celebrating the struggles and triumphs of African Americans has since become the signature work of the Alvin Ailey American Dance Theatre, bringing audiences to their feet every time it is performed.

During the 1950s the Y also hosted a long list of women who had first presented their work at the Y in the 1940s and continued to mature as artists throughout the next decade. These included Valerie Bettis, May O'Donnell, Betty Lind, Marie Marchowsky, Mary Anthony, Ruth Currier, and Natanya

THE DANCE CENTER OF THE YM-YWHA presents
THE ALVIN AILEY DANCE THEATRE
with

MATT TURNEY, guest artist

THE MUSIC MASTERS GUILD of the Harlem Branch YMCA
FRANK THOMAS, Director
NANCY REDI
GENE HOBGOOD   NATHANIEL HORNE

PROGRAM

Sunday, January 31, 1960 at 4:00 P.M.

CANTO AL DIABLO - - - - - GONZALEZ, arr.
by Anderson

An interpretation of an Afro-Brazilian fetishist ritual, exploiting the innate sense of melodrama of primitive rite.

ALVIN AILEY   NANCY REDI   MERLE DERBY
MINNIE MARSHAL   DORENE RICHARDSON   NATHANIEL HORNE
HERMAN HOWELL

SONERA - - - - - - - - CATURLA

Three abstract dances after Cuban dance forms

Sonera · Comparsa · Danza

DELORES BROWN   BETSY DIKERSON   JOY SMITH
GENE GeBAUER   JAN MICKENS   DUDLEY WILLIAMS

BLUES SUITE - TRADITIONAL-ANDERSON-RICCI

From the fields, levees and barrelhouses of the Southern Negro sprang the Blues—hymns to the secular regions of his soul.

The Blind Man   - - - -   *Gene Hobgood*
The Woman Upstairs   - - - -   *Nancy Redi*
Her Lover   - - - - - - -   *Alvin Ailey*
The Other Man   - - - -   *Nathaniel Horne*
Lady Friends   - - - -   *Joan Derby, Merle Derby,*
                                    Minnie Marshall
Their Men   - - - -   *Jay Fletcher, Herman Howell*

INTERMISSION

CREATION OF THE WORLD - - - - MILHAUD

Milhaud's early use of jazz-in-symphony inspires another look at the world's oldest love story.

ALVIN AILEY   MATT TURNEY

INTERMISSION

REVELATIONS - - - - - - TRADITIONAL

The Music Masters Guild Chorus of the
Harlem Branch Y.M.C.A.
FRANK THOMAS, Director

This suite explores motivations and emotions of Negro religious music which, like its heir the Blues, takes many forms—"true spirituals" with their sustained melodies, ring-shouts, song-sermons, gospel songs, and holy blues—songs of trouble, of Love of deliverance.

PILGRIM OF SORROW
I been buked   - - - - - - - -   *The Company*
Weeping Mary   - - - - - - -   *Nancy Redi*
Poor Pilgrim   - - - - - -   *Nancy Redi*
Round About the Mountain   - - -   *Joan Derby;*
                              Minnie Marshall, Dorene Richardson
Wonder Where   - - - - - -   *Merle Derby*
Troubles   - - - - - - - -   *The Company*
THAT LOVE MY JESUS GIVES ME
Fix Me   - - - - -   *Minnie Marshall, Herman Howell*
Honor, Honor   - - - - - - -   *The Company*
Wade In the Water   - - - - -   *Joan Derby,*
                              Jay Fletcher, Merle Derby, Nathaniel Horne
Morning Star   - - - -   *Nancy Redi, Joan Derby,*
                              Merle Derby, Minnie Marshall,
                              Dorene Richardson
My Lord What A Morning   - - - -   *The Chorus*
Sinner Man   - - - -   *Gene Hobgood, Nathaniel Horne,*
                              Herman Howell, Jay Fletcher
MOVE, MEMBERS, MOVE!
Precious Lord   -   *Gene Hobgood, Nancy Redi and the company*
God A Mighty
Waters of Babylon
Elijah Rock!

Program for Alvin Ailey Dance Theatre, 1960, with premiere of *Revelations*.
92nd Street YM-YWHA Archives.

Neumann. When Kolodney and Humphrey instituted the mixed-bill sub-scription series in 1957, many of these artists were featured on it (e.g., O'Donnell, Currier, Bettis). The majority of these dancers had not reached sufficient recognition to allow them the luxury of more elaborate settings, and they could not afford a downtown theater space on their own. For them, the Y played a central role in allowing them to continue to make and present work.

Despite this activity, the close of the 1950s saw the end of a chapter in the Y's performance history, as numerous factors both within and outside the dance world combined to drastically change the Y's place in the New York landscape. Nonetheless, over the prior twenty-five years the Y had made its mark. Kolodney's ongoing efforts to adjust to the dance community's needs had led to the success of the Y as a performance venue. He continually found ways to adapt the program to keep up with changing circumstances while re-maining as true as possible to the values and ethics at the root of his own thinking and the Jewish constituency he represented. It was this dynamic process that defined the Y's programming. At various times other venues pre-sented performers in their debut performances, but the Y remained consis-tent in promoting relative unknowns alongside celebrities and offering the public a broad range of contemporary dance. This combination had impor-tant consequences for the kinds of dances that choreographers made and the future legacy of the Y within the dance world.

The Y encouraged people to grow by shaping individual's aesthetics.
Seeing the tremendous diversity at the Y influenced the way choreographers
worked. . . . It really helped modern dance move forward.
Joe Nash[1]

(6)

CHOREOGRAPHING DIFFERENCE

The Aesthetics of Diversity

. . .

Kolodney once observed that audiences at the Y responded with an "almost ritualistic and kinesthetic response to every authentic dance movement."[2] The remark captures the raw excitement of the early years of dance at the 92nd Street Y. According to those who attended the recitals, the excitement in the air was palpable. People assembled in the Kaufmann Auditorium on a Sunday afternoon, eagerly awaiting the performance. They gazed up at the frieze of historic names circling the room, chatted with neighbors, or read their programs. Then the lights dimmed, and the "magic" began. The dancer appeared and mesmerized the audience with his or her most recent movement inventions. At intermission and after the recital there were animated discussions about the performer, along with vigorous assessments of the choreography. Such rhapsodic descriptions are characteristic from many people who attended performances at the Y and danced on its stage between the 1930s and 1950s. Although numerous famous group works were premiered there over the years, the Y remains fixed in many people's imaginations as the home of the solo dance artist and of small ensembles. The moderate size of the theater was well suited to the single performer and made for a warm and friendly atmosphere. As the African American dancer and historian Joe Nash explains, "The Y stage was perfect for intimacy and the audience was eager and willing to move with the dancers."[3]

The intimate ambiance found at the Y was especially suited to the needs of a generation of modern dancers who felt intensely about their work. The performers of the time intended to make meaningful, heartfelt statements that would be deeply experienced by the audience. They intently followed the lead of their forerunners, Duncan and St. Denis, in separating dance from its nineteenth-century association with entertainment and lasciviousness and uniting it with aesthetics and spirituality. The modern dancer Marie Marchowsky stresses how much she and others wanted to "get into the souls of people" and that they were "interested in saying something in art."[4] Sybil Shearer explains that what she believed to be important was anything that would "reflect the nobility of the spirit and produce a work of art."[5] The Y, with its humanistic interest in cultural uplift of the individual welcomed this conception of dance. Its leaders shared the influence of the progressive movements in art and adult education and embraced the aim of modern dancers to touch people in a way that would potentially transform how they saw themselves and the world. Around 1941, Kolodney wrote a short paper in which he approvingly observed, "The modern dance has, thus far, dared to be itself by doing what all the arts have attempted to do for centuries . . . to invest the body with a soul and the earth with a Heaven."[6] With Kolodney's help, as Nash recollects, "The Y was a place where the solo artist could be seen communicating something of importance."

The Y's support of certain basic values of modern dancers—to provide spiritual enrichment that seemingly cut across people's differences—allowed for an easy convergence between the dance world and the institution. At the same time at the Y what might be characterized as an aesthetics of diversity reigned; while there was an overriding desire to make meaningful work, this approach took no single form. Kolodney's commitment to democratic principles, diversity, and Jewish causes challenged those who sought to unify modern dance under the efforts of a few and to present the style as a purist activity devoid of seams that might indicate the presence of unwanted "foreign" elements. At the Y, modern dance was seen in many variations over the years, and differences were celebrated, as there was an ongoing exploration of the idiom in terms of movement vocabulary, dynamics, and subject matter. There were evocative mood pieces, finely tuned character portraits, and politically charged dances. There were works that incorporated different dance styles (tap, ballet, folk) and dances that drew specifically on people's ethnic heritage, whether African American or Jewish. Each of these received support and was considered a valuable form of expression. On their own and in combination they articulated a kaleidoscopic space defined by its ever-shifting perspectives on contemporary dance.

The convergence of Jewish interests and dance at the Y distinguished the institution from Bennington College, whose mythology had, in direct contrast, everything to do with the formation of a pure modern dance.[7] Bennington functioned as the fresh ground on which the "Big Four" of American modern choreographers danced out their difference from the orientalist and overly expressionistic European dimensions of their associates St. Denis, Shawn, and Wigman. Humphrey best voiced the battle cry when she passionately queried, "We adopted ballet, we adopted Spanish dancing, we adopted Oriental dancing—are we never to have a dance that is our own?"[8] Popularized through the work of Martin and the many who attended Bennington, a pure dance form that captured in broadly accessible terms the contemporary American experience, untainted by alien influences, was sought by choreographers working at the school. At the 92nd Street Y, in almost direct contrast to the Bennington myth, modern dance was presented as a dynamic synthesis open to multiple elements. Although there is no doubt that the Y leaders also perceived modern dance as presenting universal truths, it was from the perspective of having Jews and African Americans and other minorities dancing about their and others' experiences and celebrating the variations among these experiences rather than trying to erase them. "Fusion was already a part of modern dance," Nash has argued, and the Y understood and valued this aspect of modern dance because of its own deep interests in preserving Jewish particularity within a pluralistically defined culture.

· · ·

VARIATIONS AND THEMES

In this chapter, four choreographers who appeared at the Y—Marchowsky, Litz, Primus, and Shearer—are examined in more depth because of the ways they exemplify the aesthetics of diversity in their works. A detailed discussion of their pieces aims to bring the act of dancing to the foreground and show how the choreography of these dancers reflected two major aspects of the Y's democratic ideology: the openness to new ideas generally and its specific commitment to the blurring of stylistic boundaries. Like many of the dancers who repeatedly performed at the Y over the years, they were exploring the limits of the modern idiom as opposed to simply copying or mirroring the efforts of the Big Four. Stylistically, the pieces reflect the important breadth of ways dancers were exploring the modern idiom, whether in lyrical, humorous ways or through the incorporation of African American experience. Janet Collins is also mentioned in this regard, to emphasize the fusion experiments of the time.

These choreographers also were chosen on the basis of how representative of the Y's programming they were and the degree of accessibility of materials on their work. Marchowsky, Litz, and Primus were among the choreographers who performed frequently at the Y. While they certainly danced elsewhere during the period, the Y was of central importance to their careers. Their work paints a clear picture of the predominance of women creators through the period as well as capturing the solo form that was enjoyed at the Y. Moreover, these choreographers' works are among the better-documented through film, video, written description, and interviewing. Thematically, the dances characteristically use the female body as a means of expressing a range of emotions, from the tragic to the satirical, with a certain degree of self-reflexive commentary on modern dance. For their part, Litz and Shearer are also included to illustrate the Y's patronage of the nonconformists of the period (which would also include people like Maracci and Horton).

Clearly, Graham, Humphrey, and the other central figures who were involved at Bennington and elsewhere in the dance community performed at the Y. They affected the direction of the program and made the Y part of these broader efforts to institutionalize modern dance as they conceived it. At the same time, their influence was limited, and their agendas were recast by the Y as a result of its inclusive, multicultural mission. The dancers discussed in this chapter are just a handful of the hundreds of breathtaking and stimulating yet often overlooked performers who appeared on the Y's stage. The following analysis is meant to help in the recording of an American dance history that acknowledges the diversity of modern dance expression and the extent to which fusion elements were present in the form during the height of its popularity, despite the long-standing belief to the contrary.

Marie Marchowsky: After Toulouse-Lautrec

As observed earlier, many of the dancers who performed on the Y stage were among the second and third generations of female American modern dancers. They had been students of Graham and Humphrey-Weidman and danced in their companies. Their work was related to that of their mentors

Marie Marchowsky in *After Toulouse-Lautrec.*
Courtesy of Marie Marchowsky.

but often differed through individual choices regarding movement, form, and subject matter. The dancers were not replicating their teachers but striving to find a unique style in the face of limited resources and support. At the Y they found a unique opportunity to present their work in an affordable theatrical format to an educated audience that appreciated their efforts.

Marie Marchowsky was one such choreographer who showed her work frequently on the Kaufmann stage between 1945 and 1957. She had danced with Sokolow and Graham in the 1930s before launching her own career. Marchowsky was drawn to a stridently expressive and emotional performance style throughout her life, although in later years she added an easier, softer lyricism. She often performed dramatic solos that presented a strong woman in the face of unseen oppression. In choreographing these works she drew inspiration from celebrated paintings, using stark movement to create a cameo portrait of each character.

After Toulouse-Lautrec, based on Lautrec's *La Buveuse,* received its New York debut at the 92nd Street Y in 1952.[9] The solo was created following an inspirational trip to Europe, during which Marchowsky felt she matured greatly as an artist. It was performed along with *Odalisque,* as part of a larger piece called *Two Portraits.* The work focused on the inner turmoil of a despondent female character who is overcome with the burdens of life. Organized on a theme-and-variation structure, the piece began and ended with Marchowsky sitting slouched at a small table, her head flopped over the back of the chair, exposing her neck.[10] Her right arm rested along the table, and her left arm dangled lifeless beside her body.

The piece incorporated actions easily identified with the character's gloomy mood. In the opening phrase of the dance, Marchowsky slowly began to circle her left leg and raise it into the air. In alternate moves, the left leg circled and the right arm responded by rising and falling listlessly back onto the table. The leg and arm movements were isolated and somehow removed from the rest of the woman's body, which remained pitifully still. Suddenly, as the music became more strident, the woman sat bolt upright and, in a series of sharp moves, twisted her upper body left and right, then thrust it forward so that it slid along the table surface. As she pressed down onto the table, her left leg stretched back into a high arabesque. The sequence built in momentum until Marchowsky stood, convulsing in small jerks, letting hips and rib cage jut out in little distorted jazzy isolations.

The central section of the dance explored the character's confused state of mind more fully. In alternate pauses and bursts she moved slowly, then darted, to sit on the right side of the table. Her body slumped then tensed, as if torn between exhaustion and the desire to live. Standing again, she spun wildly, grabbing at the air with her hands. Down to the floor she collapsed and then rose again, striving to retain her composure. There was a tragicomic moment as she performed some simpering walks in imitation of a lady, but she soon lost her humor and hope and relapsed into her previously melancholy mood. Returning to the original movement theme, Marchowsky turned to the table and sat down on the chair—reaching, twisting, and sitting back in the wide slouched position. To end the piece, she once more thrust forward, sliding onto her chest, reaching across the table with her right arm in a final grasping gesture.

Marchowsky's piece was highly dramatic and conveyed the image of a woman overcome by depression and hopelessness. In the dance, sudden changes in dynamics, between slow and quick movement and relaxed and taut gesture, were used to convey her intense inner battle to shake off disillusionment and frustration. Here was a woman capable of many kinds of emotional expression. The use of theme and variation as a choreographic device revealed that no matter how much she tried to assert her will and overcome her oppression, the character was fated to return to her original lethargic state, over which she had little control.

After Toulouse-Lautrec is a character study that focuses on the details of an individual's life. As such, its content, character, and satirical edge are similar to the cameo portraits performed by Angna Enters and Valeska Gert, both celebrated dance mimes of the 1920s and 1930s. The intensity that drives the movement, as well as the use of extreme changes in dynamics, however, is Grahamesque, indicating Marchowsky's close affiliation with her teacher. The sharp attack and harsh, uncompromising nature of the movement is particularly reminiscent of Graham's early solos, such as *Lamentation* and *Frenetic Rhythm*.

The relation of the dance to others of the era suggests a certain sameness of theme and purpose, and a strong reliance on established choreographic conventions. At the same time, the use of paintings as inspiration and Marchowsky's special fusion of the mime and modern dance traditions caught the public's eye. At the time of its premiere the dance was extremely well received, suggesting that Marchowsky was successfully defining her own style. In his review in *Dance Observer,* Louis Horst wrote, "Miss Marchowsky possesses a superb technical equipment, which she employs with excellent dramatic expressiveness in her latest compositions." He wrote that her work "abounds with excellent and exciting movement phrases" and that *After Toulouse-Lautrec* "was a realistic, though extremely satiric and humorous, portrayal of a disillusioned and dissolute absinthe-drinking cafe habitue." The dance, he concludes, "proved a knock-out."[11]

Katherine Litz: The Glyph

Marchowsky's work was performed in the early 1950s when independent modern dancers were having a hard time surviving. Martin had established and promoted the Big Four approach to modern dance and was currently decrying the sorry state of the form. As Marcia B. Siegel observes: "Modern dance was no longer an open field where freewheeling experimentation could be sampled and discussed by benevolent critics. With so much local and imported ballet occupying major theaters, Martin especially began to limit the places he would go to review dance. . . . Even the sites of major dance events, the 92nd Street Y, Hunter College, Cooper Union, and the High School of Needle Trades, now lay on the fringes of his territory."[12] Martin's long promotion of Graham and, to a lesser degree, Humphrey, Weidman, and Holm, meant that dancers like Marchowsky were hard pressed to find their niche. The subtle ways that they worked within the modern idiom were submerged within a generic concept of modern dance that lumped together many female modern dancers working in the 1950s. Rather than a unique performing presence, the dancer was perceived as a copy of one of the "masters" and was largely written out of the history books.

Many of the modern dancers presented by the Y fit into this category. Another was Katherine Litz, who had danced with the Humphrey-Weidman company in the mid-1930s and early 1940s, as well as with Agnes de Mille, and made her debut as a choreographer at the 92nd Street Y in 1948. Between 1948 and 1958 she presented work in at least nine concerts there. Like Marchowsky, she was interested in dramatic characterization; however, her impulse was more buoyant and optimistic in quality. Litz's work was tenderly and appealingly witty, what Elizabeth Kendall called "ingenious interludes that prolonged a state of illogic."[13] Her heroines often provoked humor and pathos because her characters were "never quite prepared or coordinated enough to do what they are presenting to an audience . . . but they are fatally drawn to performing."[14]

The Glyph received its first New York performance at the Y on December 23, 1951. In this work, Litz was clothed in a long tube of jersey, a characteristic modern dance costume of the time, which she manipulated to great effect. The piece was divided into six sections, each one exploring the relationship between the dancer and the cloth slightly differently.[15] In between each section, the performer disappeared behind a screen standing at the upstage left corner of the space before appearing for the next part of the dance. The impression was one of mounting intrigue, as the audience wondered what would occur next.

In the opening sequence, Litz sprang from behind the screen, bouncing like a rabbit toward the center of the stage. She busily pulled at the cloth around her waist as if trying to roll it up, but with little success. The sequence was simple, with little stops and starts accompanied by a blank gaze. The character continued to exert a lot of effort to little effect until she disappeared behind the screen in preparation for part two. A few seconds later,

Katherine Litz in the *Glyph*, 1951.
Dance Division, The New York Public Library for the Performing Arts,
Astor, Lenox and Tilden Foundations. Photographer: Norman Soloman.

Litz bounded out from behind the screen more quickly than before, with small leaping runs, while again pulling at the jersey material bunched up at her waist. Then she stopped suddenly. She stood facing the audience, making undulating movements with her arms stretched overhead. She posed beguilingly and performed a short pseudo-flamenco stamping dance, which grew in momentum until Litz suddenly turned and heavily (and somewhat robotlike) strode back behind the screen. Next, Litz appeared in a sequence that contrasted a pulled-up-vertical stance, with her hands in a triangular position under her chin, and a flopped look, in which she stood in profile with her hands limp, like paws, in front of her. Litz then seemed to get caught in the jersey, pushing and pulling at it as if trying to escape, before she walked off behind the screen.

Sequence four found Litz emerging with the jersey stretched high overhead so that all that was seen were her hands and lower legs. In this concealed form, she struck a feminine pose with one hand on her hip and wiggled her hips as she strutted back and forth across the stage. Again she exited. Section five continued with the jersey stretched over her entire length. After some histrionic posturing, the creature began to discreetly scratch herself before she slumped down and scurried away again behind the screen. In the final sequence, Litz came out fully cocooned. She bent down and up, touching the floor with the top of the cloth, like a bird dipping to drink. Then, slumping onto the floor, she gradually unpeeled herself from the tube, like a snake from its skin, dragging it after her in a somewhat agitated state. In the end, it was unclear if the tube of cloth was letting go of her or she was discarding the cloth.

The Glyph is far from a conventional modern dance work. It uses an eclectic movement vocabulary that does not rely on pure technical dancing so much as gesturing, walking, and prop manipulation. Taken as a whole, the movement did not suggest a dramatic structure in the traditional sense of beginning, middle, and end but was a series of accumulations that together evoked a vaguely definable theme. By continuously appearing and disappearing behind the screen (a seeming reference to Humphrey's *The Banshee,* first performed in 1928), Litz took the idea of "variation" to the extreme, offering not one or two but a seemingly endless array of different portrayals of the basic theme of "woman with jersey." Also, Litz presented her work in a straightforward, friendly kind of way, which sidestepped the heroic performing presence often displayed by early modern dancers.

Seen in relation to the works of Graham as well as Humphrey and Limón, the piece was a whimsical commentary on the familiar symbols and personas of the modern dance world. Litz's choice of a tube of jersey cloth for the costume, for instance, resonated with the memory of Martha Graham's *Lamentation,* which was intensely emotional and serious.[16] In *The Glyph,* the costume was an entity to be explored as a sheath that transformed the dancer into different creatures. As such, it became part of a self-conscious satire of those earlier performances and no longer solely a means for expressing deep sorrow or impending doom. If Litz was directly influenced by one of her teachers, it was clearly Weidman, who was famous for his satiric portraits and mimicry of dance world celebrities.

The humor and endearing quality of this work was not lost on audiences of the time. The *Dance Observer* review immediately proclaimed the work a "masterpiece," stating, "Miss Litz inventively explores most possibilities, and has done something phenomenal through them. . . . Each variation is funnier than the preceding one, and the sum total of the work is hilarity." The reviewer proceeded to explain how Litz's cloth manipulation was different from Graham's: "Miss Litz has used it as a device to move in, to move through, to be bound in, to escape from. By rolling, unrolling, stretching, extending, and playfully dancing in it she has created a whole cross-section of patho- and patheto-comic characterizations with a minimum of means and a maximum of success."[17]

This interpretation of the work suggests why some critics and historians have labeled Litz avant-garde. In many ways her work anticipated the experiments of the 1960s, when dancers like Yvonne Rainer said "no" to the conventions of modern dance and ballet. Like Litz, Rainer and her colleagues were drawn to a more informal mode of presentation, to pedestrian movement and to new structures, especially nonlinear formats. And similar to Litz, their relentless, matter-of-fact exploration of movement and props—especially by the Grand Union collective in the early 1970s—evoked laughter through the bizarre references the juxtaposition of elements evoked.

Significantly, Litz's avant-garde explorations were an accepted part of her Y performances. *The Glyph* was one of a number of works created by Litz after she had spent the summer and fall of 1951 at Black Mountain College, a center of intense experimental activity at the time. It had its world premiere, in fact, at the college on August 24, 1951. The performance of the piece at the Y indicates the openness of the institution to new work and support of experimentation when little attention was otherwise afforded it. This is not surprising, however, since Litz was one of a long line of female choreographers who explored movement in unusual and often humorous ways at the Y. Others included the dance satirist Iva Kitchell and dance mimes like Lotte Goslar. These performers took modern dance beyond the monumentally tragic and angst-ridden domain into subtler and more whimsical territory. As late as January 1958, Kitchell performed *Soul in Search,* which was a straightforward satire of the more serious aspects of modern dance.

Sybil Shearer at the Y

Kolodney's sponsorship of young, out-of-town dancers also helped to introduce unconventional perspectives to the New York dance community. Often,
artists working in a highly personal style would alight at the Y, bringing a
fresh look at dance with them. One such person was Sybil Shearer, another
former Humphrey-Weidman dancer, who had relocated to Chicago in the
early 1940s. From there she toured the country, periodically reaching New
York, where she often profoundly startled audiences with her unique style.

In January 1944, Shearer presented a joint performance at the Y with Litz.
One of the pieces premiered on that program, *Vanity—or The Pulse of Death*,
was a good indicator of the interest that Shearer and Litz shared in social satire and humorous movement play. The critic Edwin Denby described the
piece as follows: "Two figures [Litz and Shearer] dressed in a shapeless version of Grecian robes [who] putter about the stage reciting brightly to each
other the rhymed platitudes of a poem on the Vanity of Life. The motions
they illustrate the verses with are small, careful, and absurdly domestic, and
the horrid, middle-aged stoop in Miss Shearer's back is the realistic foil to
their inane and spinsterish fussing."[18] Here, Denby pointed out how Shearer's
virtuosic use of intricate, small movements and gestures became part of a
larger human characterization. By juxtaposing these tiny movements with
the text and costume, Shearer, like Litz, played with familiar ways of interpreting a particular subject. Whereas under normal circumstances the text
on vanity and the Grecian robe would be entities considered with great seriousness and reverence (one might think of Isadora Duncan), in this situation they were made absurd through the machinations of the speakers, who,
in turn, seemed bumbling and awkward. The world was turned slightly and
subtly askew through the lens of the choreographer.

Shearer and Litz were both originally Humphrey-Weidman dancers and
shared a certain love of the unconventional, but they developed in markedly
different ways. Where Litz had a lighter, more optimistic quality, Shearer
was more extreme and confrontational in her challenge of the dance world.
She wore no stage makeup and later presented entire performances consisting of seamlessly woven works blended one into another. If she did not like
the ambiance of a particular audience, she would leave the stage and end the
performance. As a choreographer, Shearer had a highly original ability to
employ minimal movement and develop it in unusual ways through repeti-

tion and embellishment. This aspect of her work drew a great deal of admiration and inspired numerous experimental choreographers of the 1950s and beyond.

Yet in spite of this maverick behavior, Shearer's work seems to have had a stronger connection than Litz's to the romantic strain of modern dance that took itself very seriously. Her movement experimentation was often done with the intention of saying something profound about the human condition. One of the numbers presented in 1944 at the Y, *In a Vacuum*, later caught the eye of Margaret Lloyd as an example of Shearer's intensely dramatic use of minute gesture: "It was a tight, neurotic dance. The nervous tremors of lowered hands and crazily lifted feet met in an enclosing circle of light; the body angled toward these extremities, which seemed to be in a state of transposed tic; and the minute patterns of restless futility were incessantly repeated, until the spectator was all but drawn into the weird circle of meaningless motion. The drab and dowdy costume, the unkempt hair, added to the manic-depressive effect."[19] In this work, a small number of movements recurred to create a particular mood of frustration and loss of self-control. If Shearer was not interested in traditional narrative structures, she was, nonetheless, a committed portraitist.

While Shearer did not appear frequently at the Y, she believed that the "Y was an important place for a young person to perform" and that "it was good to be seen there."[20] Shearer recalls the Y as a mainstream venue largely controlled by Louis Horst, and insofar as she wished to retain her outsider status in relation to the New York dance community, in particular to Graham, she was not enthusiastic about appearing there. However, Shearer was aware that by the 1940s the Y was *the* established center for young dancers and a proving ground for the merit of one's work. Performing at the Y was needed to establish her validity as a serious artist; for this reason she went out of her way to perform on its stage.

In reality, Shearer was one of a long line of unconventional performers at the Y, and as such, her presence there does not particularly stand out. Rather, it contributed to the broadening of the modern dance aesthetic of the 1940s, which had begun with the initiation of the Dance Theatre series in the late 1930s. If anything, the appearance of Shearer at the Y displayed the flexibility of the Y's policies. Although Horst clearly played a central role in the Y's affairs, he neither completely defined its policies nor eschewed its ultimate mission to assist talented young dancers of all backgrounds.

Pearl Primus: The Negro Speaks of Rivers

Along with the Y's promotion of artists from outside New York, its sponsorship of minority artists also brought a strong awareness of the diversity of aesthetic expression, this time focusing on the "ethnic" dimension of modern dance. Beginning with Edna Guy and Katherine Dunham in the 1930s, to performances by Ailey in the late 1950s and Eleo Pomare in the 1960s, as stated earlier, the Y showcased work exploring the African-American experience. The Kaufmann stage was *the* theater where many black choreographers received their New York debut, including Dunham, Primus, Janet Collins, and Alvin Ailey. Kolodney, who was an active opponent of racism throughout his career, welcomed these performers. In a 1963 interview he acknowledged that "being a minority ourselves, maybe we are more sensitive" to minorities in general.

Kolodney's recognition of black Americans in the dance world was certainly indicated early on, as demonstrated by his invitation in 1937 to the participants of the Negro Dance Evening. In the letter he perceptively stated, "Your presence on the program will be an important contribution to the clearer understanding by our audience of the Negro dance in America, this being the main purpose of the evening." The performance itself traced a lineage of black influence through time and space. The first section, "Africa," presented the dancers Alma Sutton, Asadata Dafora Horton, and Abdul Assen in a series of dances: *Dance of Love, Dance of Beauty, Eccentric Dance, Religious Dance, Snake Dance,* and *Worship Dance.* Section two, "West Indies," consisted of *Haitian Ceremonial Dances, Biguine-Biguine* (danced by Dunham), and *Carnival Dances* (danced by Talley Beatty, Lester Harris and Group). Section three, "United States," included *Shout,* by various choreographers, and *Cake-Walk,* performed by Alison Burroughs and Clarence Yates. The fourth section, "Modern Trends," included six dances: *After Gaugin* (performed by Guy), *Composition* (performed by Burroughs), *Moorish Dance* (performed by Dunham), *Dance Spirituals* (choreographed by Guy and danced by Eleanor Clay, Odessa Johnson, Bernice Johnson, Burroughs, and Guy), *Tropic Death from "Swamp" Suite,* and *Negro Songs of Protest* (the latter two included numerous dancers and choreographers).

One of Kolodney's best-loved African American performers at the Y was Pearl Primus, who had studied at the New Dance Group with teachers such as Jane Dudley, Sophie Maslow, and Nona Schurman. Her celebrated dance, *The Negro Speaks of Rivers,* had its first concert performance at the 92nd Street Y on January 23, 1944.[21] This was Primus's second appearance at the Y

Pearl Primus in *The Negro Speaks of Rivers*.
Dance Division, The New York Public Library for the Performing Arts,
Astor, Lenox and Tilden Foundations. Photographer: Gerda Peterich.

after her formidable debut there a year earlier, and for this occasion she shared the program with Valerie Bettis, performing to a capacity audience. Following this event, Primus went on to give more than twelve recitals at the Y through 1955. Nathan, William Kolodney's son, later stressed that Primus was a particular favorite with Y audiences for her tremendous power and charisma as a dancer.[22]

The Negro Speaks of Rivers, a solo based on a poem by Langston Hughes, conjured up the African American knowledge of rivers, which flow with the pain and suffering experienced by slaves, as well as the pride and hope derived from memories of the Nile and the glories of Africa.[23] According to Joe Nash, a long-time performer with Primus, the poem would sometimes be recited before the dance and sometimes during it, showing its integral relation to the choreography. Nash explains that the dance was "about the role of rivers in a particular people—how there are conflicts, but the flow of life is ongoing."[24]

If the subject matter of the dance was clearly indicated by the poem, the dance itself was quite abstract. Primus's original choreography seems to have followed an A-B-A format, beginning and ending stage center in a deep plié in second position. Much of the intervening movement was a mixture of more technical dancing with naturalistic gesture and African dance. Movement motifs were repeated in different combination, building in intensity to a denouement. An excerpt of the dance was revived for the New Dance Group Gala Concert, held in New York in June 1993.[25] Overseen by Primus and danced by Kim Bears, this revival attests to Primus's impressionistic approach to choreography.

The New Dance Group performance begins with Bears standing still in the center of the stage. As the yearning jazz music begins, she bursts into side-to-side traveling steps moving forward, her upper body spreading and narrowing as she opens and crosses her arms.[26] Bears stops still and gradually collapses into her self, shaking and vibrating as she slowly circles around her own axis. The feeling is of pain, of a person racked by soundless sobs. The following section introduces a number of movements that are then repeated in different combinations throughout the dance. One is a low crouch, during which the dancer rolls her shoulders and contracts her torso in and out as if kneading bread. Another is a running and reaching motif in which the dancer scrambles to different parts of the stage, stretching out with her arms as if seeking aid. This run takes her into the third leitmotif, a series of gathering arm throws and spins on the diagonal, which whip the dancer through space.

These various movement phrases eventually lead to a climactic moment during which Bears performs a series of desperate leaps in a wide circle around the stage. Her upper body struggles to reach up and away as she jumps into the air. Similar movements follow, in which there are frustrated attempts at flight. One of these is a strange birdlike movement, in which the dancer stands on one leg, waves her arms by her sides and tries to take off. Another involves a wild jump in which she arches far back. The piece reaches its resolution with the first clear indication of inner strength and sense of pride. A series of spins take Bears to center stage, where she began. Facing the audience, she slowly settles into a deep, solid squat and carefully rounds her arms in front of her. Her heels thump alternately against the floor while her arms sway slowly back and forth. To finish, the dancer stands straight, bringing one arm up, and the other reaches out as she looks powerfully upward.

In *The Negro Speaks of Rivers,* Primus often uses movement metaphorically. The dancer rolls her body in imitation of a river's flowing movement. She shakes herself as if crying uncontrollably. She simulates flight to represent the desire to escape from servitude to a better life. She stretches one arm upward and the other straight out as a symbol of hope. By combining these movements, a collage of expressive moments is woven together that creates an impression of deep sadness mixed with optimism. The constant movement across the stage space—circling and crisscrossing—adds greatly to the intensity of the performance, as do the reverberating words of the poem by Hughes, "I've known rivers ancient as the world and older than the flow of human blood in human veins."

Primus's use of poetry and symbolic gesture was closely related to the choreographic approach of her teachers at the New Dance Group and other modern dancers of the time. In 1934, for instance, Dudley choreographed *Time Is Money*, a dance performed to a poem by Sol Funaroff. In this work, a dancer displayed the mechanistic movements of a worker caught in the daily drudge of employment, while another performer narrated the words from the side of the stage. Shortly before the appearance of *The Negro Speaks of Rivers,* Valerie Bettis choreographed *The Desperate Heart*, a now-celebrated visualization of John Malcolm Brinnin's poem.[27] Bettis employed sweeping kicks, spinning, scuttling, and yearning arm gestures in various combinations to create a sense of urgency that matched the poem's intensity. This piece was performed again for the shared performance with Primus in 1944, making a clear connection between the two works.

Where Primus's work differed was in her particular use of African and

African American material and strong social statements regarding black experience. Following in the steps of Hemsley Winfield, Edna Guy, and the Hampton Institute Creative Dance Group, Primus was interested in consciously incorporating this material into her choreography. Similar to Dunham, Primus's commitment ultimately took the form of extensive fieldwork and research, leading to a Ph.D. in anthropology from Columbia University. Primus did not make her first trip to Africa until the late 1940s; however, *The Negro Speaks of Rivers* shows Primus's early inspiration in African-style movement. This is seen in the rippling use of the torso and arms, rootedness to the ground, syncopation, and short rhythmic step patterns, as when she performed a series of percussive walks on the diagonal, her arms reaching upward in a V shape and then folding inward to her chest. Similar tendencies were later developed in her *Negro Spirituals*, in which she used deep multiple contractions with voluminous all-embracing arms.

Primus's appearance at the 92nd Street Y indicates her desire to be accepted by the serious dance community of the period. During 1943 – 44, Primus performed consistently at the nightclub Cafe Society but kept returning to the Y to assert her status as an earnest young concert dancer. In April 1944 she gave her first solo recitals there, both of which were sold out. The positive reviews of this concert, as well as her earlier appearances at the Y, demonstrate that Primus was extremely successful in achieving her goal. The critic Edwin Denby wrote, "Miss Primus has astonishing gifts of movement—for flow, lightness, for power; and her powerful body is beautifully plastic on the stage. With constant stage experience, her stage personality grows sweeter and more direct. Though the dance effect of almost any young dancer's solo recital is repetitive and strained, Miss Primus's seemed varied and easy."[28]

Primus's success was closely tied to the particular openness of the Y community to African Americans. Around the time of her first concerts there, internal documentation shows that blacks were welcomed at the institution. In 1945 a group of approximately thirty black boys and girls applied to join the Y under the auspices of a volunteer group called Youth Builders. The minutes of the board's meeting to discuss the request recorded: "The Y has never discriminated against applicants for membership on the basis of race or creed and does not do so now despite terribly overcrowded conditions. . . . In fact . . . at our lectures and our musical and dance recitals, the number of Negro visitors is considerable." Based on the egalitarian traditions and ideals of the Y, the board agreed to consider the applications for membership on the same basis and subject to the same conditions as applied to all applicants.

They concluded: "The ideal should be to take the matter in stride, without fanfare or fuss, and without publicity."[29]

Over the years this policy of acceptance remained solidly in place. Edith Valentine, an African American pianist for the Merry-Go-Rounders in the 1950s, observed that at the same time that she was finding it nearly impossible to rent an apartment in New York for herself and her husband, because of racist sentiments, she never encountered any discrimination at the Y. This was a feeling expressed by many dancers working at the institution, who also pointed out that the New Dance Group was the other haven for interracial acceptance in the dance world.

· · ·

FUSION FORMS AND STYLISTIC DIVERSITY AT THE Y

Following Primus, other African American choreographers to benefit from the Y's open policy included Donald McKayle and Alvin Ailey. Choreographically, these dancers further experimented with the modern idiom, incorporating ballet and jazz as well as African dance into their compositions. This eclecticism was noticed early on in the case of Janet Collins, whose broad interests even embraced Judaism, making her a prime example of the extreme kind of cultural and choreographic fusions possible at the Y.

Collins was the cousin of Carmen de Lavallade, who had studied with Maracci and Horton in California. On February 20, 1949, Collins made her debut in New York on the annual Audition Winners' Concert at the Y. In this concert she performed only two numbers: an abstract work, *Rondo,* and *Spirituals,* an emotionally charged work in two parts that contrasted the lament of "Nobody Knows the Trouble I've Seen" with the exhortation of "Didn't My Lord Deliver Daniel." No film record of these dances seems to exist, but their unusual character was sufficient to draw a glowing review from Martin, who so rarely covered the Y's events. He announced that Collins was the "most exciting young dancer who has flashed across the current scene in a long time." He then went on to observe, "Her style is basically eclectic; its direction is modern and its technical foundation chiefly ballet. The fusing element is a markedly personal approach which will undoubtedly come sooner or later into complete control of all the divergent influences and emerge as a style of its own."[30]

Collins's particular interest in Jewish themes appears to have stemmed from her interest in the Bible. In 1951 she returned to the Y for two recitals as part of the Dance Theatre Series. One of the pieces on Collins's program was

Janet Collins.
Dance Division, The New York Public Library for the Performing Arts,
Astor, Lenox and Tilden Foundations. Photographer: Gerda Peterich.

Three Psalms of David. The note stated, "For years she has done research on Negro and Hebrew dance material, working with Ernest Bloch, the celebrated composer and authority on Hebrew music." In 1956, Collins returned to the Y to perform *Three Psalms* on a program organized on biblical themes with Noami Aleh-Leaf and the Merry-Go-Rounders. Deborah Pritzker, writing in the *Y Bulletin,* described the work as "conceived as a triptych depicting the growth of man's spirit, the work—choreography and dancing—distilled the intrinsic meaning of the psalms; from inarticulate bewilderment and longing . . . to peace and acceptance . . . to full realization."[31]

Collins's debut at the Y launched her successful career as the first black premiere danseuse of the Metropolitan Opera Ballet. While she might have

Paul Draper.
92nd Street YM-YWHA Archives.

advanced without the Y's patronage, the numerous parallel examples of Primus's and Ailey's rise to fame suggest that the Y played a key role in her acceptance. The broader Y policy, plus Kolodney's personal commitment to nonsectarian programming and his desire to aid the young, struggling artist, made it possible for African Americans to perform at the Y. This in turn permitted experiments in combining different dance styles and concerns under the broader African American perspective.

In addition to these African American choreographers, others performed at the Y who were not always directly associated with modern dance but were extremely interested in stylistic mixing. These included Paul Draper, who combined ballet and tap, and Maracci, who brought together ballet and Spanish dance. Such artists consistently demonstrated that the Y, far from being associated with one particular style, was open to a diversity of expression that eschewed the narrow definitions of modern dance promoted by a Big Four approach. During an interview in 1979, Valerie Bettis remarked on the unique character of the Y to promote dancers outside this framework: "When they had auditions at the 92nd Street YW-YMHA [*sic*] for their tremendous dance series, I at the time thought that, because I was not Graham or Humphrey, I would never win anything. Well, they put me on a program with that marvelous lady Sybil Shearer who was, you must know, like Miss Genius of All Time! And Erick Hawkins, can you believe that? And then later that year they had another program for me with Pearl Primus. And the Y from that point on was amazing."[32]

The openness of the Y's Jewish constituency to new dance works is significant for the writing of dance history. Like the other institutions of the time, such as the New School and Bennington, the Y was active in validating modern dance and weaving a mythology of the greatness of that period in dance history. At the same time, the constant promotion of new work on its stage challenged the role of the mythology that claimed sole supremacy for Graham, Humphrey, Weidman, and Holm. Such a challenge had important implications for the subsequent history of the 1960s and postmodern dance, when many of the choreographic experiments nurtured on the Y stage found wide-scale recognition.

(7)

SYNTHESIZING THE

UNIVERSAL & PARTICULAR

Producing "Jewish Dance" at the Y

. . .

At the heart of the convergence of the dance and Jewish communities were the Jewish dancers who lived between both worlds. If the Y's presentation of dancers from different backgrounds supported an aesthetic of diversity and a democratic context in which to view dance, it was its producing of Jewish dancers—specifically, their choreographic endeavors, which mapped out the complex and varied ways in which the Y's Jewish constituency sought to maintain its distinctiveness within this broader vision of cultural pluralism. For although he was intent on assisting a range of dancers and on embracing general American culture, Kolodney devoted special attention to the work of Jewish choreographers and dancers. Over the years he also encouraged the creation of a new dance style, which would incorporate aspects of Jewish experience in different ways. Under the loose label of Jewish dance, such work ranged from modern dances based on Jewish themes to Israeli folk dancing.

Although many of the dancers discussed below have already been mentioned, examining in a cohesive manner the particular ways Jewish choreographers either avoided or strove to incorporate consciously defined Jewish themes into their dances provides an opportunity for a closer examination of how modernist dance conventions and theories intersected with the needs of a particular ethnic/religious minority—in this case, a sector of the Jewish community. How did modern dance practices, which tended to simplify, abstract, and stylize, and theories that validated female expression—individuality, creativity, and universalism of communication—intersect with an ethnic/religious community's need to refer to long-lasting traditions and locate quintessential, uplifting images of itself that could act as marks of distinctiveness? In the case of Jewish dance as it appeared at the Y, these two sets of impulses were often combined in a highly supportive manner, not only to enhance a new conception of Jewishness being formed in America but also to support the aim of modern dance to give expression to the contemporary experiences of all Americans. In many ways the efforts of Jewish dancers, especially in the postwar period, crystallized the Y's efforts to fight the potential ethnocentrism and racism in the dominant view of modern dance, providing as they did ongoing public, visceral manifestations of Kolodney's desire to synthesize the universal and particular in human experience.

• • •

JEWS AND EARLY MODERN DANCE IN NEW YORK

In his role as a producer, Kolodney presented Jewish dancers whose efforts went beyond the Y's walls. Understanding the institution's particular role in the lives and work of these dancers is therefore closely connected to a recognition that different people worked in New York during the period, and their relationship to their Jewishness shifted over time. Discussion of the Y, therefore, begins with an analysis of a broader connection in New York between Jews and dance and examines how early efforts at making a specifically Jewish dance practice reflected the influence of discourses from both modern dance and a large-scale movement to re-create Jewish life in the Diaspora and Palestine.

Although it is rarely acknowledged, in the late 1920s and the 1930s a large number of modern dancers were Jewish.[2] It is impossible to name all those involved, but the following gives some indication of the people active during the period. Helen Tamiris (born Helen Becker), one of the most prominent choreographers of the time, was the daughter of Russian Jewish immigrants. Many early members of Graham's company also were Jewish: Frieda Flier, Nina Fonaroff, Lili Mann, Marie Marchowsky, Sophie Maslow, Lily Mehlman, Freema Nadler, Mary Radin, Florence Schneider, Lillian Shapero, Ger-

Freema Nadler in Graham-inspired Poses, ca. 1930.
Courtesy of Freema Nadler.

trude Shurr, and Anna Sokolow. The same held true of students at Hanya
Holm's school, such as Miriam Blecher and Nadia Chilkovsky. Other Jewish
dancers and writers included Ruth Freedman and Rose Levy (early members
of Sokolow's Dance Unit); Beatrice Seckler, Eva Desca, Eve Gentry, Saida
Gerrard, and Marion Scott (members of the Humphrey-Weidman group);
the critic Edna Ocko; and radical dancer Edith Segal.

The majority of these young women were the daughters of Eastern European immigrants; they grew up in working-class families with left-wing leanings. Maslow, for instance, was raised in Brooklyn by Russian Jewish parents.
Her father was an ardent Socialist, belonging to the Workmen's Circle, a Yiddishist fraternal institution with close ties to the Jewish unions and Jewish
labor press. Sokolow's mother, Sara Sokolowski, worked in the garment trade
and was active in the Socialist Party. Freema Nadler, who danced with Graham in 1931–32, grew up in predominantly Jewish neighborhoods in New
Jersey, Brooklyn, and the Bronx. Her parents were from Ukraine and had
moved to America to escape the pogroms. In the Bronx the family lived in a
cooperative; they were left-wing and completely nonreligious. Their ideological commitments led the family to move to Russia in 1932.[3]

These young women were participating in a widespread movement of the
time that sought to radically transform American society. In his book *Jews
and the Left*, Arthur Liebman demonstrates that a significant "Jewish Left

subculture" existed in America during the twentieth century.[4] Liebman uses the term *Left* "to designate a political ideology that is in some way or to some significant extent informed by Marxism. In this sense it is used to describe the politics of individuals, groups or movements."[5] He then traces the roots of an American Jewish Left to the status of Jewish workers in Russia in the nineteenth century, suggesting that it was largely as a reaction to their dual status as an impoverished class and oppressed people that many turned toward radicalism. In America, Liebman argues, Russian Jews were highly represented in national left-wing organizations, such as the Socialist Party of America and the Communist Party during the first part of the century. These Jews tended to be working-class, nonreligious, and intimately connected with other Jews through an elaborate network of Jewish institutions and associations. Liebman writes: "They were sharing common experiences and problems in the context of their shops, neighborhoods, and voluntary, self-created organizations. The channels of communication for the sharing of defined grievances was thus highly developed among them."[6]

This ferment of leftist activity provided the larger context in which many Russian Jewish immigrants experienced the arts. In the case of dance, many in the 1920s were attracted to the work of Isadora Duncan, who seemed a symbol of people's radicalism and socialist ideals. Duncan disseminated a utopian vision of a better world through dance, promoting a mass revolutionary dance that would educate the mover about the workings of the body, thereby expanding individual consciousness and creating a more just society.[7] Duncan's enthusiasm for Russia was particularly compelling. As she wrote in *My Life,* she "actually believed that the ideal State, such as Plato, Karl Marx and Lenin had dreamed it, had now by some miracle been created on earth. With all the energy of my being, disappointed in the attempts to realize any of my art visions in Europe, I was ready to enter the ideal domain of Communism."[8] Such ideas resonated with many Jewish radicals of the 1920s. Maslow's mother "was an enthusiast" of Duncan, as were the parents of most Jewish dancers of the time. Maurice Bakst, who as a young man had studied with Humphrey and Weidman, reminisced that people were moved by her tremendous courage: "Duncan broke from tradition."[9]

Whether exposed to modern dance through their Eastern European parents or on their own, the younger generation was mesmerized with it. Young women, in particular, were drawn to the Graham style because of its spiritual base, powerful movement, and seeming embodiment of contemporary life. Many were captivated by Graham at the Neighborhood Playhouse, where most of her Jewish dancers were introduced to her. Established by the German-Jewish sisters Irene and Alice Lewisohn to improve the quality of life of immigrant children through training in the performing arts, the Playhouse was a ripe space for the intersection of Jews with the new modern dance. Graham has been associated with the more "bourgeois" segment of modern dance, owing to the abstract, individualistic nature of her dances and the distance she assumed from political causes.[10] Her dancers, however, found in her fanatical approach to dance an intrinsic passion that not only fired the new Graham vocabulary but also ignited their revolutionary fervor. Nadler spoke of Graham's tremendous inspiration as "a kind of fire" that made you "get to the core of everything" and "express what was inside."[11] Sophie Maslow reminisced, "Even though I was an adolescent, I felt that everything Martha was doing was right. All of her movements were meaningful."[12] The result was that in the 1930s these young dancers marched from the Workers Book Shop to the Graham studio in no time, equally committed to her work and their own revolutionary causes.

Because of their focus on class inequality, during the 1930s and early 1940s few of these Jewish dancers were consciously interested in their Jewishness as it related to dance. Instead, they were drawn to the social concerns of the poor and working class, factors that reflected the major focus of left-wing circles. While they continued to perform for their mentors (Graham, Humphrey, Holm), they also launched out on their own. Sokolow formed her Dance Unit; Chilkovsky and Blecher helped to establish the New Dance Group as a collective modeled after the Communist cell. The dancers discussed politics and made dances about the impoverished and downtrodden workers, slum childhood, and juvenile delinquency. Sokolow's *Case History No. —— *(1937), for instance, concerns the dismal fate of someone born to unfortunate circumstances. The program note quotes a juvenile court record, stating, "H—— R—— followed the usual pattern, beginning with unemployment. From street corner to pool room, from mischief to crime." As the 1930s ended, the focus shifted away from the specifically urban experience to express the struggles of "the people" in rural, agrarian communities.[13] In 1941, Sophie Maslow choreographed *Dust Bowl Ballads*, which presented the plight of people struggling to survive the Great Depression and the Dust Bowl, and in 1942, she created *Folksay*, a dance performed to verses from Carl Sandburg's "The People, Yes," interspersed with folk ballads and stories. In each of these dances, Maslow freely adapted American folk songs and dances.

These dancers represented one particular way that members of the Jewish community drew on the universalistic discourse of modern dance to make a space for themselves and other underrepresented members of society. Modern dance, as Martin and others defined it, was closely associated with the generic American dancer who could transcend his or her particular experience and create work that had universal significance. This perspective implied that a person could transcend his or her ethnicity (and even gender and race) in the act of representation. If one was no longer tied to one's cultural and religious traditions, one could, at least theoretically, dance about "others'" experiences. And if one could transform the particular into the universal, one could present what might otherwise be perceived as purely the concerns of a small local group as of importance to the general American population.

At a fundamental level, the radical Jewish choreographers capitalized on the rhetoric of openness basic to modern dance to make room for themselves in the American cultural landscape. They could transcend their particular Jewish, urban, female identities to assume the cause of, for instance, an Oklahoma migrant farmer, as Maslow did in *Dust Bowl Ballads*. This situation well suited a particularly nonobservant, contemporary-minded sector of the Jewish community, that wanted to fully embrace general culture. Their efforts outlined a new form of Jewishness in America defined by constituency and association, rather than manifestly "Jewish content." For although the dances did not directly refer to Jewish experience, most of the dancers involved were Jews and worked in close association with each other. In the mid-1930s the majority of soloists of the Workers Dance League, a left-wing organization sponsoring concerts, were Jewish: Sokolow, Segal, Blecher, Mehlman, Chilkovsky, and Maslow.[14] In some ways, radical dance *was* a kind of Jewish dance.

The openness of modern dance to individual transcendence was, however, not simply reproduced in the dances of the choreographers: they did not assume the safe characters of fluttering birds or standard heroes. As Blecher said, "In our dances, we do not chase a butterfly across the stage."[15] Rather, Jewish radicals took the lead in stretching the definition of modern dance to make a place for minorities in American mythology. As Ellen Graff observes, through dances like *Ballads* and *Folksay*, Maslow effectively "reconstructed historical America" to include "not only the descendants of the Mayflower but all the tired, hungry, and poor who had arrived since then." She notes, "Appropriating the folklore of rural culture, artists on the left demonstrated their kinship with the historic Americans who also had been left out of the American dream. Performing the experience of Okie farmers, or untutored country musicians, dancers located an urban—and essentially foreign and socialist—vision within the larger American experience."[16] The implication here is that modern dance and America were in flux; Maslow and other Jews from socially conscious backgrounds were passionately engaged in redefining these entities, even as they joined them. It was not a straightforward matter of assimilating to American culture but of reshaping art and society in line with egalitarian views at the root of Jewish ethics and the historical experience of persecution.

• • •

THE NEW "JEWISH DANCE"

While most Jewish dancers were involved with broad social concerns of American life, some, like Benjamin Zemach, Lillian Shapero, Lasar Galpern, Dvora Lapson, and Corinne Chochem, were growing interested in what was consciously being called Jewish dance. This term was used to refer to dancing that in some way intentionally involved Jewish experiences. These dancers functioned as part of a wide-scale effort to revitalize Jewish life in the Diaspora and Palestine, both as the Zionist cause grew in fervor and as America's Jews created new outlets of cultural expression in places like the Yiddish Theater. In their choreography, initial experiments were made in combining modernist conventions (individual expression, use of abstraction, belief in universal truths) with traditional sources of Jewish identification (namely, the Bible, ritual, custom) to create positive images of Jews.

In a 1934 article the author Naum Rosen observed the new trend, stating, "In recent years there has been in America a growing interest in Jewish dancing."[17] Rosen explains that by Jewish dancing he means "dancing that suggests and portrays that which is peculiarly Jewish." It arises from the creative dancer's delving deeply into the Jewish people's emotions and expressing them in a form of his own. According to Rosen, the clearest example of Jewish dance is seen in Maurice Schwartz's production of *Yoshe Kalb*. In this work, he explains, movement drawn from Chassidic life, and worship is used as the basis for the choreography. Rosen also briefly mentions the dances in the Moscow Habima's production of *The Dybbuk* and the work of Benjamin Zemach.

The idea of a contemporary Jewish dance is most clearly traced to Zemach, who popularized it in America in the late 1920s.[18] Zemach was one of the first to establish a connection to Zionism and to create his version of Jewish

Benjamin Zemach.
Courtesy of Naima Prevots.

dance within that context. In Russia, Benjamin had grown up under the influence of his brother, Nahum, who believed that Jewish survival involved settlement of Palestine and revival of Hebrew as a spoken language. As a founder of the Habima, Nahum oversaw the production of plays in Hebrew, using Jewish material, all of which the younger Zemach was intimately involved with. The most famous of these was *The Dybbuk*, based on the work of S. Ansky, which was first presented in 1922 and toured America in 1926. In pursuing the Zionist project, Nahum and his colleagues conceived of Jewishness in mythic terms, suggesting the timeless power of Jewish spirituality. Rather than following a naturalistic theater, which would focus on the variety and detail of Jewish life, Nahum was drawn to the work of Stanislavsky, which used symbolic characterization, costumes, and stage sets. Yevgeny Vakhtangov, Stanislavsky's top pupil, worked closely with the Habima in their staging of *The Dybbuk* to create a highly stylized production, in which Chassidic behavior was greatly exaggerated and distorted. The process of abstraction was used to construct a representation of Jews as living in a world of unsettling forces, superstition, and spirits.[19]

Benjamin Zemach was greatly influenced by the Habima's conception of Jewishness, which he brought with him to the United States in the 1920s. In creating his dances he used a process of abstraction to create powerful images of the Jewish spirit—crystallized, timeless images of the praying Jew, the devout Yeshiva student, and the wandering Jew who fights for justice in the world. In 1929, John Martin wrote a lengthy article on Zemach, stating that "[Zemach] admits a great debt to that profoundly stimulating theatre which for the first time turned the thought of the Jewish dramatic arts away from naturalism to the more elusive realm of stylization and pure theatre."

Zemach's choreographic vision is captured well in Martin's detailed 1929 article, which begins by stating that "Benjamin Zemach has set the wheels in motion to establish the first Jewish ballet in history." The example provided is Zemach's ballet-pantomime in three scenes, *Lag-Boymer*, based on the work of Sholom Aleichem. The event, Martin writes, marks "the beginning of a movement new both to the art of the dance and to the culture of the Jewish people." The article reports that, for Zemach, there are two principal sources to which to turn in creating Jewish dance: "the actual physical movements of the Jewish folk in their daily life and . . . their religious practices, such as those especially of the Chassidic sect." Characteristic daily movement is described as shortened and sharpened by the "rhythm of city living." Examples of movement from religious life include the "attitudes of the student before his

tomes of learning, when he is perplexed, when he has perceived some difficult point, when he is pacing the floor in doubt or when he is lost in meditation—all are of such intensity that they provide the choreographic delver
with much fuel for his fire." Martin continues: "[Zemach] would discover
also the secret of what he himself calls 'Bible movement,' that great, heroic
breadth of the Psalms and the Song of Songs, that serene elevation of the pa-
triarchs and prophets." No further description is given of biblical dance except to note that Zemach was leaving in a few weeks for Palestine, where "recent archaeological discoveries invite him."[20] The implication was that such
discoveries could shed light on ancient movement practices.

In locating the essence of Jewishness in Chassidic and biblical sources,
Zemach was making specific and highly significant choices. The biblical lore,
for instance, was useful to him because it created a link with the ancient Jewish past and infused his contemporary creations with a feeling of authenticity and validity, both significant for creating a sense of a unified community
with a common heritage. Turning to the Bible represented a search for prece-
dents and origins. Zemach wanted to establish that there was a long history
of Jews dancing and that it was an activity sanctified by the most sacred of
Jewish texts. Moreover, the Bible offered timeless archetypal characters and
narratives that clearly portrayed the fortitude and spirituality of the Jewish
people. In *Ruth*, Zemach created a work about the strength of Ruth and
Naomi; and in his dance *The Prophets*, Zemach refers to the passage "From
second to second their Union grew greater, And their spirit spread forth, ever
higher and higher."

In America, Zemach used biblical passages as a familiar reference point for
educating a broad audience about the Jews and their right to rebuild a nation
in Palestine. According to dance historian Naima Prevots, Zemach was interested in stressing the universal messages in his dances that would make the
work accessible to non-Jews as well as Jews. She writes of *Ruth*, "Although the
dance was based in part on the Judaic heritage, Zemach was concerned with
making a universal statement. . . . The dance had something to say about
women that would speak to everyone. Zemach abstracted the essential inner
quality of these three relationships and the strength that carries women
through their various roles and accompanying hardships."[21] When com-
menting on his dance *Fragments of Israel*, which contained biblical scenes
and images of Palestine, Prevots reiterates that the dance "was intended to
convey a universal plea for all people to maintain their identity and right
against oppression."[22]

The appeal of Chassidic material, on the other hand, lay in its aura of mysticism, which could represent the emotional intensity and mysterious nature of Jewish spirituality. Like his colleagues in the Habima, Zemach was aware of the power of a mythic representation of Jews being connected to supernatural forces. The Chassidim were a perfect vehicle for such an image. A particular sect of Judaism that evolved in eighteenth-century Europe, the Chassidim turned the stern God into a merciful God who desired to be worshipped with singing, festivity, joy, and dancing. Chassidim were well known for their ecstatic dancing in prayer and overall enthusiastic acceptance of bodily movement as a form of worship. In his signature work, *Farewell to Queen Sabbath*, Zemach portrayed this ecstasy by depicting an Orthodox Jew celebrating joy at the coming of the Sabbath.

Zemach's work set the precedent in locating a Jewish essence in the religious community as a means of signifying the timeless Jewish spirit and in using modernist practices of abstraction, stylization, and simplification to convey his message. During the 1930s several Americans interested in Jewish dance followed his lead in creating rarefied, stylized images of Jews from religious sources and traditional daily life. The Chassidic connection was particularly strong because Chassidic lifestyle seemed to be the one place where a clearly definable Jewish folklore had been kept alive.

A prime example of an American Jewish dancer working along these lines in the 1930s is found in Lillian Shapero, who was born in New York on the Lower East Side and lived with her Chassidic Polish grandparents, who encouraged her to participate in singing and dancing at the synagogue. This experience led Shapero to a love of dance; like the women discussed earlier, she attended the Neighborhood Playhouse, where she was introduced to Graham. Shapero danced with Graham's group from 1929 to 1935, during which time she also worked in the Yiddish theater. In 1933 she choreographed the dances for Maurice Schwartz's production of *Yoshe Kalb*. From then on she was associated with both the Yiddish Art Theatre and the Artef (Workers Theater Group).[23] In these productions, Shapero created theatrical dances out of movement from Chassidic sources. Martin's review in the *New York Times* of her choreography for *Yoshe Kalb* described it as "consisting of folk movement and carefully devised synthetic folk movements arranged in simple but dramatically effective design."[24]

Shapero's choreography was part of the larger movement that sought to portray Jews in an uplifting light, however, for her the emphasis was more on maintaining and developing a strong sense of Jewish cultural continuity in

Lillian Shapero.
Courtesy of the Shapero family.

the New World than on looking toward Palestine, like Zemach. In New York the Yiddish theater was often a place where families went to be reminded of their Eastern European roots.[25] It was a space where Jews could be immersed in familiar sounds, sights, stories and gestures and feel secure from the surrounding world. David Lifson observes in *The Yiddish Theatre in America*,

"The Jewish life which had become diffused due to infiltration, to a new gentile environment, to a new culture and language, this Jewish life was seeking wholeness, identity, and completeness in the Yiddish theatre."[26]

At the same time, the desire to create a modern Jewish culture in America continued to be closely connected, both in the Yiddish theater and outside it, to developments in Palestine. Dvora Lapson, who performed and wrote about Jewish dance in New York in the 1930s, framed her discussions of biblical, Chassidic, and Palestinian source materials in terms of the "return of the Jew to Palestine."[27] According to Lapson, "the dance has begun to play a new role in the life of the Jew." As an example, she refers to the hora and the fact that it has "become so closely coupled with the message of the new Palestine that wherever you come upon a group of Chalutzim [settlers], whether it be in Palestine, or in the training farms of Poland, Germany or America, you are sure to find the Hora danced by all."[28]

In New York, dance was specially featured by the Hebrew Arts Committee (HAC), part of the Zionist Organization of America. Formed in 1936 under Mordecai Kaplan's inspiration at the Jewish Theological Seminary, the aims of the HAC were to transmit Jewish values through the arts. Leaders such as Rabbi Moshe Davis wished to express distinctive Hebrew culture, develop Jewish artists, and build a home in America for the Hebrew arts. Davis saw the arts as central to the success of the Zionist movement: "The theater, dance, choral, painting (and later orchestral) units [of HAC] were not aesthetic appendages to an otherwise integrated program of propaganda but rather became the warp and woof of the organizational and ideological aspects of the movement."[29] Corinne Chochem was initially in charge of the dance unit of the HAC, directing a group called Rikkud Ami Dance Troupe, or Dance of My People. Chochem taught folk dancing at the Seminary School of Jewish Studies and wanted to reawaken interest in the Hebrew dance and create for it a suitable form by drawing on both ballet and modern dance techniques as well as "Biblical, Chassidic and Palestinian themes."[30]

The work of Chochem, along with that of Zemach and Shapero, indicates the way several dancers of the 1930s and early 1940s were consciously struggling to create a new view of Jewish identity mediated, to some extent, by the conventions of the contemporary dance world. Their work was not widespread but nonetheless remained an important part of the larger dance scene, which also included the highly active left-wing Jewish dancers. It was not uncommon for there to be, in fact, overlaps in performances between the so-called radical and Jewish causes, as in the case of Shapero, who performed numerous dances with left-wing subjects alongside her dances based on Jewish themes. One of her dances, *Crisis*, included the note: "All differences become insignificant when the moment arrives to unite against the fascist menace."[31] On the whole, though, the efforts to create a Jewish dance practice were on the fringe of general dance activity in the 1930s and not particularly widespread. It would take the disastrous effects of the Nazi regime to bring their efforts to the attention of mainstream Jewish audiences of America.

• • •

JEWISH DANCE AT THE Y IN THE PREWAR PERIOD

Having examined the broader landscape of Jewish concerns, it is possible to return to the 92nd Street Y, where both of these manifestations of American Jewish identity were found in the pre–Second World War period. Leftist sentiments, for instance, were represented by Sokolow and her dancers, who performed more or less annually at the Y during the late 1930s. Sokolow's performances there on February 28, 1937, and March 20, 1938, included many leftist pieces, including the satirical *Excerpts from a War Poem,* critical of Fascist Italy, to the words of the Italian poet F. T. Marinetti. Maslow's *Ragged Hungry Blues* and *Two Songs about Lenin* and Mehlman's *Spanish Woman*, motivated by the civil war in Spain, appeared on a program on November 21, 1937. Shapero performed *Casualty List* and *Crisis* on her December 26, 1937, recital. Marchowsky appeared in *A Moral for Workers—Horatio Alger* in a mixed-bill concert that included, among others, an early member of the Workers Dance League, Fanya Chochem, in *Strike Agitation.*

Similarly, the more religious, Chassidic variety of Jewish dance was evident at the Y in the work of Shapero and Zemach. Shapero's performance in 1937 included *Wedding Ritual, Chassidic Sketches,* and *Purim Shpiel.* In his performances at the institution, Zemach presented *Ruth, Farewell to Queen Sabbath, The Prophets,* and *Benyomen the Third.* The latter was described in the program note as a story of a Jewish Don Quixote whose wandering leads him to the realization that he must "fight for justice, here and now, together with his fellowmen." The Russian dancer and ballet master Lasar Galpern presented an evening of dance on Jewish themes on November 7, 1938, including *Chassidic Dance.* The newly emerging Palestinian dance also could be seen at the Y in Zemach's and Galpern's work as well as through the teaching of Rose Blumkin and Noami Aleh-Leaf in the late 1930s. Zemach performed pieces titled *Palestinian Folk Songs* and *The Worker's Dance on the Soil;* Galpern performed *The Earth Is Calling*, a "Palestinian Chalutz Dance about the tilling of the soil and the joys of life." Blumkin's course of 1939 stated that students would experience dance movement based on Hebrew and Palestinian themes: "This will be carried out, at first, through the learning of Palestinian folk dances with constant analysis of the forms of each dance and the possibilities of development through exaggeration, rearrangement, and various other devices to illustrate the means by which an art form is crystallized from the raw material of the peasant folk."[32]

However, while Jewish dancers and the new Jewish dance were being patronized at the Y, during the middle to late 1930s their presence was limited. Even though Kolodney made a concerted effort to shape the institution as an outlet for a Jewish consciousness, his energy remained directed toward promoting involvement in the general contemporary arts as the preferred mode of being an American Jew. Coming to the Y to take classes in modern dance, poetry, theater, philosophy, and psychology would be more or less sufficient; by doing these activities within the framework of a Jewish institution and socializing with other Jews, one was already expressing one's Jewishness. As seen earlier, such a perspective well suited the Y's constituency of wealthier, mostly nonreligious Jews interested in participating in American culture. They were not particularly engaged in either highly political, religious, or Yiddishist concerns.[33] To these people such matters had little to do with their new middle- and upper-class American lives.

For this reason, neither left-wing Jewish dancers nor the new Jewish dance were particularly successful at the Y before the war. In a 1991 interview the radical Jewish dancer Edith Segal stated that she never performed at the Y because her work was "too left" for the organization; and when Kolodney tried to organize a Jewish Dance Evening in September 1939, with Miriam Blecher, Chochem, Belle Didjah, Galpern, Aleh-Leaf, Pauline Koner, Shapero, and Zemach, he had to cancel it because there was "insufficient response," apparently on the part of the Y community.[34] Rather than finding outstanding patronage at the Y, the radical Jewish dancers performed at union halls and Communist gatherings, and the performers who were more particularly interested in Jewish dance, like Shapero, worked for the Yiddish theater. Zemach, for his part, was busy with many other ventures. From 1937 on he performed and directed in New York and Los Angeles, as well as in Canada. Among other endeavors, he directed *Natural Man* for the American Negro Theatre and was the dance director for a few Hollywood films before moving to Israel in 1971.

. . .

POSTWAR TRANSFORMATIONS:
THE Y AS THE HOME OF THE
NEW JEWISH CONSCIOUSNESS

The Second World War brought about a major change in American Jewish consciousness that brought the Y into a much more central role in patronizing modern dance based on Jewish themes and Jewish folk dancing. As the horrors of the war became more evident to people in America, important contemporary artists and intellectuals who had previously stood aloof from their Jewish identity began consciously to make work based on Jewish themes. In the modern dance world this was particularly the case with Sokolow and Maslow, both of whom started to create more works that had Jewish subject matter. In addition, the efforts of performers to create dances based on Palestine began to gain greater visibility as momentum built around the founding of the state of Israel. Israeli folk dancing in particular became extremely popular in America as a symbol of nationalist pride. As the home of largely middle-class and affluent second- and third-generation American Jews embracing a particular kind of contemporary, secular Jewish culture, the Y became the showcase for both kinds of Jewish dancing. Its constituency reflected the same kind of reevaluation of identity being experienced by the larger Jewish population, with the same desire to pay greater attention to a unique Jewish heritage.

Beginning around 1939, there was a much more conscientious attempt to fuse the "Jewish" and "general" programs at the Y. Kolodney gave an impassioned speech on the need for the Y to focus on Jewish culture and began to implement his theory in his various programs. In 1940, for instance, special emphasis was given in the Poetry Center to the contribution of Jewish poetry in contemporary times. Readings were given of poets writing on Jewish themes in English verse and Hebrew poets in English translation. In 1943, Kolodney and the current rabbi of the Y, Max Vorspan, worked on organizing various joint cultural activities. One of these was the Jewish Folk Art Nights, held under the auspices of the Adult School of Jewish Studies.

The Y's programming, moreover, perfectly reflected the somewhat conflicting efforts of the broader American Jewish population in reimagining and re-creating their Jewish identity. On the one hand, there was a move to locate Jewishness in traditional Judaism and the religious community; on the other, an interest in remaining true to contemporary American society and its support of individual expression and secular humanism. The characteristic result of the way these strands were combined was exhibited in the efforts of choreographers like Maslow and Sokolow, who carried on the tradition of Zemach in constructing quintessential images of Jewishness that were uplifting, timeless, and spiritual yet largely purified of any negative associations of the Old World, immigrant life, or actual Orthodoxy. In their work, modern dance helped to reinforce as well as shape the new perspective of Jewishness, working against the traditional religious narratives through the conventions of the modern style, which validated female expression, individuality, and creativity. The increased intersection of Jewish interests with modern dance focused the challenge to a purist, apolitical definition of modern dance, reframing it as an expression of social/ethnic/political consciousness and as a hybrid style with disparate influences.

Sophie Maslow: The Village I Knew

Through the postwar period the Y became a central showcase for the newly reflective group of Jewish modern dancers and their contemporary constructions of Jewish identity. Maslow's *The Village I Knew,* for instance, received its New York premiere at the Y in 1951.[35] The dance consisted of seven vignettes loosely based on the stories of Sholom Aleichem, the paintings of Marc Chagall, and events of significance in Jewish lives drawn from ritual and oppression. The seven sections were, briefly, "Sabbath," celebrating the coming of the Jewish Sabbath; "It's Good to Be an Orphan," showing an older woman giving a pair of boots to a young girl; "A Point of Doctrine," about a verbose housewife who presents the details of her domestic difficulties at such length that a rabbi faints; "Festival," a communal dance of celebration; "The Fiddler," depicting a girl who is in love with a poor fiddler against her mother's wishes; "Why Is It Thus?" concerning three studious men; and "Exodus," portraying Jewish villagers fleeing persecution. Periodically, a linking line of dancers, reminiscent of the paintings of Chagall, wove through the stage space, providing a unifying leitmotif for the dance.

The identification of Jewishness, at least in part, with more traditional narratives is identifiable in Maslow's attempts to capture a particular moment in the Jewish past, specifically life as it was lived in a small Jewish village in czarist Russia at the end of the nineteenth century. This interest in reliving a specific period in Jewish history is clear from program notes and from the numerous articles and reviews of the dance from the time, which clarify that

Sophie Maslow's *The Village I Knew*.
"Mother" (Jane Dudley), "Young Woman" (Sophie Maslow), and "Fiddler" (Ronne Aul).
Dance Division, The New York Public Library for the Performing Arts,
Astor, Lenox and Tilden Foundations. Photographer: Walter E. Owen.

the *The Village I Knew* "celebrates the homely little episodes of life in the im-
probable village of Vasrilevka, the ecstatic Sabbath ritual, the over proud ma-
tron who thinks her daughter much too good for the village fiddler, the apple
cider drinking Rabbi who also loves to dance."[36] Here Maslow also plainly
connects Jewishness to life in a religious community. In the dance, women
cover their eyes and circle their arms as they perform the blessing over the
candles in "Sabbath," while five men *daven* (praying with a rocking back and
forth motion) upstage. In another section, students appear engaged in study
(this is mimed) of the great books of Judaism (the Torah and the Talmud),

Sophie Maslow's *The Village I Knew.*
Donald McKayle (left), Irving Burton (middle), and William Bales(right).
Dance Division, The New York Public Library for the Performing Arts,
Astor, Lenox and Tilden Foundations. Photographer: Walter E. Owen.

during which they assume expressions of meditation, questioning, and insight. A rabbi character, moreover, appears numerous times, with his own spirited solo in "Festival."

That these kinds of references might have been problematic in the hands of a modern dance choreographer seems to have been briefly, but not seriously, considered. Maslow realized that saving Eastern European culture from the devastation of the war was not an easy task, but she presented what she considered a sensitive and accurate representation. An extensive article in *Jewish Life,* November 1949, supports Maslow's intentions for *The Village I*

Knew (which at the time was yet to be fully completed) within the larger context of the difficulties facing someone creating a dance on Jewish themes. One section of the article describes the breadth of Jewish culture, both geographically and historically, that artists could look to for inspiration. Another, "Some Common Pitfalls," outlines the various dangers facing a choreographer in working with Jewish themes. These include simplistic surface treatment of subject matter and character and the reliance on stereotypes that fail to grasp the subtleties of Jewish life: "And worst of all: how often have we seen, hidden under the fig-leaf of the finest 'folksy' intentions, the hackneyed, false, so-called 'Jewish gesture.' Dancers who cling to a trite and outworn stereotyped style are not correctly interpreting that segment of Jewish culture with which they are concerned; and are presenting their audiences with a counterfeit instead of a gem."[37] The author continues: "None of these pitfalls will threaten the dancer who will not compromise with surface treatment," proposing that just such a dancer is Sophie Maslow.

With the final dance, many people, both Jewish and non-Jewish, seemed to believe that Maslow was largely successful in portraying Russian Jewry. Walter Terry remarked in the *New York Herald Tribune*, "Its glimpses (sharply focused and knowingly selective) of Jewish community life in czarist Russia are amusing, touching, colorful and intensely human." The immediate Y dance community shared these sentiments. Deborah Pritzker stated in the *Y Bulletin* that the piece "rendered the flavor of Jewish life in Czarist Russia with warmth and humor." According to her, the piece avoided being a caricature despite its touch of sentimentality. "That it veered at times toward hilarious pantomime did not jar; rather, the juxtaposition of caricature and sweetness rounded out the interpretation."[38]

Despite the glowing assessments, however, the way Jewishness was constructed in the dance was far from straightforward, resulting instead from a desire to create images of a positive Jewish identity that were emotionally compelling yet relatively simple and untainted by religiosity. The idealized nature of the dance is evident in the way it locates Jewishness in the narrow, fictionalized world of the shtetl, a postwar construct resulting from the desire to recover the inner life of Eastern European Jewry.[39] The dance is based on selected tales from Sholom Aleichem, and it portrays the Russian Jewish community as a place full of quaint, endearing men, women, and children who live simple lives of worship, love, study, sorrow, and celebration. The various members of the community are represented by generic character types, such as Mother, Daughter, Rabbi, Student, Housewife, and Orphan, and their behavior is frequently stiff and repetitive, with a naive, doll-like quality that suggests a charming fairy tale.

The section called "A Point of Doctrine," for instance, is based on Sholom Aleichem's story "The Little Pot" and consists of simplistic characterization and gesture. In this part of the dance the Housewife stands stage left of the Rabbi, who is seated in a high-backed chair facing upstage with his back toward the audience. She gestures boldly with her arms in a mimelike manner as she "speaks" to him of her troubles. Other more specific mime gestures include crying and cradling a baby. The Housewife character repeatedly lifts her arms and legs stiffly as a unit, adding dancerly movements such as leg extensions and turns to the central gestures of the hands. The section ends with the Rabbi comically sliding to the floor beside the chair in apparent exhaustion from listening to her chatter.

The extent to which the dance did not conform to any actual "heritage" was borne out by the response of members of the religious community to the dance. In 1951, Kolodney arranged for a group of rabbis to see a performance of *The Village I Knew,* intending to show off the choreography as a wonderful example of Jewish art. According to Maslow, however, the piece was met with reproach for the inappropriate and irreverent use of ritual movements, such as when the dancers kneel on the floor for the blessing of the Sabbath candles during the opening section of the piece.[40] In other sections, kneeling or rolling on the floor was considered poor judgment, not only because it went against tradition but also because it showed the women's legs, which was seen as indecent. The rabbis also complained that Maslow had the women dance with scarves, but not when they danced with the men, which is where the scarves were needed to hinder the sexes from touching. Their comments reveal how modern dancers' attempts to locate Jewishness in the religious community were mediated by the conventions of "contemporary American woman" and "dance as art," which moved constructions of Jewish subjectivity toward individual freedom and away from ancient tenets. The extent to which Maslow's work was influenced by modern dance theories and practices can be seen in her reaction to the rabbis' comments. Maslow made it clear that the rabbis were at fault in their response by not understanding that her work was "modern dance." Her perspective indicates just how extensive modern dancers' approaches to choreography reinforced the new understanding of Jewishness in its individualized and aestheticized form.

It is well established that many modern dancers of the period advocated the free adaptation of folk forms through a process of abstraction and artistic manipulation. In his writings, John Martin summed up this attitude in his distinction between dancing that has gone through a process of artistic transformation (modern dance) and that which has not (ethnic dance). In *Introduction to the Dance* (1939), Martin writes that contemporary dance is defined by its "individuality" and "consists in extracting a certain essence from authenticity and employing it to give flavor to the whole, with no notion of archeological or ethnological accuracy."[41] On the other hand, "dance arts of the East" and "Spanish dance" (among many others) are said to be "intricately interwoven with religion and social custom."[42]

Such an outlook had important implications for Jewish dancers working in the modern idiom. If dancers wanted to reflect their heritage, they needed to transform their source material. Such a situation is highlighted in *America Dancing* (1936), where Martin praises Shapero for the way she has used "Chassidic and other Jewish dance forms," observing that "she has had the good judgment to make use of in *free adaptation* rather than in *any authentic sense* [my emphasis]."[43] As it happened, this was easy for Maslow, who had long advocated this position and been involved in adapting folk dancing to the concert stage, as evidenced in *Dust Bowl Ballads* and *Folksay*. In *The Village I Knew* the same kind of modern dance conventions for manipulating folk and everyday movement intervene to reimagine Jewishness. Naturalistic gestures of the hands and arms are extended into the whole body and linked to basic dancelike movement. For instance, a pointing motion may lead into an *attitude*, or playing with a kerchief may lead to an unfolding of the leg in a *développé* to the side. In other cases, the use of unison, precise spacing and timing create a dancy version of everyday activities, such as in "Sabbath" when the men pretending to *daven* do so in unison and in two carefully positioned lines. Other modern dance conventions include dancing in bare feet and incorporating floorwork through kneeling and sitting.

These practices and ideas, however, were not the only aspects of modern dance to affect Maslow's views. Modern dancers also upheld the ability of an artist to uncover the essences of existence through their process of choreographic manipulation. Modern dance was a point of view, in which the artist drew on his or her own experience but abstracted from it to arrive at an underlying truth of an emotional (as opposed to cerebral, or conventionally religious) nature. Again, Martin voiced these assertions when he wrote that, "the artist must take away from his material those aspects of it which attach it to his exclusive personal experience, and must confine himself to those aspects which are of more universal experience."[44] Later he stated, "Not repre-

sentation but interpretation is his business, his duty to nature itself; abstract-
ing into essences of those deep-rooted experiences of human living which
appearances, surface truths, naturalism cover and deny."[45]

Maslow, again, was an articulate and passionate spokesperson of this perspective from early in her career. In many instances she spoke passionately
about the possibility for modern dance to grasp universal truths. A 1944 article announces, "Sophie Maslow Looks for Concept of Universal Emotion in
Dancing," with the observation "She has studied in a serious way for many
years to make her dancing express a basic concept of universal emotions that
touches the level of everyone's experiences."[46]

Such a perspective meant that, when modern dancers like Maslow began
working with Jewish themes from the 1940s onward, they by no means believed that they were fabricating a fictional Jewish life. Rather, they sincerely
believed that they were getting to the essence of Jewish experience, which
had a universal message.[47] And they believed that carefully chosen gestures
could evoke an entire epoch, mood, and character: "This deep search [by
Maslow] does not aim at a mechanical authenticity. On the contrary, it leads
to a fuller, more inspired use of herself as an artist and of the potentialities of
her art. To a dancer whose language is so potent, so magic, so special and at
once so universal, to translate this truth into terms of her art, is the gist of
her work."[48] What this suggests is that while some Jews of the postwar period
might not have realized that they were searching for a timeless, quintessential
Jewish mode of expression, for modern dancers it was a natural path in line
with their theories. The *Village I Knew* shows the compatibility of modern
dance with the project of postwar Jewry, since the quest for a crystallized
identity rooted in a cozy "folk" community fit perfectly with modern
dancers' quest for essences and their empathy with "the people."

Anna Sokolow: Kaddish

Such compatibility also is evident in the dances of Sokolow, although in a
different form. Her work shows how dancers' ideas about "essences" and free
adaptation of folk movement varied from person to person and work to
work. Dances did not always offer quaint depictions of Russian life; in other
cases, they were involved in a much more solemn reimagining of Eastern European Jewry. Such an intensely serious conception of Jewishness is evident
in the choreography of Sokolow, who performed regularly at the Y until the
early 1960s. Her first pieces based on Jewish themes appeared there beginning

in the early 1940s. In a 1940 program, for instance, she performed *The Exile,* which depicted the Nazi regime as a beast in the garden of Jewish life. For a 1943 program at the Y she included *Songs of a Semite,* from a book of poems by Emma Lazarus, and in 1946, *Images from the Old Testament, Kaddish,* and *The Bride.* The Y was also the site of the 1961 world premiere of *Dreams,* Sokolow's now celebrated dance on the horrors of the Holocaust.

Sokolow's piece *Kaddish,* which focuses on the Jewish mourning prayer traditionally performed on the death of a loved one, received its New York premiere at the Y on May 12, 1946.[49] The program note stated simply: "Prayer for the Dead." The dance seems to have been a eulogy to those who had died in the war, expressing the anguish and spiritual unrest caused by the tragedy. In the original performance, Sokolow wrapped an Orthodox Jewish prayer box around her head and arm (tefillin), reproducing the everyday practice of Orthodox Jews. Early reviews lacked clear movement description of the dance, stressing instead the power of Sokolow's individual presence. David Zellmer briefly observed in *Dance Observer* that the piece "was emotionally compelling; all the movements flowing directly from the inspirational source."[50] In 1948, when the work was repeated at the Y, Martha Coleman noted that "*Kaddish* was one of the high spots of the program. Here Miss Sokolow moves in a style so completely her own that she projects a great authority and conviction. Her movement was completely definitive throughout."[51]

In 1974 the dancer Deborah Zall performed a revival of the work that omits the original prayer box.[52] This version of the dance is characterized by the extreme tension infusing the performer's body and the shifting use of the dancer's focus between the audience and an evoked higher presence. A feeling of spiritual questioning and grief is conveyed. The piece begins with Zall standing still, directly facing the audience. Slowly she looks up as her arms bend in front of her and her palms turn to face the ceiling. Then, sharply, her head jerks down, and her arms are thrust to her sides. She moves in halting, rigid steps forward toward the audience. Again she moves sharply, bending over with her left arm clutching her head, her hand spread wide. She kneels and arches back (both hands holding her head), then slowly curls forward. In the next sequence, Zall stands up, looking upward, then begins a sequence of spins and heavenward reaches. These appear to be movements of prayer, but they are direct and intense in quality, as the dancer whips back and forth, holding her head in anguish. Finally, Zall quiets down and gravely beats at her breast with her hands before falling prostrate onto the floor. After regaining her composure, she once again quietly beats her chest before haltingly walking backward, as in the beginning of the piece.

Anna Sokolow in *Kaddish*.
Courtesy of Lorry May.

Sokolow's piece is interesting in the way it both embraces the mystical spiritualism of an imagined Jewish tradition and reimagines that same past within the context of contemporary art and growing female liberation as experienced in modern dance. Her intense and serious performance style, her reaches and falling prostrate evoke the image of the timeless pious Jew in close communion with his Maker. At the same time, the dance marks the distance from what it is striving to depict, since a woman dancing around a stage wearing tefillin would be anathema to any actual Jewish heritage. Such a vision would have been deeply offensive and polluting to those who actually observe the practice.

At the same time, Sokolow's conception of Jewish tradition is far from being a literal or stereotyped representation of Eastern European Jewry. Sokolow did not try to play a specific character or tell a story. Rather, *Kaddish* is shaped by her particular modern dance aesthetic, in which a few carefully chosen movements are used to evoke powerful and varied feelings. In the dance, stark oppositions are established between upward and downward and between forward and back, in a way that suggests a person being torn between faith, sadness, and anger. For instance, the palms, which are slowly turned upward at the beginning of the dance, offer a simple but effective gesture that at once suggests hope (facing heaven) and despair (the hands are empty). Similarly, when the dancer walks backward at the end of the dance, beating her breast, the weary submissiveness implied by the gesture is immediately counteracted by the intense glare in her eyes, which fiercely challenges the audience. Throughout, the shift in gaze pushes and pulls the audience from being a spectator to the dancer's grief and her dialogue with God to being implicated in the grieving process and all that it involves.

In general, the fact that Sokolow did not see her dance as sacrilegious had much to do with her attitude toward emotion in art, drawn from the modern dance tradition. Sokolow believed that a chief purpose of dance is to express the otherwise impenetrable feelings of humanity, and she was greatly concerned that her dancers move from a deep emotional impulse. In *Kaddish* this quasi-mystical attitude allowed for an easy merging with the passion and spiritualism she was locating in Orthodox Jewry. Although religious Jews might find the work bizarre, for Sokolow and her followers the convergence felt natural and extremely powerful. Other Jewish dancers made pieces in a similar vein, seeing the spiritualism of Orthodoxy as complementary with the deep expressive impetus of modern dance. Hadassah's *Shuvi Nafshi* (1947) was a dance of ecstasy in prayer based on an excerpt from Psalm 116: "Return O my soul." The dance was a deeply spiritual expression in which a woman wearing a prayer shawl costume used spins, palm-to-cheek, and upward reaching gestures in an emotional declaration to God.

Similarly, many of the dances of Pearl Lang, whose company premiered at the Y on May 4, 1952, drew on the ecstatic tradition in Jewish religion as an inspiration for contemporary choreography. Pieces on this first concert consisted of *Song of Deborah*, *Legend*, *Moonsung*, and *Windsung*. Lang was known for combining lyricism with extreme intensity in her dancing, and

Hadassah in *Shuvi Nafshi*, 1951.
Collection of the author. Photographer: John Lindquist.

she once stated, "People dance for many reasons. I think mine came from an ecstatic religious one."[53] Lang, whose association with the Y was greatest after the 1960s, choreographed many dances on Jewish themes, including her own passionately felt version of the Dybbuk tale, *The Possessed*, which enjoyed multiple performances at the Y in 1974–75 and 1976. In her review of the work in *Eddy*, Susan Reimer Sticklor commented on the way everyday life of the Chassidim is permeated by forces flowing from hidden realms and on how this is carried over to the dancing: "The world Pearl Lang brings to the

Pearl Lang in *The Song of Deborah*, ca. 1955.
Choreography by Pearl Lang, music by Sergiu Natra. Courtesy of Pearl Lang.
Photographer: Walter Strate.

stage is transfused with an immanent presence hovering around the dancers, impelling them with silent urging. The very air sets Leye's (Pearl Lang) elbows knocking, hands vibrating, chest contracting sharply."[54] Anna Kisselgoff captured the emotional intensity conveyed by the piece in her description of Lang's solo as she becomes possessed by the spirit of her dead beloved: "There is a flamelike quiver, a shiver of both pain and ecstasy in this solo. The threshold between the supernatural and the real world—an underlying theme of the play—is piercingly suggested here as Miss Lang, a picture of purity in white, is swept into a vortex of movements that seem beyond her control. The foot is flexed, the leg is up, the torso jerks backward, the leg repeatedly revolves up and down, the palm of the hand is drawn to the chin tremblingly, the spent heroine collapses on her knees."[55]

As a place interested in promoting contemporary forms of Jewish expression, the Y was a perfect venue for these Jewish dancers to showcase their work. They provided a fitting illustration of the fusion of Jewish and modernist creative impulses that Kolodney so much desired. The portrayal of Jewish identity was at once particular in its allusion to the goodheartedness and intense spiritual legacy of Eastern European Jewry and universal in its representation of Jewish characteristics as commonly valued aspects of the human experience. In their aim to create an American Jewish identity that depended on this kind of synthesis of the general and particular, modern dance played a significant role, since it claimed that individuals could draw on their own particular traditions and present them as meaningful to a broad-based audience. Significantly, this belief reflected that aspect of the modern Jewish psyche that sought to unify people from different backgrounds, thereby leading to acceptance of Jews as equals and erasing the possibility of discrimination.

Most people educated in modernist conventions accepted that it was possible for Jewish artists to abstract from their particular experience to present general truths, and their work was widely appreciated and accepted. Characteristic responses to *The Village I Knew* reveal the extent to which audiences were willing to welcome dances on Jewish themes as having a transcendent message. Terry claimed that Maslow's dances "represented valuable additions to the expanding repertory of America's modern dance,"[56] and Nik Krevitsky of the *Dance Observer* observed that "[the dance] is conceived throughout in terms of flowing movement, which in dance quality makes the work universal and timeless. It might be Breughel as well as Chagall, Boccaccio or Mark Twain as well as Aleichem. One need not be an authority on Jewish life in Czarist times to appreciate its obvious good humor."[57] The ability of Maslow and Sokolow to fuse the dance and Jewish worlds brought Jewish experiences into the limelight to a greater degree than had existed before.[58] Their blend of modern dance and Jewishness was accessible to the general dance community and to the component of the Jewish community that was embracing a newly modernized Jewish culture.

. . .

JEWISH FOLK DANCING AT THE Y

During the 1940s and 1950s the Y also became the focal point for another widely successful but different kind of Jewish dance. This was the teaching and performance of Jewish folk dancing inspired by activity in Palestine. Following their earlier work of the 1920s and 1930s, dancers in Palestine began a unified, wide-scale movement in the 1940s to create a new folk dance.[59] In 1944, at the Festival of Shavuot, the first major gathering of dancers took place in the kibbutz Dalia in the Meggido region. That night, four dance groups, comprising two hundred dancers, performed twenty-two folk dances, most of which originated in Europe. There were about 3,500 spectators.[60] The initial Dalia meeting greatly inspired dancers living in Palestine. One of the leaders of the new movement, Gurit Kadman, encouraged people to blend the older, established steps with their own creative impulses to make new folk dances that conveyed the spirit of life on the land. Other founders included Lea Bergstein, Ze'ev Chavatzelet, Shalom Hermon, Yardena Cohen, Rivka Sturman, and Sara Levi-Tanai. As a result of the efforts of these leaders, in 1947, at the second Dalia Festival, only newly created folk dances were performed. The foundation had been laid for an original folk dance movement.

In America the new developments were felt intensely at the 92nd Street Y. After the official formation of Israel in 1948, the new dances were brought to America largely through the efforts of Fred Berk, who, although trained as a modern dancer, had danced with Benjamin Zemach after first arriving in the United States in 1942; he began to experiment with Jewish themes in his own choreography in the mid-1940s.[61] During this time, he and his partner, Katya Delakova, performed numerous times at the Y. In 1947 they were presented by the Adult School of Jewish Studies in their own concert and for "Palestine Nite" (a benefit evening for the reconstruction of a Zionist training farm destroyed by fire). In December, Berk's newly formed Jewish Dance Guild also performed there.[62]

A press release posed the question, "What is a Jewish dance?" Delakova and Berk's answer was "a dance which reflects the philosophy of the Hebrews."[63] While Berk and Delakova's early dances drew more on Chassidic and biblical material, other pieces increasingly referred to contemporary Israeli life and culture. In a 1949 performance at the Kaufmann Auditorium the couple concluded with a piece called *Songs Come to Life* in three sections: "Pioneers," "How Beautiful Are the Nights," and "Hora." The program note

Fred Berk and Katya Delakova, 1940s.
92nd Street YM-YWHA Archives.

Fred Berk's Hebraica Dancers, ca. 1966.
92nd Street YM-YWHA Archives. Photographer: Sosenko Studio.

states, "Israeli folksongs throb with a new life and rhythm, which derive from the utterly novel experience of a people rehabilitating itself in its historic homeland."

From 1950 onward, Berk began to focus on disseminating Israeli folk dance in America. His Jewish folk dance classes began in earnest at the Y in 1951, and in 1952 he became involved in staging a yearly Israeli Dance Festival in New York.[64] In 1955, after returning from a trip to Israel, Berk formed the Hebraica company at the Y. Kolodney gave him $2,000 to start the company plus a closet for costumes and properties. The group consisted of six teenage couples drawn mostly from Berk's classes at the Y, who rehearsed once a week for a couple of hours.[65] Berk choreographed suites of dances portraying Israeli holidays and everyday life, which included *From a Fishing Village*, *The Market Place*, *The Vineyard*, and *The Desert*.

The titles of these works illustrate the way in which Berk was reflecting as well as contributing to the key images of Jewish nationalism. The dances concerned "the land," a certain rustic simplicity, and the constant joy of existence. As observed earlier, in Berk's most frequently performed work, *Holiday*

Folk Dancing at the Y, 1955.
92nd Street YM-YWHA Archives. Photographer: Herbert Sonnenfeld.

in Israel, there was the additional focus on unification in spite of diversity. During the hora portion of the dance, all of the diverse settlers joined hands in a symbolic moment of shared Jewishness. *Holiday in Israel* was originally performed for the Merry-Go-Rounders, but it often appeared on performances by Hebraica and other Jewish dance programs.

The attraction of such dancing to Jewish Americans was tremendous. The folk dances symbolized Israel and a unified Jewish people and did so in a manner that seemed to bridge all differences. Religious or secular, rich or poor, young or old, you would be caught up in the circle of dancers. At the Y, Jewish youth gathered to take part in the Zionist fervor that was capturing America's youth. The space pulsed with the euphoria of a newly discovered source of communal identification, in which all were happy and dedicated to a common vision. One participant recalled, "What I loved was the Israeli spirit; we all wanted to learn Hebrew and go to Israel . . . [the leaders] either had all been to Israel and had come back to train Jewish youth, or they were just waiting until they were old enough to get there. They all danced at the Y: the fervor was high."[66]

No doubt many of the young people involved with folk dancing traveled to Israel and fell in love with the new state. From a larger perspective, however, the Y represented a broader Jewish-American perspective that asserted that Zionism need not entail making aliyah but maintaining a strong awareness of Israel in the Diaspora: at the Y, people frequently experienced the "Israeli spirit" but from a comfortable, American, middle-class distance. In her book *American Jews and the Zionist Idea*, Naomi Cohen writes that, in the 1950s, American Zionists "could not be persuaded that aliyah suited American needs or that there was something wrong about feeling rooted in the United States or believing that American Jews could sustain their separate cultural institutions."[67] According to Cohen, postwar Jews fit comfortably into an increasingly urban, middle-class America. Although they responded positively to Israel and the need for its survival (the creation of the state had assured them that they were no longer members of an uprooted, persecuted people), they felt the rootedness of the Jewish community within American society.

The Y was a prime example of a well-established American institution interested in maintaining a close link with Israel but from a primarily cultural perspective.[68] This can be seen in the words of William Kolodney, who stated early on, "The Jewish Center believes in Palestine as the most significant single constructive cultural force in Jewish life." To Kolodney the implications of this premise were "While maintaining neutrality with reference to Zionism, especially its political and nationalistic phases, the Jewish Center should favor Palestine above all other areas as the most logical physical center for landless Jews and should support and keep in intimate touch with Jewish cultural and religious life there."[69] Kolodney's words reflected the desire of many American Jews to stay in close contact with the Israeli ethos yet remain somewhat separate from its actual political status as a developing nation. The Y's role in Israeli affairs was confined to the work of Berk and to its general support of Zionism. Although Berk's efforts were important, Zionist activities were not a dominant part of the Educational Department in the 1950s.

At the Y, Israeli folk dancing was one of a number of ways that American Jews chose to express their Jewishness. Taken individually, the views of Jewishness were potentially restrictive, but the diversity of the activity at the institution shows that many forms of Jewishness were experienced there as a result of the convergence of Jews with dance. Such variety offered a flexible approach to Jewish identification. Jews expressed themselves through the general arts, through modern art with a Jewish twist, or through Israeli folk dance—or through all three. In each case, the dancing provided an aesthetic mediation through which sponsors, artists, and their audiences negotiated their relationship to their Jewish identity from more to less conscious awareness of themselves as a distinct ethnic/religious group.

What unified all the above efforts was a belief in the ability to combine the uniquely "Jewish" with the "general." Such an approach made it easy for the Y to partake of and uphold mainstream modern dance practice, which so clearly emphasized the "universal" aspect of art. At the same time, by maintaining the "Jewish" connection, the Y's programming, constantly offered as a possibility the idea that modern dance was explicitly, not implicitly, about cultural fusion. Moreover, the work of Jewish dancers like Maslow challenged the double standard of much mainstream modern dance discourse. While Martin and others had suggested that anyone could be a modern dancer, with all that such a perspective signified regarding transcendence of one's individual experience, in practice there was often a contradictory state of affairs, in which Martin understated the ethnic/racial dimensions present in dances by white, Anglo-Saxon, Protestant choreographers like Graham, but not necessarily by minority artists. When Graham choreographed *Primitive Mysteries*, for instance, it was simply considered modern dance, although it was strongly influenced by Native American traditions. However, when Dunham or Primus performed, it was regularly labeled Negro dance. In other words, when it came to the "other," it seemed as if ethnicity and race were often read as significant and by implication subtly dismissed as less "pure" than the modern dance of the Big Four. From this perspective, the very label, "Jewish dance," in a way exists as a subtly deprecating term.

One way that Maslow (and others) challenged this double standard was in hiring black dancers to perform in her pieces when it was relatively uncommon. Early performances of *The Village I Knew,* for instance, included Ronne Aul and Donald McKayle. McKayle later recalled his enjoyment and appreciation of working with Maslow as a beginning modern dancer. He also remembered an incident that underscored the way African American dancers, in particular, were faced with a mixed message in the modern dance world. According to McKayle, Martin had "said he didn't understand why there was a black boy in a Russian Jewish Village." McKayle "wrote to him . . . and said well if he really was interested in why there was a black boy in a Russian Jewish village he should ask the question why there wasn't a Russian Jew in that whole Russian Jewish village because there wasn't one on stage . . . because that didn't seem to bother him only that there was one that was black."[70] According to McKayle, Martin responded that with McKayle present on stage the work lacked verisimilitude. Clearly, blacks were not always allowed to represent others, despite the openness espoused by Martin.

The significance of Maslow's efforts for the modern dance world was great. Along with her, Jewish patrons, dancers, and audiences at the Y highlighted, on a highly visible, institutional scale, the potential of the modern dance framework for expansion to include and validate difference. Like the educational programming, the Y's progressive orientation in its producing led to a continuing challenge of modern dance to embrace racial, religious, and ethnic diversity. Such an effort affected the way modern dance was conceived by its practitioners and had a lasting importance for the evolution of postmodern dance in the latter part of the century.

*The analysis and history of the new educational program at the
92nd Street Y is the story of an attitude and a mood. The attitude toward adult
education was conditioned by the feeling that the private life of the individual,
lost in the mass, should be recaptured and made more meaningful.*
William Kolodney[1]

(8)

𝒜 POSTMODERN PRECURSOR

The Y's Legacy beyond the 1960s

• • •

On October 20, 1957, Paul Taylor gave a concert at the Kaufmann Auditorium that is considered by many to mark the beginning of a new era and the fall of an old era. At this recital, Taylor presented a work called *Epic*, in which he stood in different static positions while a recorded female voice repeatedly read off the time. Apparently this piece, as well as others on the program, was so offensive to certain members of the audience that they got up and left the theater. Taylor later recalled that "immediately following [the performance] I go to my dressing room, where the manager of the concert hall has been waiting to inform me that if I should ever rent the theater again, it will be over his dead body."[2] The concert received poor assessments by John Martin and Walter Terry, and Louis Horst published his now famous blank review in *Dance Observer*—a square of empty space in the middle of the page labeled with the dance recital title and signed with his initials, "L. H."

Whether, in fact, the Y's manager ever threatened Taylor remains un-likely considering Kolodney's deep respect for individual expression, not to mention his diplomatic demeanor.[3] Nonetheless, Taylor interpreted the events of that evening as a sign of the closed-mindedness of the modern dance community. The negative response demonstrated the need for young

Far from depicting a cycle of life, it merely strung together loosely a few academic steps and some vague pantomime. Her performance was also weak and heavy, though it would be unfair to judge her capacities in choreography so lacking both in organization and stylistic point. Long before the work was over, she was tired and so were we.

But credit is due to both choreographer and composer for experimenting in a field which is destined to grow rapidly in the coming years, if I am not mistaken, for dance should find a larger place for itself in our concert life.

R. S.

An Evening with Ruth St. Denis

Theatre Marquee
Sept. 20-22, 27-29, 1957

ONE of the most distinguished of this season's dance events was the all too rare New York appearance of Ruth St. Denis in a program consisting of two of her historic solo dances—*The Gregorian Chant* and *White Jade* —as well as a new "plastique," *To A Chinese Flute.* As always, Miss St.

Denis was transcendent in her dances, moving as beautifully and lyrically as always. This rare program highlighted the first public showing of the new color film of four of Miss St. Denis' solos (reviewed in our October 1957 issue) as well as a series of color stills of this dance artist taken by photographer John Lindquist during various of her appearances at Jacob's Pillow. In addition, Barbara Andres appeared in two dances, *The Javanese Court Dance* and *The Peacock,* both choreographed by Miss St. Denis. The first series of these three evenings was sold out before the premiere necessitating a second series of week-end performances that were also played to capacity audiences, and deservedly so, for this is one of the rare and most deeply rewarding dance talents in our time.

A. T.

Paul Taylor and Dance Company

Y.M.-Y.W.H.A.
October 20, 1957

L. H.

Louis Horst's blank review for Paul Taylor's 1957 Y recital.
Dance Observer.

choreographers like himself to find new supporters and venues for their work. It meant that he had to dig in and continue to pursue his dreams. As Taylor put it in his autobiography, *Private Domain,* "I won't get mad, I'll get even." This phrase indeed seems to have become the rallying cry of a new generation of dancers and critics in the 1960s, who sought to redefine themselves in opposition to what had come before. To this generation, modern dance was controlled by and identified with Martin, Horst, Graham, Humphrey, Weidman, and Holm, and in their eyes the 92nd Street Y was firmly regarded as the performing outpost of the establishment. They did not understand the Y's complex and innovative status in the dance world. Nor did they grasp Kolodney's vision of the cultural program there as providing a much needed opportunity for individuals to (re)create themselves in a world of mass and oppressive ideologies, materialism, and conformity; for the younger generation the Y was simply a performance space sanctioned by the mainstream dance world.

With the evolution of postmodern dance, the mythology of its rejection of and difference from modern dance continues. In the 1980s and 1990s the newness and radical nature of postmodern dance is constantly theorized through a variety of issues, some of which concern the form and some the content of dance works. In Gay Morris's introduction to *Moving Words: Rewriting Dance,* "the 'shifting ground' of a postmodern world" is contrasted with "modernist formulas where boundaries are fixed and forms pure."[4] Such books include multiple essays on the mixing of high and low dance cultures, the work of minority and other marginalized artists, the intricacies of stylistic/intercultural fusions, social and political commentaries on hegemonic forces, and the radical nature of "boundary art" made on the fringes of society. While some acknowledgment is given to the reliance of postmodernism on the modernist legacy, it is more in terms of a place from which to start a fundamental critique, rather than as a source of postmodernist concerns.

Challenging such a conceptualization of postmodern dance is the case of the 92nd Street Y, which functioned for many years as a proto-postmodern institution. As a recreational sectarian institution beyond the theater district, the Y supported the meeting of high and low cultures, the work of minority artists, and the fusion of different movement styles. The liminal status of Jews within American culture and their struggle to define a place for themselves and others as fluid, multiple entities at once particular and universal in their identification entailed a profound, if not frequently subtle, critique of any purist values of the mainstream discourse of the dance world. Jewish efforts at the Y marked what Susannah Heschel has called "the methodology of counterhistory and its usefulness in formulating a radical challenge to hegemonic forms of knowledge."[5] Rather than being newly invented with Taylor or the Judson generation and their followers, many of the progressive policies and diverse choreographic ideas that arose during the postmodern period have a history of anticipation in places like the 92nd Street Y. While such progressive practices migrated to new areas during the 1960s and 1970s, they flowered and found widespread recognition during the 1980s and 1990s when postmodernism in dance officially became identified with diversity, multiculturalism, and stylistic fusion.

The beautiful ironies implicit in examining the Y's place in American dance history are not to be missed. First, in their desire to be accepted by the modern dance world, Jews at the Y and elsewhere played an important role in laying the groundwork for the postmodern era. Jews like Kolodney, as the "other" in society at that time, made a space for all minorities and underrepresented constituencies partly as a way of being accepted themselves. In other words, to some extent they developed policies and practices now associated with postmodernism in order to expand the modernist framework so that Jews could be included in it. Second, this book's very perspective of the Y, which is to reflect on its contribution to a pluralistic, democratic view of American culture, relies on the very postmodern atmosphere it critiques. Without the prevalence in the 1990s of the emphasis on diversity and writings on the unique offering of particular groups, this study would likely not be as meaningful or find a sizable market.

Yet such ironies do not mask the lasting, very real impact of the Y on people's lives, both in the past and in the present. As a precursor of some of postmodernism's central concerns, the Y delineated a clear path toward the kind of world it advocated. Today there are two opposing poles of postmodernism with contrary ethics: one advances the idea of a pluralist, egalitarian America that is both cultured and tolerant; the other, an America where an identity politics of resentment thrives. The first view fosters an inclusive, cosmopolitan America that integrates difference into itself: the second acclaims difference to the exclusion of all else. The first takes the newer insights of cultural theory and poststructuralism regarding the mechanisms of cultural production and dissemination of power as a means of creating a world of greater equality and compassion. The second revels in the gaps, holes, fissures, and fragmentation of so-called cultural texts to decry the reality of individuals, meaning, truth, and even history. Given these differences, it is clear that the Y acted as a forerunner of the first mode of postmodernism, reflecting as it did a humanist tradition in Jewish thought and ethics that strove to create a framework for equity and for individual and social betterment, rather than a space of separation, nihilism, skepticism, or lack of meaning.[6]

· · ·

THE 1960S: CHANGING TIMES

The particular perception of the Y as an outpost of the mainstream dance world is well represented by Don McDonagh in his popular book *The Rise and Fall and Rise of Modern Dance*, which champions the experimental choreographers of the 1960s. In his 1990 introduction to a reprint of the book, McDonagh aggressively characterizes the Y as a venue where dancers were carefully auditioned, reviewed, and supported by the interests of Martin and the "Big Four": "In Manhattan, it was commonly held that a Broadway Theater or the YM & YWHA at 92nd Street and Lexington Avenue were most suitable venues." McDonagh complains, "Reviewers did not cover concerts in the outer boroughs or outside of the[se] preferred venues," ignoring the fact that for many years the Y was also off the reviewers' beaten track.[7] He then refers to the Taylor incident as a way of demonstrating the narrowness of the modern dance community of the late 1950s: "The 'Y' instituted an audition process to select those lucky choreographers from among all who applied. Paul Taylor was welcomed and in 1957 did an 'unacceptable' program and was informed that he would never be invited to appear in the house again. That was akin to expulsion from the 'family.'"[8]

For McDonagh, this moment foreshadowed the search of the new generation for other venues in the 1960s: "The Kaufmann Concert Hall at the 'Y,' which had seen the growth of a modern dance generation in the 1930's, found itself continually bypassed by the generation of the 1960's, which favored churches and other free halls that had shown themselves to be accommodating to dance. In addition to being free, they possessed most importantly an enthusiastic and open attitude toward experimentation."[9] In McDonagh's partisan reading, the Y was portrayed as the mean parent that closed its doors to a wonderful new breed of young dancers. For him, the "churches came to the rescue" and with their more "open" attitude happily permitted the expansion of the new work that was to take the world by storm. In this way, McDonagh argues, a new kind of dancing was able to come of age.

McDonagh's interpretation of historical events, like most dramatically satisfying accounts, sounds good but is misleading in both detail and substance,

Saturday Evening, December 20, 1958 at 8:30

PAUL TAYLOR AND DANCE COMPANY

TOBY ARMOUR   PHENA DARNER   VIOLA FARBER

DONYA FEUER

music   MORTON FELDMAN   DAVID HOLLISTER

artistic collaboration   BOB RAUSCHENBERG

lighting   THARON MUSSER

piano   DAVID TUDOR

cello: Sterling Hunkins. clarinet: John Huggler. percussion: Warren Smith.
management: Isabelle Fisher. 17 Minetta St., New York 12, New York.
personal representative: Ruth Schneidman. sound technician: Jan Syrjala

Steinway

Staff for the YM-YWHA:
DAN BUTT, Stage Manager   JOHN WORKMAN, Assistant Stage Manager
YM-YWHA, 92nd Street and Lexington Ave., New York 28, N. Y., Box Office: AT 9-2400

Program for Paul Taylor and Dance Company, 1958.
92nd Street YM-YWHA Archives.

failing as it does to depict accurately the Y's policies and changing role in the New York dance world. To begin with, Taylor did not audition to present his work at the Y, since by that time the Dance Teachers Advisory Committee had been dissolved. Rather, he reserved the hall under the same conditions by which it was made available to everyone in the late 1950s—by paying a $100 deposit for the desired date. Despite his own remarks to the contrary, Taylor

PROGRAM

REBUS* ....David Hollistei

decor and costumes by Bob Rauschenberg

cello .... Sterling Hunkins

clarinet .... John Huggler

percussion ....Warren Smith

TOBY ARMOUR, PHENA DARNER, VIOLA FARBER, PAUL TAYLOR

Intermission

EPIC ....Time Signals
PAUL TAYLOR

EVENTS 2 ....Rain
TOBY ARMOUR, DONYA FEUER

Intermission

IMAGES AND REFLECTIONS** ....Morton Feldman

The music is extension #3, intermissions, #1, #2,

#3, #4, #5 and illusions #1, #2, #3, #4.

decor and costumes by Bob Rauschenberg

piano ....David Tudor

WHITE AND SULPHUR ....PAUL TAYLOR

TRELLIS ....TOBY ARMOUR, PHENA DARNER, VIOLA FARBER

CLOCK ....PAUL TAYLOR

MAY APPLE ....VIOLA FARBER, PAUL TAYLOR

SHELL ....TOBY ARMOUR

BLUE AND COPPER ....PAUL TAYLOR

ENVELOPE ....FULL COMPANY

*First performed at New Brunswick, N. J., March 1958 for the Rutgers University
series on communication in the arts.

**First performance.

performed at the Y once more, with a similar program, on December 20,
1958, that is, just fourteen months after he was supposedly banished from the
Y stage. *Epic* was again performed, along with *Events 2* and a premiere of *Images and Reflections,* among other works. Clearly, the previously negative
publicity had served Taylor well since "every seat in the house was occupied
and many prominent [*sic*] people in the dance world were present." The reviewer in the *Y Bulletin* thought the choreography was "too static" but "exhibited creative potential."[10] In *Dance Observer,* Jill Johnston, who was to

become a major enthusiast for the avant-garde, wrote a largely favorable review, noting that although "*Epic* requires a greater projection of presence than Mr. Taylor can now muster, *Events 2* succeeds in creating a hypnotic mood of suspended action, of spaces and distance."[11] Taylor made a profit of $252.89 from the evening.

But the Taylor scandal does show that an extensive shift was occurring in the dance world in the late 1950s, a shift that profoundly diminished the status of the Y as a place for studying and viewing dance. The Y's increasing loss of visibility, however, was far from being the result of a simplistic reaction of one superior generation of choreographers against the ideas of an outdated older regime (as McDonagh and many others might have it). Instead, the alteration of the Y's status arose from large-scale changes occurring throughout America and especially in New York. In the 1930s and 1940s a crystallization of economic needs, as well as aesthetic and educational values, had occurred, which allowed for a convergence of interests between members of the Jewish community and the modern dance world. The Y was able to provide economic and institutional support at a time when the majority of modern dancers needed it, and from an aesthetic point of view there was the shared desire for excellence and for artistic works that were deeply meaningful expressions. Modern dancers and artistically sensitive Jews were committed to cultural uplift and educating the human being through the arts. Throughout the 1960s, conditions changed so drastically that this close connection between the dance world and the Y was no longer possible.

As the larger culture was thrown into turmoil with the civil rights movement, the counterculture, and the Vietnam War, economic circumstances changed in the dance world, as did the philosophy of the avant-garde. The result was a *new* crystallization in the realm of experimental dance, around a different cluster of individuals, institutions, values, and movement concerns. It is this new crystallization, occurring through the decades of the 1960s and 1970s, that has since been theorized as the early stage of what is now called postmodern dance.

One of the first changes concerned the economic dimension of performing. Throughout the 1930s and 1940s the 92nd Street Y provided young, emerging dancers with an inexpensive yet elegant theater in which to perform, one of the few places in New York City to do so. Extending from the late 1950s through the 1960s, however, there was an explosion of new venues and sources of funding. In 1959 the West Side Young Women's Christian Association (YWCA) appointed Alvin Ailey its first artist-in-residence, and in

1962 its Clark Center for the Performing Arts launched a New Choreographers Concert Series. Also, in 1959, a Rockefeller Foundation grant enabled the Riverside Church to install a small theater, which was made available to young choreographers. Three years later, Judson Memorial Church at Washington Square offered itself for use by emerging dancers. To the participants, "the church seemed a positive alternative to the once-a-year hire-a-hall mode of operating that had plagued the struggling modern dancer before. Here we could present things more frequently, more informally, and more cheaply."[12] In 1963, Hunter College began a showcase for modern dance, and in 1965, Jack Moore and Jeff Duncan launched Dance Theater Workshop as a dancers' collective. For many dancers such spaces offered inexpensive options with potentially larger performance areas than were available at the Y.

John Kalas writes in *The Grant System* that during the 1960s "a virtual torrent of new federally mandated programs appeared."[13] The change began in 1964, when President Johnson signed a bill establishing the National Council on the Arts, an advisory body of citizens prominent in the arts. In 1965 the National Foundation on the Arts and Humanities was established, along with the National Endowment for the Arts (NEA) and the National Endowment for the Humanities (NEH). Through the NEA a dance program began in 1966, offering support for several touring efforts and choreographers' fellowships. In 1968 a Dance Touring Program was initiated. At the same time Congress passed the Elementary and Secondary Education Act (ESEA). This promoted the use of art groups and cultural resources in education.

The overall effect of this new federal aid, plus the establishment of the influential New York State Council on the Arts (which also occurred in the mid-1960s), was that the huge gap in adult and arts education, formerly filled by benevolent institutions like the 92nd Street Y, was increasingly assumed to be a government responsibility. Kalas observes that "the federal government became the major actor in the grant system in the 1960s and overwhelmed the foundations' investment capabilities."[14] There was a decline in the impact of private foundations and individual donors on social change: "During the early period, foundations were decisive on many important social fronts: establishing public libraries, museums, galleries, and cultural and artistic centers; providing opportunities to minorities; building schools and colleges. . . . The result [of government funding] is that foundations no longer play the 'comprehensive' role that they once did."[15] In this way, the Y, like other privately run institutions, began in the 1960s to lose its unique place in the cultural geography of New York.

If economic conditions were changing, so was the philosophy of the avant-garde. From the 1930s through the 1950s, the emphasis was on making meaningful statements through dance and enriching the lives of individuals through exposure to the arts. Kolodney shared this philosophy and its accompanying aesthetic and was interested in working with dancers and critics to achieve the improvement of society. Modern dancers were pleased to find such a sympathetic patron and gravitated toward the Y because of the shared values and respect and encouragement their art form received there. In the 1960s, in contrast, a growing number of young dancers were no longer interested in making deeply meaningful statements or in artistic excellence as defined by the earlier generations of movers. They felt that most modern dances and ballets were overly emotional, idealistic, and elitist representations, having little to do with the experiences of the person in the street. Instead, the choreographers were, as the dance historian Sally Banes has written, engaged in finding "new ways to foreground the *medium* of dance rather than its *meaning*."[16] In her introduction to *Terpsichore in Sneakers: Post-Modern Dance*, Banes traces the connection of the Judson dancers to a larger trend away from meaning in art. She refers to Susan Sontag's *Against Interpretation*, explaining, "Sontag calls for a transparent art—and criticism—that will not 'mean,' but will illuminate and open the way for experience."[17]

Banes points out that this "foregrounding of the medium" was attempted by challenging the "nature, history, and function of dance as well as its structures. . . . The younger generation of choreographers showed in their dances that they departed not only from classical modern dance with its myths, heroes, and psychological metaphors, but also from the elegance of ballet."[18] Choreographers like Yvonne Rainer, Steve Paxton, and David Gordon, all of whom were involved in the Judson Dance Theatre, were engaged in saying no to everything that came before, claiming that you did not need to have virtuosic technique or use dramatic narratives in order to be a dancer or choreographer. You could be an ordinary person performing a simple task of moving a mattress from one spot to another. A person might run around in sneakers and sweatpants, spit on the floor, walk along a wall—and all that could be dance.

The natural extension of this new perspective was for postmodern dancers to bypass performance venues that were not sympathetic to their point of view. Instead, they were pleased to find a patron such as Reverend Al Carmines at the Judson Memorial Church. Carmines was their contemporary, personally involved in experimental musical theater, and aware of the bohemian subculture of Greenwich Village, with its happenings and pop art. While tied to Protestant religious concerns, he remained fiercely supportive (in a manner not unlike Kolodney) of a nonsectarian, uncensored, creative arts program as a means of opening up his congregants' lives. He once stated, "The two great doctrines of Christianity are salvation and creation. There's been too much concern with the first. Judson wants to do more about the second."[19]

The two major factors that brought the Y and the modern dance community together initially—financial need and a shared philosophy—were consequently redirected in the 1960s. Perhaps even more important, major figures who had made the convergence of interests possible dropped out of the picture. Horst's death in 1964 ended the publication of *Dance Observer,* which had been so staunch a supporter of Y activities. Martin retired from the *New York Times* in 1962, ending an epoch in dance criticism. Humphrey's death in 1958 also removed an extremely important force from the Y and the New York dance scene. As noted earlier, she had particularly grasped the importance of the Y and had helped to develop it as a school and performance space. Her humanistic perspective had perfectly complemented Kolodney's outlook and supported the diverse programming that the Y presented. Through her openness to new ideas, Humphrey was able to see the value of efforts to bring together Jewish interests with modern dance in projects such as the Merry-Go-Rounders, where she worked so closely with Fred Berk.

All of these changes were reflected in the Y's dance programming during the 1960s, which remained extremely active but focused on more traditional forms of dance, with the occasional ballet company and ethnic dancer. Between 1960 and 1969 a range of fifteen to twenty-eight dance performances continued to be offered annually. Paul Sanasardo, who had danced with Sokolow during the 1950s, presented his work at the Y frequently during the late 1960s. The other modern dancer whose choreography appeared there in more than a half dozen performances was the Graham dancer Yuriko, who formed her own company in 1960 and performed almost yearly at the Y between 1964 and 1971, presenting pieces that combined the influences of Graham and Japanese theater forms. Berk presented yearly programs of Jewish dance, while the Leonard Fowler Ballet and the Mexican ballet dancer and choreographer Gloria Contreras offered several programs. Over twenty groups from a range of backgrounds performed in one to four performances during this period. Dancers like Marie Marchowsky and Pauline Koner continued to appear there, along with Talley Beatty, Louis Johnson, and Donald

McKayle. Meanwhile, up-and-coming choreographers began to present their work, such as the rebellious African American Eleo Pomare, and Lar Lubovitch, whose newly formed company that blended ballet and modern styles performed there on October 28, 1968, and again May 26, 1969. Daniel Nagrin, Lucas Hoving, Louis Falco, Joyce Trisler, Deborah Jowitt, and Janet Soares were just a handful of the many now celebrated dance professionals who appeared on the Y's stage during these years.

While the Y was certainly not the focal point of the avant-garde of the 1960s, it is worth noting that numerous dancers who took part in the insurrection danced on the Kaufmann stage. Experimentalists Sara Rudner and Laura Dean, for instance, appeared in Sanasardo's pieces. Between 1966 and 1967, Sanasardo also presented mixed programs with new works by talented choreographers like Cliff Keuter whose early dances were often surreal, funny, and sometimes ominous, and Elina Mooney whose individual movement vocabulary explored a tension between stylization and immediacy. Kenneth King appeared as a guest dancer on February 26, 1966. Annual performances were also given under the auspices of the nonprofit organization Contemporary Dance, Inc., of shared performances of new choreography. Jeff Duncan and Jack Moore showed work on these programs, along with Soares, Hoving, and the innovative Alwin Nikolais/Murray Louis dancer Phyllis Lamhut. The organization sponsored one particular young choreographers' concert on April 25, 1963, that presented works by several of the dancers closely involved with the radical experiments of the time. The program featured dances by Vickie Blaine, Lucinda Childs, Ruth Emerson, Fred Herko, Al Huang, Elizabeth Keen, Arlene Rothlein, Gus Solomons Jr., and Judith Willis. Such performances indicate that the Y was not completely disregarded by the new generation of choreographers.

Kolodney's retirement in October 1969 significantly altered the status of dance at the Y, for when he left the institution, dance lost a major promoter.[20] His son Nathan, also a remarkable man of penetrating insight and a passionate advocate of the arts as well as Jewish center work, took over the directorship of the educational program the following few years. While the Dance Center classes remained strong, the emphasis in the Y's performance programming shifted toward film, theater, and activities that explored more of the intellectual and aesthetic dimensions of the arts. Nathan, for instance, arranged for a Film Director's Project during the 1971–72 season, which featured directors like Milos Forman and a series of conversations with the playwrights Tennessee Williams, John Guare, Edward Albee, Neil Simon, and Arthur Miller.

William Kolodney with daughter Rima, and sons Nathan and David (beard), ca. 1965.
Courtesy of Nathan Kolodney. Photographer: Richard Brown.

Throughout these years an eclectic array of dance performances featured modern, ballet, tap, flamenco, Indian, and Jewish dance. In terms of young choreographers, the Greenhouse Dance Ensemble performed new work by members of the Erick Hawkins company. Nancy Meehan, who had also worked with Hawkins, appeared in a concert in 1973 that drew high praise from the *New York Times* critic Anna Kisselgoff, who wrote that Meehan was a choreographer "bursting with ideas and surprises."[21] The Y also hosted the radical experiments of Joan Sellers, who, on a mixed program with fellow modern dancer Hava Kohav on April 5, 1973, shocked the sensibility of some viewers with her performance of dances created with the aid of a computer. Sellers had thought out timings, movements, stage areas, and spatial patterns, and the computer had then selected the possibilities at random to create a dance. This was one of the first experiments with dance and computers, marking a trend that has since evolved into a widely practiced field characterized by sophisticated experimentation in multimedia and interactive performance.

During the 1970s a number of factors contributed to a continued downward trend in dance recital programming. In 1973, Omus Hirshbein, son of the Yiddish playwright Peretz Hirshbein, was hired as education director to enhance the program of performing arts and to nurture educational programs for children and adults. At the time, Hirshbein was a professional pianist who had served as the administrator of the Hunter College Concert Bureau and briefly at Carnegie Hall as its deputy director, and he began to enliven the music series at the Y as soon as he arrived there.[22] Meanwhile, over the next several years, dance performances dropped to a mere handful. This occurred partly because of Hirschbein's love for and expertise in music and to some extent because of the difficulties in finding dance companies that were willing to perform on what was increasingly seen as a modest and unwieldy stage. The days of the solo artist had largely disappeared and had been replaced by groups that needed larger performance areas with adequate wing space and dressing rooms. The severest blow came in 1977, when the theater was unionized, and dance performances virtually ended at what was now referred to as the Kaufmann Concert Hall.[23] According to Hirshbein, dance concerts simply could not pay for themselves under the new union regulations.[24] From then on, dance performances were rarely held in the auditorium.

Nonetheless, there were important developments. The José Limón com-

Pearl Lang and Paul Sanasardo in *The Possessed*.
Dance Division, The New York Public Library for the Performing Arts,
Astor, Lenox and Tilden Foundations.

pany was in residence from 1974 to 1978, meaning that its members taught the modern technique classes, rehearsed in the Y's studios, and gave periodic performances. Don Redlich's company followed as company-in-residence from 1978 to 1979 and Marcus Schulkind from 1979 to 80, but they too failed to last, owing to the difficulty of attracting enough students to support all the classes and of confining the groups' New York seasons to the small Kaufmann stage. During the 1970s, Hirshbein also worked closely with Pearl Lang in presenting programs of dance relating to Jewish culture. The world premiere of *The Possessed* occurred in December 1974, along with other programs focused on Jewish themes. Lang's company also appeared in April 1977, featuring a new work on the Holocaust, *I Never Saw Another Butterfly,* based on biblical songs and poems written by children who died at Theresienstadt.

In 1979 a Performing Arts Division was established, separate from the Education Department. Ed Skloot was hired as the education director, and Hirshbein became director of performing arts, meaning primarily that he took over programming for the Kaufmann Concert Hall and the activities of the Poetry Center.[25] Because the Dance Center offered classes, it stayed under the educational wing. Following Humphrey's death, numerous women had assumed the directorship of the Dance Center, all of whom strove to bring the same kind of reputation and broad vision to the program but within the severe constraints of a new financial reality and changing dance world. Lucile Nathanson, who was director for the longest period, from 1962 to 1976, assumed a leadership role in teacher training and children's dance. Along with Bonnie Bird, she also helped to found the American Dance Guild, an active service organization to this day. She was, however, succeeded by a series of relatively short-lived directors, none of whom could fully revitalize the Y's dance performance programming. These included Susan Schickele (1976–78), Sharon Gersten Luckman (1978–86), Jane Kosminsky (1986–88), Ilona Copen (1988–91), and Cathryn Williams (1991–93). Each strove in her own way to find a means of presenting dance at the Y without the use of the Kaufmann theater, now outside her jurisdiction.

Schickele oversaw the José Limón Dance Company residency, and Luckman brought in the Don Redlich company. Kosminsky began an informal performance series, "Fridays at Noon," and attempted one season of fully produced work in Buttenwieser Hall, a large room used most frequently for dance classes, lectures, and special events, which Kosminsky converted into a studio theater with lights, black drapes, and a Marley floor. Called "Dance Preludes," one series was launched in March 1987 to nurture young choreographers. Active through the spring of 1988, it presented works by more than a dozen dancers, including Kate Foley, Neta Pulvermacher, Laurie Roth, John Jasperse, and Leslie Nelson. Kosminsky also presented individual programs and a "Solo Flights" series that included Judy Landis and Margaret Beals, but the theater was soon shut down because of the high costs involved in its operation. Copen, for her part, started a series of informal, curated studio showings, "Sundays at 3," featuring seasoned performers like Sokolow, Lang, and Jean Erdman, along with shared programs by new choreographers. During Williams's 1991–92 season, the series continued with performances by Peter Pucci and Dendy Dance, both up-and-coming choreographers of the time, with Douglas Dunn, Jean Erdman, and a variety of other dance companies, ranging from tap to ballroom and baroque.

• • •

MOVING BEYOND THE MYTHOLOGY

The internal and external changes that occurred following the 1960s all suggest why the 92nd Street Y lost its central place in American dance, but there are other signs, often overlooked, which suggest that the Y contributed greatly to postmodern dance even as the institution faded from view.[26] These signs refer to the entire history of the Y and its unusual role in the dance world. The Y's historical promotion of dancers with limited New York exposure, as well as movement explorations and fusions of many varieties, meant that it was far from being synonymous with the concerns of John Martin and the Big Four or from being outdated. During its heyday in the period leading up to the 1960s the constant infusion of talent made for a highly inspiring atmosphere, for many of the people in the Y's audience were themselves dance students and budding choreographers, along with established professionals in the field. These audience members were witnessing—on the same stage, in the same space—a wide variety of dance expression as well as music, poetry, and drama. They were being shown what was possible in performance and being given the opportunity to contemplate and debate the nature of contemporary art through the Y's extensive classes and lectures.

What the Y's history suggests is that, rather than disappearing with the advent of the 1960s, the diverse choreographic ideas presented on the institution's stage migrated to new areas and began to work their way back into the emerging postmodern aesthetic of the 1980s and 1990s. Character work, use of text, detailed gestural movement, parody, stylistic fusions, African American and Jewish themes—long part of the Y's and, it would seem, modern dance's history—were to continue even while economic and philosophical concerns were changing the surface topography of the performance landscape. In addition, the Y's flexible approach to identity as a fluid entity affected by social and political circumstances, cultural heritage, contemporary trends, and individual agency can also be seen as an important precursor of postmodern thinking on subjectivity, as was (is) the Y's view of community as a collective of individuals from diverse backgrounds whose experiences should be recognized, valued, and officially patronized.

Far from arising with little connection to their past, experimental choreographers of the post-1960s period continued the practices and policies of the dancers and institutions that came before them. Many of the modern dancers who performed at the Y portrayed women trying to master the expectations of society in their sometimes serious, sometimes whimsical snippets from life. Marchowsky's *Cafe Habitué* and Litz's *Glyph,* along with the satirical cameo portraits of Angna Enters, Iva Kitchell, and others, explored aspects of the female experience that remain frequent subjects of choreographic inquiry. Twyla Tharp, for instance, often pokes fun at the conventions of femininity that plague the dance world and society at large. A characteristic image of Tharp finds her meandering slouched over and poker-faced around the rehearsal studio as she throws off rounds of fancy kicks, turns, and hip gyrations that suggest technical prowess and feminine allure even as she undermines and plays with their significance. Sybil Shearer, for her part, was interested in highly developed movements concentrated on particular parts of the body. She once dressed as a southern belle at a party and faced upstage while her arms snaked and groped behind her back as though trying to extract an ant from under her dress. Such an interest in intricate movement explorations can be later traced in the abstract minutiae—the arm/hand and footwork—of Merce Cunningham and in the impressionistic gestural work of a choreographer like Martha Clarke.

Perhaps more noticeable has been the legacy of the fusion experiments that were continually displayed and promoted at the Y. Paul Draper's and Carmelita Maracci's dances with ballet, tap, and Spanish dance and Pearl Primus's and Anna Sokolow's explorations of African and Jewish themes in their works established a precedent. In the years since these performers were in their prime, choreography concerned with stylistic and intercultural fusion has received widespread recognition and theorization. Tharp has combined ballet with soft-shoe and modern dance, Fred Darsow explores flamenco and postmodern styles, and Doug Elkins has mixed contact improvisation and hiphop. Choreographers such as Bill T. Jones and Blondell Cummings continue to explore African American experiences within the framework of contemporary dance of the 1980s and 1990s, following in the footsteps of Alvin Ailey and Donald McKayle, both of whom enjoyed successful careers following their early beginnings at the Y.

Similarly, works thematizing Jewish experience have continued since the 1940s. Meredith Monk's *Quarry* (1976) suggests, among other things, "the hunting down of Jews in Nazi Germany and generalizes to warn of the necessity for victims in any dictatorship."[27] Other postmodernists working with Jewish as well as non-Jewish themes in their work include Amy Sue Rosen, David Dorfman, and Danial Shapero. Each of these choreographers has continued to explore issues of identity, religion and ethnicity. They extend a

Neta Pulvermacher & Dancers in *Five Beds/Children of the Dream*, 1998.
92nd Street YM-YWHA Harkness Dance Center. Photographer: David Hodgson.

tradition stemming back to Zemach and the early efforts of Sokolow, Shapero, and Maslow, although their work is sometimes highly critical of Jewish
tradition, as with Dorfman's *Dayeinu* (1992), which challenges the values of
religious life.[28]

Contemporary dance in the 1980s and 1990s, far from being disconnected
to the era of "traditional" modern dance, continues to explore many aspects
of the form as they appeared at the Y. Even the challenge to meaning, which
seemed so prevalent in the 1960s, returned to haunt the dancers of this later
period. Dancers from ethnic and racial minorities continue to be important
leaders in promoting a humanist desire for social transformation through
exposure to the arts. An early pioneer in this regard is the Jewish choreographer Anna Halprin, who had appeared in the Audition Winners' recital at the
Y in 1945 and went on to an influential career on the West Coast, leading
workshops and staging large community-based works dealing with healing
and global concerns. In the 1990s, Halprin has been joined in such efforts by
choreographers, like Bill T. Jones, who are extremely concerned with making
profound statements with their work and in touching people on emotional
and spiritual planes. In pieces like *Last Supper at Uncle Tom's Cabin/The
Promised Land* (1990) or *Still/Here* (1994), issues of faith, sexuality, illness

and race are explored with the aim of raising individual and collective understanding, compassion, and tolerance. Similarly, the Jewish choreographer Liz Lerman founded an extremely successful company in 1976, which is multigenerational as well as multiracial and focuses on programs that explore ethnic, racial, and sexual diversity. For the supporters of her and Jones's work, along with many others, the myriad progressive educational events and performances offered by the Y in its heyday would have made perfect sense.

Within today's postmodern context, where multicultural concerns and issues of diversity are now part of the official, mainstream discourse, it is perhaps not surprising that the Y has once more gained some visibility in the dance world. Since 1993 the Y's Dance Center has been under the direction of Joan Finkelstein. Finkelstein is a former dancer with Cliff Keuter's and Don Redlich's dance companies (among others), and also has taught at New York University's Tisch School of the Arts, the University of Wisconsin, the University of Illinois, and California State University. During her tenure at the Y, Finkelstein has overseen the reception of generous support from the Harkness Foundation for Dance. This funding led to the new naming, 92nd Street Y Harkness Dance Center and made it possible to present a small dance festival at Playhouse 91 (a few blocks from the Y at Ninety-first Street and Second Avenue) annually since December 1994.

The performance series was mandated by the multiyear grant from the foundation, the mission being (in keeping with Kolodney's earlier policy) to present new work and repertory, giving emerging companies greater exposure and more established companies an alternative to the Joyce Theater or downtown loft-type venues. Companies that have been presented include most of the leaders in the current wave of postmodern dance, including Bebe Miller, Doug Varone, Molissa Fenley, Yoshiko Chuma and the School of Hard Knocks, Urban Bush Women, Amy Rosen, and Jane Comfort.[29] The Harkness Dance Center simultaneously offers a broad range of classes, from ballet to Afro-Caribbean dance for adults and children and "Breaking Ground" interviews with the likes of Cunningham, Jones, Tharp, Judith Jamison, and Mark Morris. In addition, Finkelstein has initiated a series, "Jewish Voices," in which choreographers working with Jewish themes preview and discuss their work; among them have been Pearl Lang, Neta Pulvermacher, and Ze'eva Cohen.

In the late 1990s the Y competes with many other venues as a presenter of contemporary dance. While the Joyce Theater provides a prestigious, theatrical setting for the more established contemporary choreographers, Dance

Theater Workshop, PS 122, Dia, and the Kitchen are the most popular spaces for more experimental work. There is also the Brooklyn Academy of Music (BAM), whose Next Wave Festival brings the hottest in avant-garde performance to New York's public. Perhaps more than any other institution, BAM has usurped the Y's role as a vanguard promoter of new dance, music, and drama, with its focus on contemporary performance and offer of a subscription series that covers all the arts. BAM, however, rarely presents little-known dancers, choosing instead to focus on those who have already established a solid reputation in avant-garde circles.

At the same time, the Y as a whole continues to exert an important institutional presence in New York. The Y is well known as a major cultural center and a place where Jewish and non-Jewish interests constantly intersect. There are still people traveling there to learn Israeli folk dances on Wednesday nights and children still taking modern dance classes whose parents and grandparents went there before them. The same issues that concerned the Y in the past continue to infuse it with tension and vigor today: how to maintain Jewish identity while integrating into the wider American society, how to synthesize Jewish and non-Jewish creativity for mutual benefit. Although the answers to these questions remain in flux and are constantly being debated, the Y is committed to the idea that it is possible for people to retain their particular identities while living together in harmony. As such, it remains a tremendous source of inspiration for those of us hoping for a better life distinguished by communal trust and understanding.

APPENDIX A
Members of the Dance Teachers Advisory Committee, 1939 – 53

Following is a list of members of the Dance Teachers Advisory Committee (DTAC) for the years 1939 – 53. Note that members were rarely at every meeting. William Kolodney was also part of the committee.

1939 – 40 Mary O'Donnell, Eugenie Schein
1940 – 41 Mary O'Donnell, chair
    Christine Leahy, Genevieve McGuinness, Pearl Rotholz, Hermine Sauthoff, Eugenie Schein
1941 – 42 Louis Horst, chair
    Mary O'Donnell, Rose Koenig, Miss Satlien, Eugenie Schein, Sylvia Hirshowitz, Hermine Sauthoff, Barbara Page (Beiswanger), Ellen Adair, Muriel Stuart, Bessie Schönberg
1942 – 43 Louis Horst, chair
    Mary O'Donnell, Rose Koenig, Eugenie Schein, Sylvia Hirshowitz, Barbara Page, Muriel Stuart, Bessie Schönberg, Lois Balcom, Pearl Rotholz, Ruth Jones
1943 – 44 Louis Horst, chair
    Lois Balcom, Ruth Jones, Mary O'Donnell, Barbara Page, Eugenie Schein, Bessie Schönberg, Muriel Stuart, Anita Zahn
1944 – 45 Louis Horst, chair
    Ruth Jones, Mary O'Donnell, Barbara Page, Eugenie Schein, Bessie Schönberg, Marion Streng, Muriel Stuart, Anita Zahn
1945 – 46 Louis Horst, chair
    Martha Hill, Doris Humphrey, Ruth Jones, Elna Lillback, Mary O'Donnell, Eugenie Schein, Bessie Schönberg, Marion Streng, Muriel Stuart, Anita Zahn
1946 – 47 Same as previous year
1947 – 48 Same as previous year
1948 – 49 Same as previous year except that Mary O'Donnell did not participate
1949 – 50 Louis Horst, chair

Agnes de Mille, Martha Hill, Hanya Holm, Doris Humphrey, Richard Kraus, Jerome Robbins, Eugenie Schein, Bessie Schönberg, Marion Streng, Muriel Stuart, Antony Tudor, Anita Zahn

1950–51   Same as previous year plus Elizabeth Rockwell and Theodora Wiesner

1951–52   Louis Horst, chair

Agnes de Mille, Martha Hill, Hanya Holm, Doris Humphrey, Richard Kraus, Jerome Robbins, Eugenie Schein, Bessie Schönberg, Marion Streng, Muriel Stuart, Antony Tudor, Theodora Wiesner, Anita Zahn

1952–53   Same as previous year plus Hazel Muller

1953   Committee folded

APPENDIX B
Dance Performances at the 92nd Street Y, 1935 – 59

The following is a list of dance events held at the Y between the years of 1935 and 1959. This list does not include performances for children. It also does not cover outside events (specially negotiated situations in which a school or organization used the theater) or events that were part of Walter Terry's Dance Laboratory. Almost all of the activities listed here were presented by the Y itself in various of its spaces, especially Buttenwieser Hall and the Kaufmann Auditorium. Where possible, I have indicated whether the events were part of a subscription series. A question mark signifies that the nature of the recital was unable to be determined. No listing under the "type" category means the recital was an individual presentation by the Y and not part of a subscription series.

The Y offered various kinds of subscription series between 1935 and 1959. The first was the Major Subscription Series; the second, the Dance Theatre Subscription Series; and the third, the Dance Center Subscription Series. At one point the Dance Theatre Series was listed as a division of the Major Subscription Series. This has been indicated by "MSS/DTSS."

The information here was culled with as much accuracy as possible from a variety of sources, including the *Y Bulletin,* reviews, programs, and other archival documents.

92nd Street YM & YWHA, 1935 – 59 Dance Performances
(see table notes on p. 249)

DATE	EVENT	TYPE
1935 Season		
3/10/35	Dvora Lapson	
5/25/35	Lecture-demonstration with Horst, Humphrey, Weidman, Holm, Graham	Symposium
1935–36 Season		
10/17/35	"The Modern Dance"	Panel symposium arranged by the *Dance Observer*

DATE	EVENT	TYPE
12/7/35	Sophia Delza	
1/5/36	Martha Graham	MSS
3/8/36	Helen Tamiris	MSS
3/29/36	Benjamin Zemach	MSS
4/5/36	Anna Sokolow	MSS
4/26/36	Humphrey-Weidman	MSS
5/36	National Dance Congress	
5/16–17/36	Elsa Findlay	Sponsored by the Y Educational Council

1936–37 Season

10/31/36	Ballet Caravan	MSS
11/1/36	Ballet Caravan	MSS
11/15/36	Esther Junger	MSS
1/10/37	Martha Graham	MSS
2/28/37	Anna Sokolow	MSS
3/7/37	Negro Dance Evening	MSS
4/8/37	"The American Dance"	John Martin lecture
4/11/37	Carmelita Maracci	MSS
4/25/37	Humphrey-Weidman	MSS
5/27/37	National Dance Congress forum	

1937–38 Season[a]

10/17/37	Philadelphia Ballet Co.	DT
10/31/37	Lil Liandre, Eleanor King, Mary Radin & Dancers of the Eternal Road	DT
11/7/37	Lasar Galpern	DT
11/14/37	Hampton Institute Creative Dance Group	DT
11/20/37	Lisa Parnova	DT
11/21/37	José Limón, Sophie Maslow, Jane Dudley, Lily Mehlman, American Dance Assoc.	DT
12/12/37	Angna Enters	MSS
12/26/37	Lillian Shapero	DT
1/2/38	Ballet Caravan	DT
1/8/38	American Dance Assoc.	DT
1/17/38	Criticism and the Direction of Contemporary Dance 4th b'day celebration of *Dance Observer*	Forum
1/22/38	Mura Dehn, Roger Pryor Dodge	DT

DATE	EVENT	TYPE
1/23/38	Theatre Dance Co.	DT
2/13/38	American Dance Assoc.	DT
2/27/38	Waldeen	DT
3/5/38	Sai Shoki	DT
3/20/38	Anna Sokolow	DT
3/27/38	Ted Shawn & Male Dancers	DT
4/3/38	Edouard Du Buron	DT
4/10/38	Hanya Holm and Group	DT

1938–39 Season[b]

11/13/38	Ronny Johansson	MSS/DTSS
11/19/38	Saki	
11/27/38	Martha Graham	MSS/DTSS
12/4/38	Estelle Dennis	
1/1/39	Theatre Dance Co.	MSS/DTSS
1/15/39	Agnes de Mille	MSS/DTSS
1/29/39	Humphrey-Weidman	MSS/DTSS
2/5/39	Lotte Goslar	MSS/DTSS?
2/26/39	Carousel Theatre Co.	MSS/DTSS?
3/18/39	The Triad—Juana de Laban, Gertrude Ulmann, Erica Stolzberg	MSS/DTSS?
3/19/39	Esther Junger	MSS/DTSS?
3/26/39	Angna Enters	MSS/DTSS?
4/1/39	Louis Horst/Martha Graham Concert Group	cosponsored with *Dance Observer*

1939–40 Season[b]

1/14/40	Carmelita Maracci	MSS/DTSS
2/4/40	Pauline Koner	MSS/DTSS
2/18/40	Anna Sokolow, Alex North	MSS/DTSS
3/10/40	Esther Junger, Pauline Koner	MSS/DTSS
3/17/40	Agnes de Mille	MSS/DTSS
3/31/40	Humphrey-Weidman	MSS/DTSS
4/7/40	Hanya Holm	MSS/DTSS
4/14/40	Louis Horst/Martha Graham Group	MSS/DTSS
4/21/40	Margaret Severn	MSS/DTSS
8/7/40	Ruth St. Denis, La Meri	MSS/DTSS

1940–41 Season

11/10/40	Katherine Dunham	DTSS
12/8/40	Carmelita Maracci	DTSS
12/15/40	Carmelita Maracci	DTSS

DATE	EVENT	TYPE
12/29/40	Carmelita Maracci	DTSS
12/22/40	Argentinita	DTSS
1/12/41	Louis Horst, Martha Graham Group	DTSS
1/19/41	Angna Enters	DTSS
2/2/41	Benjamin Zemach & Group	DTSS
2/9/41	Benjamin Zemach & Group	DTSS
2/23/41	Paul Draper	DTSS
4/6/41	Hunter College, NYU Dance CLub	
4/20/41	Erick Hawkins	
4/27/41	Humphrey-Weidman	DTSS
5/4/41	Bennington College, Sarah Lawrence College	
5/18/41	Welland Lathrop and Ensemble	
1941–42 Seasonb		
11/2/41	Louis Horst/Martha Graham Group	MSS/DTSS
12/13/41	Anna Sokolow	Recital
12/14/41	Hanya Holm	MSS/DTSS
12/28/41	Carmelita Maracci	MSS/DTSS
1/18/42	Six dancers (Nelle Fisher, Nina Fonaroff, Eleanor King, Welland Lathrop, Noami Aleh-Leaf, Elizabeth Waters)	MSS/DTSS
2/1/42	Paul Draper, Larry Adler	MSS/DTSS
3/1/42	Virginia Johnson	MSS/DTSS
4/12/42	Humphrey-Weidman	MSS/DTSS
4/26/42	Hunter College, Vassar College	
5/3/42	Dudley-Maslow-Bales Trio	Presented by the *Dance Observer* under the auspices of the YMHA Dance Center
5/10/42	NYU Dance Group, Bennington College, Sarah Lawrence College	
6/17/42	May O'Donnell, José Limón	
1942–43 Seasonb		
11/1/42	Louis Horst/Martha Graham Group	MSS/DTSS
11/14–15/42	Duncan Dance Congress	Duncan Dance Guild
11/15/42	Angna Enters	MSS/DTSS
12/6/42	Valerie Bettis, Erick Hawkins, Sybil Shearer	MSS/DTSS
12/20/42	Paul Draper, Larry Adler	MSS/DTSS

DATE	EVENT	TYPE
1/7/43	Lecture on "Choreography & the Modern Dance," "Ballet and the Modern Dance"	Arranged by the *Dance Observer* Board
1/31/43	Carmen Amaya	MSS/DTSS
2/14/43	Five Dancers—(Audition winners Julia Levien, Iris Mabry, Pearl Primus, Gertrude Prokosch, Nona Schurman)	MSS/DTSS
3/14/43	Dudley-Maslow-Bales & New Dance Group	?
3/28/43	Hanya Holm	MSS/DTSS
4/11/43	Martha Graham and Co.	MSS/DTSS
5/9/43	3rd annual university dance performance	
5/16/43	Belle Rosette and Group	
6/13/43	Anna Sokolow	
1943–44 Season[b]		
10/31/43	Second Duncan Dance Congress	Duncan Dance Guild
11/28/43	Second Duncan Dance Congress	Duncan Dance Guild
11/14/43	American Concert Ballet	MSS/DTSS
12/5/43	Anna Sokolow	
12/12/43	Argentinita, Pilar Lopez	MSS/DTSS
1/2/44	Sybil Shearer, Katherine Litz	MSS/DTSS
1/23/44	Valerie Bettis, Pearl Primus	MSS/DTSS
2/20/44	Audition winners (Robin Gregory, Matti Haim, Gertrude Lippincott, Carolyn Wilson)	MSS/DTSS
2/26/44	Evening of Hebrew Theatre & Dance	Hebrew Arts Committee of Histadruth Ivrith
3/5/44	Valerie Bettis	Dance Teachers Advisory Committee
3/8/44	"Composers and the Dance"	Panel
3/26/44	Martha Graham	MSS/DTSS
3/29/44	"Dance Criticism"	Panel
4/16/44	"Dance Production"	Panel
4/22–3/44	Pearl Primus	Dance Teachers Advisory Committee
4/29–30/44	Valerie Bettis, and the American Actors Theatre	Sponsored by the Drama Dept.

DATE	EVENT	TYPE
4/30/44	Mia Slavenska and Ensemble	MSS/DTSS
5/4/44	"Dance Performers"	Panel
5/14/44	University dance demonstration	Dance Teachers Advisory Committee
	"Dance Educators"	Panel

1944–45 Season[b]

10/29/44	Duncan Dance Congress	
11/12/44	Third annual congress	Duncan Dance Guild
11/26/44	Mia Slavenska, David Tihmar & Co.	MSS/DTSS
12/10/44	Bennington College, Sarah Lawrence College	
1/7/45	Paul Draper, Arthur Ferrante	MSS/DTSS
1/21/45	Jane Dudley, Frieda Flier, William Bales Trio, & the New Dance Group	MSS/DTSS
2/4/45	Jean Erdman, Marie Marchowsky	
2/11/45	Martha Graham	MSS/DTSS
2/25/45	Pearl Primus	MSS/DTSS
3/11/45	Sybil Shearer	
3/18/45	Pauline Koner, Noami Aleh-Leaf	MSS/DTSS
3/25/45	Dudley, Flier, Bales Trio	MSS/DTSS
4/8/45	Audition winners (Jessica Fleming, Eva Desca Garnet, Rheba Koren, Joan Miller, Shirley Wimmer)	MSS/DTSS
4/22/45	Seventh annual demonstration of the work of college dance groups	
4/29/45	Nina Fonaroff, May O'Donnell	
5/20/45	Nelle Fisher, Welland Lathrop	
5/27/45	Students' demonstration	

1945–46 Season[b]

12/9/45	Charles Weidman and Co.	MSS/DTSS
12/23/45	Rosario and Antonio and Co.	MSS/DTSS
12/30/45	Audition winners (Helaine Blok, Ann Halprin, Miriam Pandor, Ethel Winter, Yuriko)	MSS/DTSS
1/13/46	José Limón, Beatrice Seckler, Dorothy Bird	MSS/DTSS
1/27/46	Anita Zahn and Duncan Dancers	
2/3/46	Jane Dudley, Sophie Maslow, William Bales	MSS/DTSS
2/10/46	Angna Enters	MSS/DTSS

DATE	EVENT	TYPE
2/24/46	Gertrude Lippincott, Iris Mabry	
3/10/46	Martha Graham and Co.	MSS/DTSS
4/21/46	Bennington College, Sarah Lawrence College	
4/28/46	Eighth annual college dance demonstration	
5/12/46	Anna Sokolow	
5/19/46	Pearl Primus	
5/26/46	Students' demonstration	
6/16/46	Pearl Primus	

1946–47 Season[b]

10/27/46	Nina Fonaroff	
11/10/46	Pearl Primus	MSS/DTSS
11/24/46	"The Function of the Dance Critic"	Panel
12/8/46	The Foxhole Ballet	
12/15/46	"Contemporary Music for Dance"	Panel
12/29/46	Charles Weidman	MSS/DTSS
1/12/47	Audition winners (Miriam Davis, Eleanore Goff, Natanya Neumann, Carrol Kobin Newman, Alix Taroff)	MSS/DTSS
1/26/47	Iva Kitchell	
2/9/47	Iva Kitchell	
2/12/47	Hadassah and Claude Marchant	
2/23/47	José Limón and Co.	MSS/DTSS
3/1/47	Eva Desca, Jessica Fleming	
3/9/47	La Meri, Federico Rey	MSS/DTSS
3/15–16/47	Katya Delakova & Fred Berk—Dances on Jewish Themes	Adult School of Jewish Studies
3/30/47	Ruth Mata, Eugene Hari	
4/13/47	Ruth Mata, Eugene Hari	
4/6/47	Marie Marchowsky	
5/4/47	Valerie Bettis and Dance Co.	
5/21/47	Sarah Lawrence Dance Group, Bennington College Dance Group	
6/3/47	Students' demonstration	
6/8/47	Students' demonstration	

1947–48 Season[c]

10/22–3/47	Asadata Dafora, Shogola Oldba Group	
11/16/47	Nina Fonaroff and Co.	
12/4/47	Ruth Mata, Eugene Hari	

DATE	EVENT	TYPE
12/7/47	Sarah Lawrence College, Bennington College Dance Groups	
12/9/47	Jewish Dance Guild	Adult School of Jewish Studies
12/14/47	Dorothy Bird, Silan Chen	
12/18/47	Arati Bose Indian Dancer	East-West Series
12/28/47	Mary-Averett Seelye, Eleanor King	
1/4/48	Maria Teresa Acuna, Juan de Leon	
1/15/48	"People of the Philippines" Music and Dance	East-West Series
1/27/48	Paula Padani	Dance Center, sponsored by Hadassah
2/1/48	Anna Sokolow	
2/15/48	Choreographers' Workshop	
2/19/48	"Slavic Peoples" Russian Folk Dances	East-West Series
2/29/48	College dance demonstration	
3/6/48	Iris Mabry	
3/7/48	Audition winners (Linda Lion, Judith Martin, Helen McGehee, Marion Scott)	
3/14/48	Mary Anthony, Joseph Gifford, Katherine Litz, Natanya Neumann	
3/18/48	"People of Mexico"	East-West Series
3/21/48	*Dance Observer* benefit concert	
3/28/48	Theatre Dance, Inc.	
4/11/48	Pearl Primus	
4/15/48	"People of Latin America"	East-West Series
5/23/48	Talley Beatty and Group	
5/26/48	"Caribbean Backgrounds" (Students from Katherine Dunham School)	East-West Series
6/5/48	Annual adult dance demonstration	

1948–49 Season

10/17/48	Rhythms of Spain	
10/24/48	Talley Beatty and Co.	
11/7/48	Nina Fonaroff and Co.	DTSS
11/13/48	"Kalpana"	Uday Shankar film with intro. by Shankar
11/21/48	Theatre Dance, Inc.	DTSS
11/28/48	American Dance Festival benefit org. by Agnes de Mille	DTSS

DATE	EVENT	TYPE
12/12/48	Carmelita Maracci and Co.	DTSS
12/19/48	Carmelita Maracci and Co.	DTSS
12/15/48	Rosario and Antonio	
12/28/48	Ruth Mata, Eugene Hari	
1/9/49	Paul Draper, Larry Adler	DTSS
1/15/49	Katya Delakova, Fred Berk	
1/23/49	Valerie Bettis and Co.	DTSS
2/13/49	Jane Dudley, Sophie Maslow, William Bales and New Dance Group	DTSS
2/20/49	Audition winners (Janet Collins, Normand Maxon, Billie Kirpich, Midi Garth, Tao Strong)	
2/26/49	Three Ballets by Todd Bolender	
3/6/49	Mary Anthony, Joseph Gifford, Katherine Litz	DTSS
3/19/49	Choreographers' workshop	
3/27/49	Theatre Dance, Inc.	
4/2/49	Janet Collins	
4/3/49	Iva Kitchell	DTSS
4/9/49	Sarah Lawrence College, Bennington College	
4/10/49	Ruth Mata, Eugene Hari	DTSS
4/16 –7/49	"Dances & Mimes"	Organized by Agnes de Mille for the benefit of the Henry George School
4/26/49	Lin Pei-Fen	Cosponsored by East-West Assoc.
5/1/49	Choreographers' workshop	
5/11/49	Dances of India & Ceylon, American India, Mexico, South Seas, Indonesia, Haiti	Cosponsored by East-West Assoc.
5/14/49	Nona Schurman, Eve Gentry	
5/22/49	Virginia Johnson	
5/24/49	Peter Hamilton	
5/28/49	Student dance program	
6/5/49	Theatre Dance, Inc.	

1949–50 Season

10/16/49	Three Ballets by Todd Bolender	
10/31/49	Three Ballets by Todd Bolender	
10/23/49	Yuriko	

DATE	EVENT	TYPE
10/24/49	Ruth St. Denis	Part of Walter Terry's Dance Lab
11/6/49	José Limón and Co.	DTSS
11/13/49	Theatre Dance, Inc.	
11/20/49	Audition winners (Ronne Aul, Rena Gluck, Nachum & Dina, Nina Caiserman, Lucas Hoving)	DTSS
12/11/49	Bennington College	
12/17/49	Choreographers' Workshop (Two Canadian Ballet Companies: Volkoff Canadian Ballet and Ruth Sorel's Montreal Ballet)	
1/8/50	Rosario and Antonio	DTSS
1/22/50	Benefit recital for Y Building Fund	House Council, sponsor
2/4/50	Carmelita Maracci	
2/6/50	Emily Frankel, Mark Ryder	
2/12/50	Jane Dudley, Sophie Maslow, William Bales	DTSS
2/19/50	Carmelita Maracci	DTSS
2/22/50	Choreographers' workshop	
2/26/50	Indonesian Dance Troupe, Pearl Primus	DTSS cosponsored with East-West Assoc.
3/5/50	Nina Fonaroff & Co.	DTSS
3/12/50	Charles Weidman	DTSS
3/25/50	Katya Delakova, Fred Berk	
3/26/50	Choreographers' workshop	
4/16/50	Ruth Mata, Eugene Hari	DTSS
4/23/50	Katherine Litz and Group	
5/13/50	American Square Dance Group (Margot Mayo)	
5/14/50	Merce Cunningham, Valerie Bettis, and Group	DTSS
5/21/50	Theatre Dance, Inc.	
5/24/50	East and West Dance Latin-American, Asian, and African	
5/27/50	Adult student concert	
6/4/50	Hadassah and Co.	

1950–51 Season

DATE	EVENT	TYPE
9/24/50	Talley Beatty	
10/14/50	Choreographers' workshop	

DATE	EVENT	TYPE
10/24/50	A Tribute to Uday Shankar, Auspices of East-West Assoc., The India League of America	Benefit for India Culture Center Fund
11/4/50	Choreographers' workshop	
11/26/50	Merce Cunningham, Jean Erdman, Katherine Litz	DTSS
11/27/50	Rosalia Chladek	Inst. of International Education, A.N.T.A., and *Dance News*
12/3/50	Bennington College	
12/9/50	Dance Film Festival	Y Dance Center & the Cinema Guild of America
12/16/50	Choreographers' workshop	
1/14/51	Pearl Primus	DTSS
1/21/51	Audition winners (Carol Barko, Jack Moore, Charlotte Griswold, Miriam Cole, Sheldon Ossosky, Marilyn Gennaro, Virginia Copeland, Glen Tetley, Marion Edelson)	DTSS
1/28/51	Jane Dudley, Sophie Maslow, William Bales	DTSS
2/26/51	Roberto Iglesias, Ballets de Espana	DTSS
3/4/51	Dance Auditions Festival (1942–1950)	DTSS
3/11/51	Charles Weidman	
4/7/51	Helen McGehee, Ronne Aul	
4/15/51	Midi Garth, Nona Schurman, Stuart Hodes	
4/15/51	Mura Dehn	
4/22/51	Janet Collins	DTSS
4/29/51	Janet Collins	DTSS
4/25/51	International Folk Dance Festival Stars	
4/28/51	Theatre Dance, Inc.	
5/12/51	Dancers Repertory Co.	
5/17/51	Lakshimi, Dances and Music of India	
5/19/51	Bar Harbor Summer Dance School Benefit	
5/20/51	Bhanumati Menon, Leticia Jay	

1951–52 Season

10/11/51	Pearl Primus	
10/14/51	José Limón, Pauline Koner	DTSS

DATE	EVENT	TYPE
10/21/51	Pearl Primus	
11/3/51	Beth Dean and Company	
11/11/51	Mara and Her Dancers	
12/1/51	Helen McGehee, Natanya Neumann	
12/3/51	Janet Collins	
12/8/51	Bennington College	
12/9/51	Theatre Dance, Inc.	
12/23/51	Katherine Litz, David Tudor, pianist (dance and music)	
1/13/52	Choreographers' workshop	
1/19/52	Emily Frankel, Mark Ryder	
1/20/52	Angna Enters	DTSS
1/21/52	Audition winners (Irving Burton, Ruth Currier, Bodil Genkel, Audrey Golub, Gloria Newman)	DTSS
2/3/52	Jane Dudley, Sophie Maslow, William Bales	DTSS
2/17/52	Merle Marsicano, Betty Lind	
2/18/52	Judith Martin and Dance Co.	
3/1/52	Marie Marchowsky, Joseph Gifford	
3/8/52	Pearl Primus	?
3/16/52	Pearl Primus	DTSS
3/23/52	Choreographers' workshop	
3/29/52	Nina Fonaroff and Co.	
4/6/52	Theatre Dance, Inc.	
4/6/52	May O'Donnell and Dance Co.	
4/20/52	Midi Garth, Stuart Hodes, Linda Margolies	
5/3/52	Ethel Butler, Myrtle Brickman, Barbara Bray	
5/4/52	Pearl Lang and Co.	
5/14/52	Mara and the Cambodian Ballet	
5/27/52	Demonstration classes, Repertory Workshop Group	
6/1/52	Ronne Aul	
1952–53[d]		
11/1/52	Helen McGehee	
11/2/52	Jean-Léon Destiné	
11/9/52	Rukmini Devi	

DATE	EVENT	TYPE
11/15/52	Sinda Iberia	
11/26/52	Choreographers' workshop	
12/7/52	Bennington College	
12/13/52	Nina Youshkevitch Ballet Workshop	
12/21/52	Danny Daniels and Group	
12/27/52	Miriam Cole, Stuart Hodes, Linda Margolies, Jack Moore	
1/18/53	Choreographers' workshop	
1/18/53	Mara and the Cambodian Ballet	
1/25/53	Dance Associates	
2/14/53	Nina Fonaroff and Co.	
2/21/53	Calypso Carousel	
3/7/53	Marie Marchowsky, Natanya Neumann	
3/18/53	Vela Montoya	
3/21/53	Juana	
3/22/53	Choreographers' workshop	
3/28–29/53	Choreo'53 Lester Horton	
4/11/53	Harriette Ann Gray and Co.	
4/15/53	Mara and the Cambodian Ballet	
4/18/53	Judith Martin and Dance Co.	
4/23/53	Curtiss James and Co.	
4/25/53	Audition winners (Alvin Schulman, John Fealy, Tom Ribbink, Gladys Bailin)	
4/29/53	Dilip Kumar Roy, Indira Devi	
5/16/53	Katherine Litz	
5/31/53	Tao Strong and Co.	
6/7/53	Dance Associates	

1953–54 Season[d]

DATE	EVENT	TYPE
12/6/53	Bennington College Dance Group	
12/10/53	Gala Dance Concert Benefit for the Merry-Go-Rounders	
12/16/53	Paul Draper	
1/16/54	Festival of Dances	Cosponsored with Southeast Asia Assoc. of America
2/13/54	Sahomi Tachibana	
2/25/54	Panegyris	Greek Folk Dance & Song Society
2/28/54	Israeli Dance Concert	
3/4/54	Inesita	

DATE	EVENT	TYPE
3/7/54	Shivaram and Priya Gopal	
3/27/54	Israeli Dance Concert (repeat performance)	
3/30/54 – 4/4/54	New Dance Group Festival	
4/21/54	Harriette Ann Gray and Co.	
4/22/54	Inesita	
4/25/54	Charles Weidman Theater Dance Co.	
4/26/54	Emily Frankel, Mark Ryder	
4/27/54	Ballet Theatre Workshop	
5/12/54	Mara and Group	
5/29/54	Robert Joffrey	
6/3/54	La Tana and Montero	
6/13/54	Asadata Dafora and African Dancers	
7/6 –11/54	New York City Summer Dance Festival (under the direction of D. D. Livingston & Hope Sheridan)	
7/6	Alexandra Danilova, Roland Vasquez, and Michael Lland, Inesita, Katherine Litz	
7/7	Danilova, Vasquez, Lland, Mara and Her Cambodian Ballet, Geoffrey Holder and Co., Alvin Schulman, Audrey Golub	
7/8	Charles Weidman and Co., Paul Draper, Lillian Moore	
7/10	Charles Weidman and Co., Louis Johnson, Nala Najan and Srimathi Gina, Albert Minns, and Leon James	
7/11	Pearl Primus, Anthony Mordente and Carol Frishman, Sahomi Tachibana, Srimathi Gina (matinee)	
7/11	Myra Kinch and Co., Robert Joffrey Ballet, Josefina Garcia, Arleigh Peterson and Co., Midi Garth	

1954–55 Season[d]

11/7/54	Mara and the Cambodian Ballet	
12/5/54	Bennington College Dance Group	

DATE	EVENT	TYPE
12/18 –19/54	An Evening of Modern Music and Dance-theatre, Choreography by Anna Sokolow	
12/26/54	Sahomi Tachibana	
1/3/55	Carola Goya and Matteo	
2/24/55	Anna Sokolow	
2/26/55	Anna Sokolow	
3/5/55	Israeli Dance Concert	
3/24/55	Robert Joffrey	
4/10/55	Mark Ryder, Emily Frankel	Presented by Dance Drama Company
4/16/55	Mark Ryder, Emily Frankel	Presented by Dance Drama Company
4/24/55	Myra Kinch	
5/7 – 8/55	Pearl Primus	
5/11/55	Bhanumathi and Co.	
5/22/55	School of Ballet Repertory	
5/31/55	William Dollar and Co.	

1955–56 Season[d]

DATE	EVENT	TYPE
11/26/55	Paul Draper	
11/27/55	Geoffrey Holder and Co.	
12/4/55	Bennington College Dance Group	
12/18/55	Geoffrey Holder and Louis Johnson	
1/15/56	Natanya Neumann and Ruth Currier	
1/18/56	The "Dance in Israel" Lecture by Anna Sokolow	
1/23/56	Contemporary dance productions	
1/29/56	Bhanumathi and Dance Co.	
2/1/56	Boston Dance Theatre	
3/17/56	Marie Marchowsky Dance Concert	
3/29/56	Bard College—music, art and dance	
3/31/56	Hadassah and Joseph Gifford	
4/14/56	Anna Sokolow	
4/19/56	Evening of Indian Arts	
4/21/56	Valerie Bettis and Dance Co.	
4/28/56	Anna Sokolow and Sophie Maslow	
5/5/56	Midi Garth and Dance Co.	
5/12/56	Eve Gentry, Marion Scott, Virginia Freeman	

DATE	EVENT	TYPE
5/13/56	Evening of Israeli Music and Dance	

1956–57 Season[d]

DATE	EVENT	TYPE
10/14/56	Betty Lind and Dance Co.	
11/11/56	Sophie Maslow and Dance Co.	
11/25/56	Geoffrey Holder and Dance Co.	
12/2/56	Bennington College Dance Group	
12/13/56	Mary Anthony	
1/13/57	Betty Lind and Dance Co.	
1/20/57	Louis Johnson and Co.	
2/2/57	Contemporary Dance Productions	
2/10/57	Three Arts Theatre in an Evening of Chamber Music and Dance (Paul Taylor)	
2/17/57	Harry Asmus Ballet Repertory	
2/27/57	Louis Johnson and Dance Co.	
3/3/57	Bill Hooks–Marvin Gordon Dance Co.	
3/18/57	Bard College Arts Festival—Dance, Drama, Music	
3/24/57	Florita Raup and Co.	
3/31/57	Edith Stephen and Dance Co.	
4/6/57	Alan Banks Dance Co.	
4/7/57	College Dance Demonstration	
5/4/57	Marie Marchowsky and Dance Co.	
5/11/57	Contemporary Dance Productions	
5/12/57	Westchester Ballet Co.	

1957–58 Season[e]

DATE	EVENT	TYPE
10/20/57	Paul Taylor and Dance Co.	
10/27/57	Geoffrey Holder and Dance Co., Daniel Nagrin, William Hug	DCSS
11/2/57	American Jazz Dance Co.	
11/10/57	Mary Anthony and Dance Co.	
12/8/57	Bennington College	
12/14/57	Joseph Gifford Dance Theatre	
12/17/57	Anna Sokolow, Valerie Bettis, Louis Johnson, and their dance companies	DCSS
12/22/57	Geoffrey Holder and Dance Co.	
1/5/58	Merce Cunningham and Co., May O'Donnell and Co., Iva Kitchell	DCSS

DATE	EVENT	TYPE
1/12/58	Contemporary dance productions	
1/26/58	The Theatre of Angna Enters	
2/2/58	Westchester Ballet Co.	
2/9/58	New Opera Theatre Society, Gypsy and Russian folk dances	
2/16/58	Juilliard Dance Theatre, Sophie Maslow & Co., Katherine Litz	DCSS
2/19/58	Anna Sokolow Dance Co.	
2/22/58	Contemporary dance productions	
2/23/58	Karen Kanner and Dance Co., William Burdick and Dance Co.	
2/24/58	Anna Sokolow Dance Co.	
3/1/58	Hebraica by Fred Berk	
3/2/58	Daniel Nagrin	
3/3/58	Ximenes and Vargas	
3/6/58	Ximenes and Vargas	
3/9/58	Louis Johnson and Dance Co.	
3/23/58	John Butler and Co., Pauline Koner, Donald McKayle and Co.	DCSS
3/30/58	Ernest Parham and Dance Co., Alvin Ailey and Dance Co., and Talley Beatty	
4/20/58	Mary Anthony and Co., Paul Curtis and American Mime Theatre, Ruth Currier	DCSS
4/26/58	Paul Draper	
5/3/58	Dick Fitz-Gerald, Eleanore Kramer, Diane and Vol Quitzow, Deborah Zall and companies	
5/10/58	Jean-Léon Destiné Haitian Dance	
5/11/58	Fred Berk Repertory Dance Co.	
5/18/58	Pearl Lang and Dance Co., Sophie Maslow Dance Co.	

1958–59 Season

DATE	EVENT	TYPE
10/12/58	Geoffrey Holder and Co.	
10/26/58	Talley Beatty and dance companies of Myra Kinch and Diane and Vol Quitzow	DCSS
11/9/58	Jean Cébron	

DATE	EVENT	TYPE
11/22/58	Louis McKenzie, George Mills, Cyril Peters	
11/30/58	Mary Anthony Co., Jean Cébron, Murray Louis Co.	DCSS
12/7/58	Bennington College	
12/14/58	Anna Sokolow Dance lecture	
12/20/58	Paul Taylor and Dance Co.	
12/21/58	Alvin Ailey and Dance Co.	
12/28/58	Marshall Stearns, Albert Minns, Leon James	Lecture-demonstration
1/18/59	Contemporary dance productions	
1/25/59	Midi Garth, Geoffrey Holder & Co., and Juilliard Dance Theatre	DCSS
2/15/59	Adelphi College Dance Group and Reader's Theatre	
2/22/59	Paul Draper, Ruth Currier and Company, Pauline Koner and Co.	DCSS
3/1/59	Westchester Ballet	
3/4/59	Contemporary dance productions	Recital
3/7/59	Hebraica	
3/9/59	Jean Erdman and Co.	
3/16/59	Jean Erdman and Co.	
3/15/59	Leon James and Albert Minns, American Jazz Dancers, May O'Donnell and Co.	DCSS
4/5/59	Joseph Gifford Dance Theatre	
4/12/59	Sophie Maslow and Co., Daniel Nagrin, Anna Sokolow and Co.	DCSS
4/25/59	Fred Berk Repertory Co.	
5/2/59	"Studio for Dance" Paul Sanasardo and Donya Feuer and companies	
5/6/59	Louis McKenzie, Rita Roitman, Deborah Zall and companies	
5/10/59	Kevin Carlisle and Dance Co., Donald McKayle and Dance Co.	
5/16/59	Bhaskar and Co. in Dances of India	
5/24/59	Eleo Pomare and Co.	
5/27/59	Contemporary dance productions	

DATE	EVENT	TYPE
5/28/59	The Making of a Dancer, works by Lucas Hoving, Diane Quitzow, and Bonnie Bird	
1959–60 Season		
11/1/59	Geoffrey Holder and Co.	DCSS
11/8/59	Daniel Nagrin	
11/15/59	Sophie Maslow and Dance Co.	
11/22/59	The Mime Theatre of Etienne Decroux	
11/28/59	Talley Beatty and Co.	
12/5/59	Hava Kohav and Co.	
12/6/59	Bennington College Dance Group	
12/13/59	Adam Darius and Dance Co.	
12/19/59	Studio for Dance, with Paul Sanasardo and Donya Feuer	
12/20/59	Aviv Theatre of Song and Dance	DCSS
12/27–30/59	National Dance Conference; Humphrey-Weidman Technique	Sponsored by Dance Center

Notes:

MSS = Major Subscription Series
DT = Dance Theatre
DTSS = Dance Theatre Subscription Series
DCSS = Dance Center Subscription Series

a. Initiation of the Dance Theatre concept.
b. Dance Theatre Subscription Series, a division of the Major Subscription Series.
c. Dance Theatre Subscription Series was not held. An East-West Series was held in cooperation with the East and West Association.
d. No subscription series was held. Except where noted, all events were presented by the Y Dance Center as individual recitals.
e. Subscription series resumes under the name Dance Center Subscription Series.

NOTES

Introduction

All primary documents (letters, reports, proposals, minutes) held in the
92nd Street YM-YWHA Archives unless otherwise noted.

1. David Biale, Michael Galchinsky, and Susannah Heschel, "Introduction: The Dialectic of Jewish Enlightenment," in *Insider/Outsider: American Jews and Multiculturalism* (Berkeley: University of California Press, 1998) 8.

2. Of the few studies that have been written on dance at the Y, the most informative is found in Margaret Lloyd, *The Borzoi Book of Modern Dance* (New York: A. A. Knopf, 1949). This text, which provides an overview of dance activity at the time, contains a chapter in which the Dance Center is discussed.

3. See Deborah Dash Moore, *At Home in America: Second Generation New York Jews* (New York: Columbia University Press, 1981).

4. The distinction between Jewishness and Judaism indicates the difference between Judaism, the religion, and Jewishness, which may but need not be based on religious identification.

5. The Haskalah refers to a Jewish ideological movement initiated in the eighteenth century that aimed at modernizing Jewish life and thought. *Haskalah* was the Hebrew term for "enlightenment" (literally, "rationalization"). The ideals of the Haskalah included reason (Judaism as rational belief), tolerance, and human perfectibility.

6. C. Urbont, interview by author, 1994. Urbont was assistant executive director of the Y 1951–56; executive director, 1956–1975; and executive vice president, 1975–78.

7. See, for instance, Gerald E. Myers, "Ethnic and Modern Dance," in American Dance Festival, *The Black Tradition in American Modern Dance*. ([Durham, N.C.]: American Dance Festival, 1988), 24–5.

8. Frances Hawkins to William Kolodney, 10 December 1936.

9. See Marcia B. Siegel, *Days on Earth: The Dance of Doris Humphrey* (New Haven,

Conn.: Yale University Press, 1987), 226, and Pauline Koner, *Solitary Song/Pauline Koner* (Durham, N.C.: Duke University Press, 1989), 149.

10. Ellen Graff discusses the complex, fluid nature of the relation between dancers in the left-wing movement and the modern dance movement in *Stepping Left: Dance and Politics in New York City, 1928–1942* (Durham, N.C.: Duke University Press, 1997), and see Mark Franko, *Dancing Modernism/Performing Politics* (Bloomington and Indianapolis: Indiana University Press, 1995).

11. Emily Bilski, "Seeing the Future through the Light of the Past: The Art of the Jewish Museum," in *The Jewish Museum, New York,* by Vivian B. Mann with Emily D. Bilski (London: Scala Books, in association with The Jewish Museum, New York, 1993), 17.

12. See John O. Perpener III, "The Seminal Years of Black Concert Dance" (Ph.D. diss., New York University, 1992), and Jennifer Dunning, *Alvin Ailey: A Life in Dance* (Reading, Mass.: Addison-Wesley, 1996).

13. YMHA *Bulletin,* 23 May 1941, 1.

14. See Naomi Cohen, *American Jews and the Zionist Idea* (New York: Ktav, 1975), 114–15.

15. Quoted in Marian Horosko, *Martha Graham: The Evolution of Her Dance Theory and Training, 1926–1991* (Pennington, N.J.: A Cappella Books, 1991), 51.

16. Quoted in S. Josephs, "Ageless Movement" (*Jewish Week,* 7 June 1996), 45.

17. Thanks to Nathan Kolodney for making this observation.

18. Barbara Kirshenblatt-Gimblett, introduction to *Life Is with People: The Culture of the Shtetl,* ed. Mark Zborowski and Elizabeth Herzog (New York: Schocken Books, 1995), ix.

19. Ibid.

20. See *The Invention of Tradition,* ed. Eric Hobsbawm and Terence Ranger (New York: Cambridge University Press, 1983).

21. Kirshenblatt-Gimblett, introduction, ix–xlviii.

22. Ibid., xviii.

23. Graff, *Stepping Left,* 139.

24. See Oscar I. Janowsky, *The JWB Survey* (New York: Dial Press, 1948).

25. Biale, Galchinsky, and Heschel, "Introduction," 8.

26. Ibid., 7.

27. Ibid., 8.

28. See Karen Brodkin Sacks, "How Did Jews Become White Folks?" in *Race,* ed. Steven Gregory and Roger Sanjek (New Brunswick, N.J.: Rutgers University Press, 1994).

29. David Biale, "The Melting Pot and Beyond," in *Insider/Outsider: American Jews and Multiculturalism* (Berkeley: University of California Press, 1998), 18.

30. Like folklorists Daniel and Jonathan Boyarin, in their article "Diaspora: Generation and the Ground of Jewish Identity" (*Critical Inquiry,* 19 [summer 1993]), this book seeks to articulate a Jewish subject-position as "a perpetual, creative, diasporic tension"

in which Jews living in different democratic countries find a way of fully engaging with their surroundings without losing their distinctiveness.

31. Bonnie Bird, interview by author, 1995.

1. Jews and American Culture

1. Harry L. Glucksman, "Tendencies in the Jewish Center Movement," in *Proceedings* (National Conference of Jewish Social Service, Albany, N.Y., 1923), 153.

2. The first board of directors consisted of Lewis May, S. Newton Leo, Sol B. Solomon, Julius J. Frank, I. S. Isaacs, Mark Blumenthal, Morris S. Wise, J. J. Lyons, Oscar S. Straus, Arnold Tanzer, Adolph S. Sanger, William Strauss, William Bennett, J. P. Solomon, and George Samuels. Refer for the early history of the Y to Benjamin Rabinowitz, *The Young Men's Hebrew Associations, 1854–1913* (New York, National Jewish Welfare Board, 1948).

3. Jack Nadel, "Our Seventy-Five Years," in *Building Character for 75 Years, 1874–1949: Y.M. & Y.W.H.A.*, ed. Alfred Stern (New York: Robin Hood Press, 1949), 11.

4. See, for instance, the prospectuses of the Young Men's Hebrew Association of the City of New York, 1879–80 and 1882–83. The board of directors' House Committee was in charge of classes until 1878, when a standing Committee on Library and Classes was established. This committee lasted until 1897, when a separate Class Committee was formed.

5. See Deborah Dash Moore, *At Home in America: Second Generation New York Jews* (New York: Columbia University Press, 1981).

6. There was, however, ongoing debate in certain circles regarding the mission of the Y and its commitment to Jewish topics. In the pages of *American Hebrew,* for instance, criticism raged in the 1880s over the Y's emphasis on non-sectarian programming. See Charles Wyszkowski, *A Community in Conflict* (New York: University Press of America, 1991), 42–44.

7. See C. Howard Hopkins, *History of the Y.M.C.A. in North America* (New York: Association Press, 1951).

8. Joseph Hart, *Adult Education* (New York: T. Y. Crowell, 1927), 175.

9. Nadel, "Our Seventy-Five Years," 12.

10. Ibid., 14. It should be noted that Schiff was involved in a parallel development in contributing to the Jewish Theological Seminary, which was founded in New York in 1886 to educate rabbis in modern research.

11. Jacob Schiff to Percival S. Menken, 20 December 1898.

12. *Encyclopaedia Judaica* ed., s.v., "New York City."

13. Mel Scult, "Becoming Centered: Community and Spirituality in the Early Kaplan," in *The American Judaism of Mordecai M. Kaplan,* ed. Emanuel S. Goldsmith, Mel Scult, and Robert M. Seltzer (New York: New York University Press, 1990), 59.

14. Ibid., 60.

15. Moore, *At Home in America*, 131.

16. Ibid., 131.

17. At the same time, it is important to note that the Y was not as committed to "Jewish" concerns as Kaplan would have liked. According to Mel Scult, "Kaplan was discouraged by the secular character of the YMHA and the lack of respect for Jewish law that was frequently in evidence"(Scult, "Becoming Centered," 134).

18. For the history of the Jewish center and synagogue movement, see David Kaufman, *Shul with a Pool: The "Synagogue-Center" in American Jewish History* (Hanover, N.H.: University Press of New England, 1999).

19. See Oscar I. Janowsky, *Change and Challenge: A History of 50 Years of JWB*. New York: National Jewish Welfare Board, 1966.

20. *Encyclopaedia Judaica*. ed., s.v. "United States of America."

21. See Moore, *At Home in America*.

22. A 1928 report by Harold H. Levin in the Y's archival files states that, c.1913, 90 percent of the Y's members came from within a radius of a mile, whereas in 1928 less than 20 percent lived in the vicinity, the others coming from the Bronx, Queens, Brooklyn, and other places in the New York metropolitan area.

23. Beth Wenger, *New York Jews and the Great Depression* (New Haven, Conn.: Yale University Press, 1996), 95.

24. Ibid., 94.

25. Ibid.

26. From 1914 to 1942 the YWHA had its headquarters on 110th Street, although women were permitted to attend certain activities, such as dance classes, at the 92nd Street Y.

27. The old structure, which included a pool dating from 1911, was pulled down to make room for the expanded building.

28. Kaufmann's donation was specifically earmarked for the auditorium, as part of the larger building fund campaign.

29. Abraham Wolf Binder was appointed director of the Music Department in the fall of 1917. In 1919, Binder established the Y's Music School as one component of the Music Department, along with choral and symphonic groups. Binder remained as director until 1966, overseeing its various educational and performance activities.

30. The terms "general" and "Jewish activities" sporadically appear earlier, especially in the literature of the late 1920s. In 1927, for instance, the title "Religious Director" was changed to "Director of Jewish Activities" for a short time.

31. The Ethical Culture movement originated under Adler's leadership in New York in 1876, based on the conviction that moral tenets need not be grounded in religious or philosophical dogma.

32. In 1942 the women's YWHA building was appropriated for army use, and YWHA members were invited to share the 92nd Street Y. In 1945 the organizations joined and the name was changed to YM-YWHA. From then on the 92nd Street Y became the home for both men and women.

33. Herman Jacobs, "Basic Plans for 'Y' Courses and Classes," 1930.

34. Everett Martin, *The Meaning of a Liberal Education* (New York: W. W. Norton & Co., 1926), viii.

35. Ibid., 2.

36. Ibid., 3.

37. Eduard C. Lindeman, *The Meaning of Adult Education* (New York: New Republic, 1926), 7.

38. Hart, *Adult Education*, 306.

39. Lindeman, *Meaning of Adult Education*, 107.

40. Elizabeth Wells Robertson, "Art Training in Preparation for Adult Leisure," *Proceedings of the Seventy-first Annual Meeting of the National Education Association of the United States* 71 (1933):282.

41. Lorado Taft, "Enrichment of Adult Life thru Art," *Proceedings of the Seventy-first Annual Meeting of the National Education Association of the United States* 71 (1933):285.

42. Beth Wenger observes how Jewish social workers of the Depression era underlined the importance of education, recreation, and cultural programs, not simply relief and employment assistance, to strengthen ethnic culture and commitment. See *New York Jews and the Great Depression* (New Haven, Conn.: Yale University Press, 1996), 159.

43. Due to Kaplan's influence, dramatics, arts and crafts, and music were taught at the Jewish Theological Seminary as of 1929.

44. Mordecai Kaplan, "The Place of Adult Study in Jewish Life," *The Jewish Center* 5(2) (June 1927):15.

45. Mordecai Kaplan, *Judaism as a Civilization: Toward a Reconstruction of American Jewish Life* (Philadelphia: Jewish Publication Society of America and the Reconstructionist Press, 1981), 203.

46. Isadora Duncan–style dancing was offered at the experimental school of Kaplan's Jewish Center, a secular community organization he established in 1916 with a synagogue as its nucleus.

47. "Statement of a Tentative Cultural Program for the Season 1932–33."

48. Naima Prevots, *Dancing in the Sun; Hollywood Choreographers 1935–1937* (Ann Arbor, Mich.: UMI Research Press, 1987), 203.

49. For a detailed consideration of Zemach's choreography, especially in relation to Zionism, see chapter 7, this volume.

50. Naima Prevots, "Benjamin Zemach: From Darkness to Light," in *Israel Dance* (Tel Aviv: Israel Dance Society and Friends of the Dance Library of Israel, 1986), 24.

51. "Statement of a Tentative Cultural Program."

52. Minutes, Cultural Activities Committee, 4 April 1932.

53. Naaman choreographed and had a school located at West Fifty-fifth Street in New York in the late 1920s, and in 1931 she choreographed the dream sequence in Ernst Toller's *Bloody Laughter* on Broadway (49th St. Theater).

54. *Educational Bulletin.*

55. For examples of Slavson's work see *Character Education in a Democracy* (New York: Association Press, 1939) and *Recreation and the Total Personality* (New York: Association Press, 1946).

56. *YMHA Bulletin,* 26 September 1933.

57. "Proposed Program for 1933 –1934," 9 May 1933.

58. *Dance Observer,* March 1934, 19.

59. Jack Nadel to Joseph Klein, 7 October 1934.

60. *YMHA Bulletin,* 12 October 1934, 3.

61. Letter from Nathan Kolodney to author, June 1998.

62. It is unclear exactly what happened with Kolodney's studies during this time. Mention of this thesis topic is given in a letter from Jack Nadel to Joseph Klein, 7 October 1934.

63. *YMHA Bulletin,* 12 October 1934.

64. Nathan Kolodney to author, June 1998.

65. "The Purpose of the Educational Program of the 92nd St. YMHA," January 1936.

66. Ibid.

67. The work is not particularly scholarly, lacking footnotes and bibliography. Nonetheless, it is a rare piece of self-examination and interpretation of his life's work.

68. William Kolodney, "History of the Educational Department of the YM-YWHA" (Ed.D. diss., Teachers College, Columbia University, 1950), 9.

69. Ibid., 28.

70. Ibid., 29.

71. Ibid., 162.

72. "Purpose of the Educational Program."

73. "Outline of Educational Program for the Season 1936 –1937."

74. *YMHA Bulletin,* 12 October 1934, 1.

75. William Kolodney to Frederick A. Blossom, 30 October 1935.

76. Carl Urbont interview by author, 1994.

77. William Kolodney, "History of the Educational Department," 137.

78. Ibid., 30.

79. *YMHA Bulletin,* 12 October 1934, 1.

80. William Kolodney, "Paper by William Kolodney," in *Proceedings and Papers of the Annual Conference of the National Association of Jewish Center Workers* (National Association of Jewish Center Workers in Cooperation with the JWB, 1940), 87.

81. See Kolodney, "Paper by William Kolodney," where he argues for the continued need of a "neutral" arts program at the same time as he promotes greater support of Jewish artists.

82. *Educational Bulletin,* 1935 –36.

83. *YMHA Bulletin,* 24 April 1936.

84. For a detailed account of theater at the Y, see Nancy Friedland, "The 92nd St. Y and Anglo-Jewish Theatre" (M.A. thesis, New York University, 1993).

85. See Frederic Cople Jaher, *A Scapegoat in the New Wilderness: The Origins and Rise of Anti-Semitism in America* (Cambridge, Mass.: Harvard University Press, 1994), and Donald Stuart Strong, *Organized Anti-Semitism in America: The Rise of Group Prejudice during the Decade 1930–40* (Washington, D.C.: American Council on Public Affairs, 1941).

86. Herbert Kline to William Kolodney, 2 May 1936. Kline refers to a previous conversation he had with Kolodney regarding a Jewish theatre, and this statement recounts their shared opinion.

87. Peter M. Rutkoff and William B. Scott, *New School: A History of the New School for Social Research* (New York: Free Press, 1986), 62. The authors also make a connection between pragmatism and Jewish entry into American academic life (p. 78). This suggests that there was a strong link between Jews and the spread of progressive education theory.

88. Minutes of the Board of Directors, 92nd Street YM-YWHA, 20 November 1951, 4.

2. Founding the YM-YWHA Dance Center

1. John Martin, quoted in William Kolodney, "History of the Educational Department of the YM-YWHA" (Ed.D. diss., Teachers College, Columbia University, 1950), 144.

2. *A Gala Evening of Dance* (at the Theresa L. Kaufmann Concert Hall on 21 April 1974, in celebration of the 100th anniversary of the 92nd Street YM-YWHA, New York). Videotaped by Judith Mann and Walter Benjamin for the Jerome Robbins Film Archive.

3. Minutes, 7 November 1930.

4. Marnie Katzman, "Dance at the Y," 1990. Collection of the author.

5. In a 1951 *Dance Magazine* article on the Y, Doris Hering notes that Mr. Kolodney "credits his wife, Leah, with the actual idea for opening the doors of the Y and its theater to modern dance." *Dance Magazine,* 14 November 1951, p. 2. Kolodney married Leah Rothaus on 21 March 1935. She was born in Pittsburgh to a Russian-Jewish family and attended the Carnegie Institute of Technology, where she received a degree in social services, but she was also a potter and loved the arts. She died of cancer in 1955.

6. Margaret Lloyd, *The Borzoi Book of Modern Dance* (New York: A. A. Knopf, 1949), 308.

7. Little is known regarding this meeting, which is mentioned in Walter Terry's remarks in *The Nineteenth Annual Capezio Dance Award,* honoring William Kolodney (New York: Vincent Astor Gallery of the Library for the Performing Arts, 1970).

8. John Martin to William Kolodney, 26 November 1934.

9. *Y Bulletin,* 15 December 1954, p. 2.

10. The Blue Laws (or the Sunday Blue Laws) required theaters to be closed on Sundays in the state of New York. However, a bill legalizing dance concerts on Sundays was passed in April 1932 as a result of efforts by the Concert Dance League.

11. See Lloyd, *Borzoi Book of Modern Dance,* 307.

12. Dancers for this series were chosen by audition. Judges included the Dalcroze instructor and conductor Paul Boepple, Martha Hill, the folk dance expert Mary Wood Hinman, the critic and editor Paul Love, and Louis Horst. Seven performances were held the first season featuring little-known dancers. A similar series was given the following three springs.

13. John Martin, *America Dancing: The Background and Personalities of the Modern Dance* (New York: Dodge Publishing Co., 1936), 186.

14. Ellen Graff, *Stepping Left: Dance and Politics in New York City, 1928–1942* (Durham, N.C.: Duke University Press, 1997), 10–11.

15. Ibid., 171.

16. William Kolodney to Martha Graham, 7 January 1935.

17. William Kolodney to John Martin, 11 March 1935.

18. John Martin to William Kolodney, 9 April 1935. It is unclear how the custom concerning what spaces would and would not be reviewed was established. Scrapbooks of Martin's writing during the period between 1934 and 1936, located in the Dance Collection of the New York Public Library, suggest that he covered the Broadway theaters (including the Adelphi, Ambassador, Guild, and Ritz), Radio City Music Hall, and Town Hall but not the Students Dance Recitals series at Washington Irving High School. Later, when the Humphrey-Weidman Studio Theater opened on Sixteenth Street in 1940, he expanded his coverage to include it.

19. Ibid.

20. *YMHA Bulletin*, 17 May 1935, 3.

21. William Kolodney to Martha Graham et al, 27 May 1935.

22. Letter from John Martin to William Kolodney, 13 June 1935.

23. No date is listed on the proposal.

24. Marcia B. Siegel, *Days on Earth: The Dance of Doris Humphrey* (New Haven, Conn.: Yale University Press, 1987), 143.

25. Ibid., 146.

26. New School for Social Research, spring 1933 course catalogue.

27. See Claudia Gitelman, "Dance, Business, and Politics: Letters from Mary Wigman to Hanya Holm, 1930–1971," with translations by Marianne Forster, *Dance Chronicle* 20(1) (1997): 18.

28. Susan Manning, *Ecstasy and the Demon: Feminism and Nationalism in the Dances of Mary Wigman* (Berkeley: University of California Press, 1993), 261.

29. Bonnie Bird, interview by author, 1995.

30. Selma Jeanne Cohen, *Doris Humphrey: An Artist First* (Middletown, Conn.: Wesleyan University Press, 1972), 135.

31. Larry Warren, *Anna Sokolow: The Rebellious Spirit* (Princeton, N.J.: Princeton Book Co., 1991), 67.

32. Kolodney had planned a recital by Paul Haakon for 29 March and an evening of "Men of the Dance" for 5 April 1936, with Roger Pryor Dodge, William Dollar, José

Limón, Harry Losee, Gene Martell, William Matons, and Demetrius Vilon, but both were canceled for no documented reason.

33. Proposed Program for the Educational Department, 1935–36.

34. Frances Hawkins, "The Cost of a New York Recital," *Dance Observer,* December 1934, 85.

35. An educational and cultural budget records a federation appropriation of $2,945 for 1935. Additional information is given in minutes of the board of directors meeting of 21 May 1935; it states that the board accepted Kolodney's new program along with a projected deficit of $2,000. It seems that the board agreed to give Kolodney the extra $2,000 to get his entire educational program off the ground.

36. "The Purpose of the Educational Program of the 92nd St. YMHA, January 2, 1936," 92nd Street Y Archives.

37. Jack Nadel, transcript of interview by Steve Siegel, 11 February 1980, p. 92.

38. *Dance Observer,* February 1936, 17.

39. Ibid., October 1935, 74.

40. Ibid., June–July 1936, 66.

41. "Program of Events."

42. *New Theatre* 3 July 1936, 23.

43. Lois Balcom, "Joseph Mann and His 18-Year Dance Series at Washington Irving," *Dance Observer,* August–September, 1942, 94.

44. It seems as if Martin later reconsidered. In a letter dated May 19, 1937, he wrote to Kolodney about the upcoming 1937–38 season projected for the Y: "I am afraid I cannot promise to review your series at the Y, because I would be getting myself in for too much. However, if there proves to be anything on it that is of unusual interest, I can probably manage to cover that." And from this period on he occasionally reviewed performances at the Y.

45. William Kolodney to Charles Weidman, December 1947.

3. Democracy in Action

1. Nona Schurman, interview by author, 1995.

2. *Dance Observer,* February 1938, 26.

3. Weidman offered one course in modern dance in the fall, and Holm taught two lessons in a course otherwise run by Henrietta Greenhood.

4. Bonnie Bird, interview by author, 1995.

5. From 1938 course description of "Technique of the Modern Dance," offered by Henrietta Greenhood, with Hanya Holm, supervisor.

6. *Educational Bulletin,* 1938–39.

7. YMHA *Bulletin,* 12 October 1934, 2. The topic of this paper seems to have been an incarnation of Kolodney's Ph.D. dissertation that was never realized in finished form.

8. William Kolodney, "History of the Educational Department of the YM-YWHA" (Ed.D. diss., Teachers College, Columbia University, 1950), 28–29.

9. For a detailed analysis of *The Eternal Road,* see Atay Citron, "Pageantry and Theatre in the Service of Jewish Nationalism in the United States, 1933–1946" (Ph.D. diss., New York University, 1989), 133–275.

10. Naima Prevots, "Benjamin Zemach: From Darkness to Light," in *Israel Dance* (Tel Aviv, 1986), 24.

11. Frieda Maddow, quoted in Prevots, "Benjamin Zemach," 25.

12. For more on the Yiddish Art Theatre, see Nahma Sandrow, *Vagabond Stars: A World History of Yiddish Theater* (New York: Harper and Row, 1977), 261–67; and David Lifson, *The Yiddish Theatre in America* (New York: Thomas Yoseloff, 1965), 313–95. Note that a more extensive discussion of Shapero's work appears in chap. 7, this volume.

13. Also listed but ultimately canceled was Lil Liandre's Theatre Dance Group, designed to "heighten technical proficiency for theater use." *Educational Bulletin.*

14. For a fuller discussion of "Jewish dance," see chap. 7.

15. "Proposed Program for 1939–40."

16. William Kolodney, "Paper by William Kolodney," in *Proceedings and Papers of the Annual Conference of the National Association of Jewish Center Workers* (National Association of Jewish Center Workers in Cooperation with the JWB, 1940), 87.

17. Ellen Graff, "Stepping Left: Dance and Politics in New York City, 1928–1942" (Ph.D. diss., New York University, 1992), 89–90.

18. "Proposed Educational Program 1940–41."

19. Ibid. In advertising prepared for the *Dance Observer* in September 1937 it was further indicated that tuition fees for all classes during the 1937–38 season would include a year's subscription to *Dance Observer* and a free subscription to the Dance Theatre Series, which Kolodney was currently establishing.

20. The Selective Training and Service Act was signed by President Franklin D. Roosevelt on 16 September 1940. It was amended in 1941, and after 1942 men were required to register with their local board on attaining their eighteenth birthday. Through the course of 1942, monthly calls for the armed forces rose from 99,929 in January 1942 to 450,000 in December 1942.

21. Minutes of the Board of Directors, 92nd Street YMHA, 6 July 1942.

22. "Annual Report of the Educational Department, 1943."

23. In May 1942, Kolodney indicated that he was finding himself incapable of directing the center's many activities and was considering hiring Barbara Page, a leader in the recreational and educational dance world who had taught previously at the University of Colorado, Hunter College, and New York University and who, in the late 1930s, was national chairman of the Dance Section of the American Association for Health, Physical Education and Recreation. The hiring of Barbara Page (Beiswanger) would have drastically changed the nature of modern dance training at the Y, taking it from a dance-oriented, to a more fitness-oriented program. As it turned out, at the last minute she was

hired as the social director of the Central YWCA at Fifty-second Street and Lexington Avenue and never worked at the Y.

24. *Bulletin of Educational Activities,* 1943.

25. *Bulletin of Educational Activities,* 1944.

26. It should be noted that Humphrey also acted as an adviser to the growing children's department, which began to blossom after 1951 under the chairmanship of Bonnie Bird.

27. No choreography classes were offered in 1947–48 and 1952–53. Nona Schurman taught beginner courses in choreography at the same time that Humphrey offered her advanced class during 1946–47 and 1953–54.

28. Doris Humphrey to Mrs. Helen Robinson, October 1947. Dance Collection, New York Public Library.

29. Marcia B. Siegel, *Days on Earth: The Dance of Doris Humphrey* (New Haven, Conn.: Yale University Press, 1987), 226.

30. The 1937 Polish film of *The Dybbuk* was directed by Michal Waszynski.

31. According to Fibich, a director of an orphanage in Paris who greatly admired their work arranged for them to perform in New York for the Congress of Jewish Culture.

32. Felix Fibich, interview by author, 1994. All following quotes attributed to Fibich are from that interview.

33. Humphrey's observations regarding movement are documented in her book. Doris Humphrey, *The Art of Making Dances* (New York: Grove Press, 1959).

34. Weidman taught at the Y between 1944 and 1948; Limón taught there between 1945 and 1947.

35. See Nona Schurman and Sharon Leigh Clark, *Modern Dance Fundamentals* (New York: Macmillan, 1972).

36. Observed in technique class given by Nona Schurman, 1995.

37. Registration form, 1947.

38. Nona Schurman, interview by author, 1995. All following quotes attributed to Schurman are from that interview.

39. *Y Bulletin,* 4 November 1959, 2.

40. Documents suggest that no labs were offered for the period 1956–58.

41. From taped Dance Laboratory session "Eroticism and the Dance," 4 November 1951.

42. Ibid.

43. *Bulletin of Educational Activities,* 1947–48. Listed in the same catalog is a workshop course, "The Use of Poetry in Modern Dance," directed by John Brinnin.

44. *Bulletin of Educational Activities,* 1951–52.

45. Audiotapes of these and many other laboratory sessions are available at the Dance Collection, New York Public Library.

46. For a more detailed examination of Berk and "Jewish dance," see chap. 7.

47. See Judith Brin Ingber, "Fred Berk: The Metamorphosis of a European Dancer,

1939 –1949," *Dance Chronicle* 7(1) (1984), and *Victory Dances: The Story of Fred Berk, a Modern Day Jewish Dancing Master* (Tel Aviv: Israel Dance Library, 1985).

48. See chap. 7 for a discussion of Zionism. For a historical overview of Israeli folk dance, see Gurit Kadman, *Am Roked* (Tel Aviv: Schocken Publishing, 1969), and Judith Brin Ingber, "Shorashim: The Roots of Israeli Dance," *Dance Perspectives,* no. 59 (autumn 1974).

49. *Bulletin of Educational Activities,* 1955.

4. Audience Building, Jews, and Global Culture

1. Merry-Go-Rounders scripts, Dance Collection, New York Public Library.

2. Judith Brin Ingber, *Victory Dances: The Story of Fred Berk, a Modern Day Jewish Dancing Master* (Tel Aviv: Israel Dance Library, 1985), 84.

3. Manon Souriau, one of the original cast of the company, is tracing the Merry-Go-Rounders' origins and influence in a forthcoming book about the company.

4. Bonnie Bird, interview by author, 1995. All other Bird quotes from that interview.

5. Ibid.

6. Press release.

7. Nikolais loaned the piece to the company for the first season.

8. Bonnie Bird interview.

9. *New York Herald Tribune,* Sunday, 18 January 1953.

10. Bonnie Bird interview (her emphasis).

11. Bunny Mendelsohn, interview by author, 1995.

12. Press release.

13. *New York Times,* 27 March 1954.

14. Fred Berk, *Holiday in Israel* (New York: Dance Notation Bureau Press, 1977), vi–vii.

15. I use the term "inspired" here to denote that the dances were theatricalized renditions of the folk forms. A more detailed examination of this process of artistic adaptation and its significance can be found in chapter 7.

16. According to dance ethnographer Jill Gellerman, there are different versions of this dance, depending on the community that performs it. Often, however, there is a mimed fight between two women or two men, during which the couple shakes handkerchiefs in pretended anger before becoming reconciled. The dance apparently originated to display the reconciliation of the mothers-in-law of the betrothed couple. For a discussion of dancing at Jewish weddings, see Gellerman's upcoming dissertation on *Simkhe* dancing in the New York community. Also see collected papers of "Dancing into Marriage: Two-day Conference on Jewish Wedding Dance," sponsored by CORD and the Minneapolis Jewish Community Center, Minneapolis, June 27–28, 1982; and Zvi Friedhaber, "The Dance with the Separating Kerchief," *Dance Research Journal,* 17(2) and 18(1) (fall 1985/spring 1986): 65 – 69.

17. Berk, *Holiday in Israel*, vi.

18. Ibid.

19. Ibid., vi–vii.

20. Ingber, *Victory Dances*, 84–85.

21. The term *ethnic*, as found in the writings of John Martin and other dance writers of the time, was used to denote dance forms that were closely tied to the cultures in which they originated and that had not gone through a process of creative manipulation by an individual choreographer. "Ethnic" and "folk" dance were defined in contrast to ballet and modern dance. This nomenclature was not seriously challenged until the late 1960s, when anthropologists began to question its accuracy and validity. See Joann Kealiinohomoku, "An Anthropologist Looks at Ballet as a Form of Ethnic Dance," in *What Is Dance*, ed. Roger Copeland and Marshall Cohen (Oxford: Oxford University Press, 1983), 533–49.

22. A fuller discussion of the relationship between dance and Zionism is offered in chap. 7.

23. *Dance Observer*, March 1953, 42.

24. Shirley Ubell and Manon Souriau, interviews by author, 1995.

25. Berk, *Holiday in Israel*, xvii.

26. Ingber, *Victory Dances*, 84.

5. Producing on the Edge

1. Merle Hirsh to the YMHA, 17 October 1937.

2. This figure also does not include the many canceled recitals.

3. Agnes de Mille, *Martha: The Life and Work of Martha Graham* (New York: Vintage, 1992), 170.

4. Music recitals were added to the Major Subscription Series for the 1936–37 season. From then on, music was the central focus of the Major Subscription Series.

5. The relationship between the Dance Theatre Subscription Series and the Major Subscription Series is not clear. Sometimes the Dance Theatre Subscription Series was listed as a subset of the Major Subscription Series, and occasionally it was listed independently. It also seems that in at least one instance dance was still included on the Major Subscription Series, as with Angna Enters during the 1937–38 season.

6. Since then there have been various series attempted by the successors of Kolodney. Some of these are further described in chap. 8.

7. Lee Freeson, interview by author, 1996.

8. Ibid. Freeson does not believe a contract was made.

9. Agnes de Mille, *Portrait Gallery* (Boston: Houghton Mifflin, 1990), 59. It is important to realize that de Mille's account of Maracci's first trip to New York is not accurate. Maracci performed at the Y on her initial trip to New York, as opposed to returning later

for her debut. Lee Freeson has also stated that Moore did not give her $35,000 to come to New York. Instead, she loaned Maracci about $750, and Maracci made her own way to New York. Lee Freeson interview.

10. The timing here is unclear. Lee Freeson recalls that Maracci did not have plans to perform at the Y prior to her arrival in New York. It appears that her agreement to perform at the Y occurred during and following the problems with Grisman.

11. *Dance Observer,* May 1937, 55.

12. Lee Freeson to William Kolodney, 26 April 1937. According to Freeson, in a 1996 interview, Maracci felt so strongly about the Y that, even after she became successful, she demanded that her manager secure performances at the Y.

13. Carmelita Maracci to William Kolodney, 26 June 1937.

14. Carmelita Maracci to William Kolodney, 2 April 1938.

15. "Proposed Program for the Educational Department, 1937–1938."

16. The Major Subscription Series from then on focused on music until 1943, when the series was discontinued and music concerts were held either individually or on newly organized series.

17. The conditions under which dancers could perform at the Y were complex and forever changing. Better-known dancers were offered a negotiated fee; others entered the cost-sharing agreement.

18. William Kolodney to Martha Hill et al., 29 April 1937.

19. William Kolodney to John Martin, 30 April 1937.

20. It should be noted that Graham herself at this time believed in the concept of dancer-choreographer and insisted that her dancers study choreography with Horst. See Janet Soares, *Louis Horst: Musician in a Dancer's World* (Durham, N.C.: Duke University Press, 1992), 117.

21. Margaret Lloyd, *The Borzoi Book of Modern Dance* (New York: A. A. Knopf, 1949), 304.

22. "Proposed Program for the Educational Department, 1939–1940."

23. This relationship went two ways, with Kolodney often speaking up for dance in education. For instance, in 1942, when the dance program at Columbia's Teachers College seemed in danger of being cut, Kolodney wrote a strong letter of defense of the program. He stated, "I should certainly hate to see my Alma Mater give up its leadership of many years standing in the field of education through the arts by eliminating so vital an art as the dance" (4 May 1942).

24. Nancy Palmer to Miss Lipschutz, 1 May 1942.

25. *Dance Observer,* June–July 1945, 72.

26. It is rather unclear just how much input the committee had. On the one hand, extant minutes from their meetings suggest a large role, but it also appears that Kolodney constantly negotiated with dancers independently.

27. William Kolodney to Sybil Shearer, 30 April 1942.

28. *New York Times,* 21 February 1943.

29. *Dance Observer,* March 1949, 37.

30. William Kolodney to Katherine Rivett, 5 January 1942.

31. From press release.

32. YMHA *Bulletin,* 6 March 1942, 2.

33. Letter from Lucille Ricker, 17 March 1942.

34. Note that the American Concert Ballet, an early incarnation of New York City Ballet, appeared at the Y on 14 November 1943.

35. Muller organized dance recitals at the museum starting around 1940. The dance programs were free until 1949, when admission was charged and they became part of a more formalized series.

36. Doris Hering, "Ulysses in Tights," *Dance Magazine,* October 1951, 42.

37. "Proposal to the Board for 1947–8."

38. Larry Warren, *Lester Horton: Modern Dance Pioneer* (Princeton, N.J.: Dance Horizons/Princeton Book Company, 1977), 171.

39. Ibid., 184.

40. Minutes of the Board of Directors, 92nd Street YM-YWHA, 19 January 1954, 8.

41. William Kolodney to members of the Dance Teachers Advisory Committee, 13 October 1953.

42. Minutes of the Board of Directors, 92nd Street YM-YWHA, 1954.

43. John Martin, "The Dance: Policy—The 'Y' Takes a Breather from Performances," *New York Times,* Sunday, 1 November 1953.

44. Walter Terry, "New Theatre Policy at the Y.M.H.A," *New York Herald Tribune,* 1 November 1953, 4.

45. Anatole Chujoy, "Regrettable Change of Policy," *Dance News,* December 1953, 6.

46. Ibid.

47. Minutes of the Board of Directors, 92nd Street YM-YWHA, 1954.

48. *Dance Observer,* August–September 1951, 103.

49. Marie Marchowsky, interview by author, 1995.

50. It is not clear from the documentation how this transfer occurred or who initiated it. Humphrey may have been too busy with the Juilliard Dance Theatre to continue, or Kolodney may have asked her to take a less central role. Either way, Humphrey remained an important adviser to Kolodney, and no break occurred between them.

51. Minutes of the Board of Directors, 92nd Street YM-YWHA, 22 May 1956.

52. Copy of contract for Rahel Nadav and Bracha Klausner, ultimately canceled, 1956–57 season.

53. Doris Humphrey to William Kolodney, dated June 16, 1957. It is likely that Humphrey did not expect to personally pay for the series but was willing to help to seek outside support in case there was a deficit.

54. *Dance Observer,* December 1957, 153.

55. Both parties ultimately paid $941.90 to cover the cost of the deficit.

56. Jerome Robbins to Doris Humphrey, 25 May 1958.

6. Choreographing Difference

1. Joe Nash, interview by author, 1995.

2. William Kolodney, "Does the Modern Dance Have a Future?" unpublished paper, c. 1941.

3. Joe Nash, interview.

4. Marie Marchowsky, interview by author, 1995.

5. Sybil Shearer, "Looking Back," *Ballet Review,* fall 1984, 25.

6. Kolodney, "Does the Modern Dance Have a Future?"

7. See Susan Manning, *Ecstasy and the Demon* (Berkeley: University of California Press, 1993), 261.

8. Quoted in Manning, *Ecstasy and the Demon,* 261.

9. *La Buveuse* was also known as *Gueule de Bois.* The work was published in *Le Courrier Francais* in 1890.

10. Analysis based on a 1950s film of *After Toulouse-Lautrec* directed by Fran Allan and performed by Marie Marchowsky, Dance Collection, New York Public Library.

11. Louis Horst, *Dance Observer,* April 1952, 55.

12. Marcia B. Siegel, *Days on Earth: The Dance of Doris Humphrey* (New Haven, Conn.: Yale University Press, 1987), 264.

13. Elizabeth Kendall, "Katherine Litz: Daughter of Virtue," *Ballet Review,* 7(2–3) (1978–1979): 1.

14. Ibid., 3.

15. Analysis based on a video recording of the dance performed by Litz in 1977. Videotaped by Johannes Holub in performance during the New York Dance Festival, September 1977. Dance Collection, New York Public Library.

16. *Lamentation* was first performed in New York at the Maxine Elliott Theatre on 8 January 1930.

17. *Dance Observer,* January 1952, 25.

18. Review dated 9 January 1944. Edwin Denby, *Dance Writings* (New York: Alfred A. Knopf, 1986), 190–91.

19. Margaret Lloyd, *The Borzoi Book of Modern Dance* (New York: A. A. Knopf, 1949), 233–34.

20. Sybil Shearer, interview by author, 1995.

21. The work had previously been performed at the nightclub Cafe Society.

22. Nathan Kolodney, interview by author, 1994.

23. Langston Hughes was one of the five poets listed on the first poetry series of Kolodney's Poetry Center in 1939.

24. Joe Nash, interview by author, 1996.

25. Analysis based on a revival of the dance for The New Dance Group Gala Concert

held in New York in June 1993. Video directed by Johannes Holub, 1994; dancer: Kim Y. Bears. Available on videotape from the American Dance Guild.

26. Music for the gala by Onwin Borde; the original 1944 score was by Sarah Malament.

27. The world premiere of *The Desperate Heart* was at the Humphrey-Weidman Studio Theatre, 24–26 March 1943.

28. Edwin Denby, *Dance Writings* (New York: Knopf, 1986), 222.

29. Minutes of the Board of Directors, 92nd Street YM-YWHA, 20 March 1945.

30. *New York Times,* 27 February 1949.

31. *Y Bulletin,* 4 April 1956.

32. Valerie Bettis, interview by Wendy Laakso, 1979, Dance Collection, New York Public Library.

7. Synthesizing the Universal and Particular

1. Quoted in press release on Delakova and Berk, January 1947.

2. It should be noted that there were Jewish male modern dancers in the 1930s, including Maurice Bakst and Lee Sherman, both of whom worked with Humphrey-Weidman.

3. Freema Nadler, interview by author, 1996. Nadler remained in Russia until 1991, when she returned to the United States with her daughter.

4. Arthur Liebman, *Jews and the Left* (New York: John Wiley & Sons, 1979), 26.

5. Ibid., 2.

6. Ibid., 144.

7. For a detailed look at Duncan's political ideas, see Ann Daly, *Done into Dance: Isadora Duncan in America* (Bloomington: Indiana University Press, 1995).

8. Quoted in Ilya Ilyich Schneider, *Isadora Duncan: The Russian Years* (New York: Da Capo Press, 1968), 9.

9. Maurice Bakst, interview by author, 1996. Bakst studied and rehearsed with Humphrey and Weidman in the early 1930s; he stopped in 1932 because of heart problems. He also worked with Benjamin Zemach and rehearsed the dances for *The Eternal Road.*

10. Ellen Graff, *Stepping Left: Dance and Politics in New York City, 1928–1944* (Durham, N.C.: Duke University Press, 1997), 9.

11. Nadler, interview, 1996.

12. Quoted in *Martha Graham: The Evolution of Her Dance Theory and Training 1926–1991,* comp. Marian Horosko (Chicago: A Cappella Books, 1991), 51.

13. See Graff, *Stepping Left,* 138–40.

14. From poster titled "Soloists of Workers Dance League."

15. Quoted in Joseph Mitchell, *New York World-Telegram,* 13 December 1934.

16. Graff, *Stepping Left,* 146–47.

17. Naum Rosen, "The New Jewish Dance in America," *Dance Observer,* June–July 1934, 51.

18. The origins are unclear. Lasar Galpern claimed that his "Hebrew Dance" (performed at the Y on 7 November 1937) was the first "Hebrew dance" ever created, in 1919 in Moscow (program note). Among his various achievements, Galpern was the ballet master of the Jewish State Theatre in Moscow; dance director and instructor at the Municipal Drama School, Operetten Theatre, and Municipal Theatre in Leipzig; ballet master of the Municipal Opera House in Dusseldorf; ballet master and instructor at the Opera House and Conservatory of Music in Cologne. He was brought to America to be ballet master at the Radio City Music Hall in the 1930s.

19. For an interesting analysis of *The Dybbuk,* see Debra Cash, "The Dybbuk: A Study of the Theatrical Use of Ritual Gesture," manuscript, 1978, Dance Collection, New York Public Library.

20. John Martin, "The Dance: A Unique Art Ballet," *New York Times,* 9 June 1929.

21. Naima Prevots, *Dancing in the Sun: Hollywood Choreographers, 1935–1937* (Ann Arbor, Mich.: UMI Research Press, 1987), 204.

22. Ibid., 209.

23. Shapero continued to work with the Yiddish theater, choreographing movement for productions of Maurice Schwartz for as long as he was head of the Yiddish Art Theatre (1932–52). She also choreographed for Chanukah Festivals at Madison Square Garden and assisted with the Jewish Pavilion at the 1939 World's Fair.

24. John Martin, "The Dance: In the Drama," *New York Times,* 2 April 1933.

25. For a more detailed examination of the Yiddish theater see Nahma Sandrow, *Vagabond Stars* (New York: Harper and Row, 1977).

26. David Lifson, *The Yiddish Theatre in America* (New York: Thomas Yoseloff, 1965), 333.

27. Dvora Lapson, "Modern Hebrew Dance," *American Dancer,* April 1934, 9.

28. Ibid.

29. Moshe Davis, *The Hebrew Arts Committee, 1945,* Master Institute Theatre, (spring, 1945), 6. Pamphlet held in the Jewish Theological Seminary library, New York. Davis wrote numerous unpublished papers on the new committee. In "A Jewish Arts Orientation" (1943) he was highly critical of American Jewish leadership for failing to promote Jewish culture and lamented the undeveloped audience for Jewish art.

30. "Hebrew Arts Program in Full Swing," *New Palestine,* 3 January 1945.

31. *Crisis* was performed on Shapero's December 1937 concert at the Y.

32. *Educational Bulletin,* 1939.

33. Nancy Friedland examines the failure of the "Jewish American Theatre" experiment at the Y in the 1930s in her M.A. thesis "The 92nd St. Y and Anglo-Jewish Theatre," New York University, 1993. Friedland explains that Y audiences were not supportive of the experimental, artistic forays into "Jewish theatre."

34. See Edith Segal, interview by Leslie Farlow, 1991, Dance Collection, New York

Public Library. See also William Kolodney to Lasar Galpern, 12 November 1939. The wording is brief, and it is unclear whether Kolodney did not hear from the performers or was unable to gain support from the Y's membership.

35. The dance received its initial premiere on 18 August 1950 at Palmer Auditorium, New London, Connecticut, as part of the American Dance Festival. The piece was an expanded version of an earlier dance, *Festival,* which had been presented by the company at ADF the previous summer.

36. H. Dzhermolinska, "The Village I Knew," *Dance Magazine,* March 1951, 12.

37. V. Platon, "Thoughts on a Dance in Progress," *Jewish Life,* November 1949, 34–36.

38. Deborah Pritzker, "Maslow Dancers Blend Two Eras in Concert Form Here," *Y Bulletin,* 28 November 1956, 1.

39. See Barbara Kirshenblatt-Gimblett, introduction to *Life Is with People,* ed. Mark Zborowski and Elizabeth Herzog (New York: Schocken Books, 1995), xviii.

40. S. Maslow, interview by author, 1995.

41. John Martin, *Introduction to the Dance* (New York, W. W. Norton & Co., 1939), 107–8.

42. Ibid., 105.

43. John Martin, *America Dancing: The Background and Personalities of the Modern Dance* (New York: Dodge Publishing Co., 1936), 285.

44. Ibid., 91.

45. Ibid., 105.

46. E. Hickman, "Sophie Maslow Looks for Concept of Universal Emotion in Dancing," *Asbury Park (New Jersey) Sunday Press,* 24 September 1944. Dance Collection, New York Public Library.

47. This implies that while some Jews of the postwar period might not have realized that they were searching for quintessentially Jewish images (such as the shtetl), modern dancers continued to be propelled in that very direction by the theories they espoused. Maslow's quest for her Jewish roots fit beautifully with modern dancers' search for "essentials." In both cases there was a desire to discover timeless truths that epitomized one's existence.

48. V. Platon, "Thoughts on a Dance in Progress," 36.

49. The dance originally premiered in Mexico City in 1945.

50. *Dance Observer,* June–July 1946, 76.

51. Ibid., March 1948, 32.

52. A black-and-white recording of the dance as performed by Deborah Zall is in the Dance Collection, New York Public Library.

53. Tobi Tobias, "Two Essays for Pearl Lang," *Dance Magazine,* September 1974, 48–54.

54. Susan Sticklor, "Pearl Lang's 'The Possessed' (The Dybbuk)," *Eddy,* no. 6, spring 1975, 44.

55. Anna Kisselgoff, "Dance: 'The Possessed,'" *New York Times,* 16 January 1976. Dance Collection, New York Public Library.

56. Walter Terry, "A Jewish Community in Dance," *New York Herald Tribune,* 28 January 1951.

57. Nik Krevitsky, "American Dance Festival," *Dance Observer,* August-September 1950, 102.

58. Both Maslow and Sokolow continued to contribute to Jewish culture. Maslow created dances for the annual Chanukah Festivals at Madison Square Garden from 1955 to 1967, and Sokolow was heavily involved with dance in Israel from 1953 onward.

59. See Judith Brin Ingber, "Shorashim: The Roots of Israeli Dance," *Dance Perspectives,* no. 59, autumn 1974.

60. Dan Ronen, "Fifty Years of Israeli Folk Dance, 1944–1994," *Israel Dance,* no. 4, October 1994, 123.

61. As a student in Vienna, Berk was introduced to Jewish themes in the work of Gertrud Kraus. At the time, however, he did not relate to the Jewish subject matter. See Ingber, *Victory Dances: The Story of Fred Berk, a Modern Day Jewish Dancing Master* (Tel Aviv: Israel Dance Library, 1985), 20.

62. The Jewish Dance Guild was formed by Berk and Delakova around 1946 out of teaching they were doing at the Jewish Theological Seminary. See Ingber, *Victory Dances,* 61–64.

63. Press release on Fred Berk and Katya Delakova, 1947.

64. Over the years, the Israeli Dance Festival was held at Hunter College, the 92nd Street Y, Carnegie Hall, the Felt Forum, and Philharmonic Hall. Ingber, *Victory Dances,* 96–97.

65. Some crossover existed with the Merry-Go-Rounders since Manon Souriau was one of the company members and Beatrice Rainer played the piano.

66. Carolyn Strauss, quoted in Ingber, *Victory Dances,* 81.

67. Naomi Cohen, *American Jews and the Zionist Idea* (New York: Ktav Publishing, 1975), 114–15.

68. In the 1930s the National Jewish Welfare Board took no official stand on Zionism, although by the early 1940s the majority of Jewish centers and YM-YWHAs were becoming pro-Zionist. Samuel Halperin, *The Political World of American Zionism* (Detroit: Wayne State University Press, 1961), 263.

69. William Kolodney, "Paper by William Kolodney," in *Proceedings and Papers of the Annual Conference of the National Association of Jewish Center Workers.* (National Association of Jewish Center Workers in Cooperation with the JWB, 1940), 87.

70. *Speaking of Dance: Donald McKayle, Conversations with Contemporary Masters of American Modern Dance.* Produced by American Dance Festival (ADF) Video, 1993. Producer/director: Douglas Rosenberg. Note that members of the initial cast, as listed on the program for the January 1951 92nd Street Y recital, included Jane Dudley, William Bales, Alvin Beam, Rena Gluck, Billie Kirpich, Donald McKayle, Muriel Manings, Anneliese Widman, and David Wood.

8. A Postmodern Precursor

1. William Kolodney, "History of the Educational Department of the YM-YWHA" (Ed.D. diss., Teachers College, Columbia University, 1950), 152.

2. Paul Taylor, *Private Domain* (New York: Knopf, 1987), 80.

3. Taylor may have been referring to Dan Butt, listed on the program as the stage manager for the recital.

4. Gay Morris, ed., *Moving Words: Re-Writing Dance* (New York: Routledge, 1996), 11.

5. Susannah Heschel, "Jewish Studies as Counterhistory," in *Insider/Outsider: American Jews and Multiculturalism* (Berkeley: University of California Press, 1998), 111–12.

6. David Hirsch, *The Deconstruction of Literature: Criticism after Auschwitz* ([Providence, R.I.]: Brown University Press, 1991), brilliantly links the antihumanist strand of poststructuralist theory with the Nazi regime, revealing the extent to which Jewish history and postmodernist thought are intimately connected.

7. Don McDonagh, *The Rise and Fall and Rise of Modern Dance* (Pennington, N.J.: A Capela Books, 1990), x.

8. Ibid.

9. Ibid., 172.

10. *YMHA Bulletin,* 31 December 1958, 1.

11. *Dance Observer,* February 1959, 25.

12. Sally Banes, *Terpsichore in Sneakers: Post-Modern Dance.* (Hanover, N.H.: University Press of New England/Wesleyan University Press, 1987), 12.

13. John Kalas, *The Grant System* (Albany: State University of New York Press, 1987), 30.

14. Ibid., 26.

15. Ibid.

16. Banes, *Terpsichore in Sneakers,* xvi; my emphasis.

17. Ibid.

18. Ibid., xvii.

19. *Current Biography,* 1972, s.v. "Carmines."

20. Shortly following his retirement, Kolodney fell seriously ill with Parkinson's disease. He died in 1975 following heart complications.

21. Anna Kisselgoff, "Dance: 'Live Dragon,'" *New York Times,* Sunday, 25 March 1973.

22. Hirshbein remained at the Y until 1993, during which time music recitals and poetry readings flourished. He left the Y for the National Endowment for the Arts, where he directed the Music, Presenting, and Opera/Music Theatre programs.

23. The unionizing of the hall supposedly came about because of the start of a resident orchestra at the Y. With the new orchestra, a reliable and skilled crew was consistently needed, so the Y arranged to have a union house.

24. Omus Hirshbein, interview by author, 1994.

25. As changes occurred at the Y during the 1980s and early 1990s, Hirshbein's title and responsibilities shifted several more times.

26. The situation described is specific to the dance world. In the fine arts, the 1960s proved a successful period for the Jewish Museum, which was celebrated as a patron of contemporary art.

27. Banes, *Terpsichore in Sneakers,* 157–58.

28. See Naomi Jackson, "Searching for Moving Metaphors: Jewishness in American Modern and Postmodern Dance," *Jewish Folklore and Ethnology Review,* in press.

29. Susan Josephs, "Dancing All the Way Uptown," *Jewish Week,* 14 December 1995.

BIBLIOGRAPHY

Banes, Sally. *Terpsichore in Sneakers: Post-Modern Dance.* Hanover, N.H.: University Press of New England/Wesleyan University Press, 1987.

Berk, Fred. *Ha-Rikud: The Jewish Dance.* New York: Union of American Hebrew Congregations, 1973.

———. *Holiday in Israel.* New York: Dance Notation Bureau Press, 1977.

———. *The Jewish Dance.* New York: Exposition Banner Press, 1960.

Biale, David, Michael Galchinsky, and Susan Heschel, eds. *Insider/Outsider: American Jews and Multiculturalism.* Berkeley: University of California Press, 1998.

Carlson, Reynold E., Theodore R. Deppe, and Janet R. MacLean. *Recreation in American Life.* Belmont, Calif.: Wadsworth Publishing Co., 1972.

Chochem, Corinne. *Jewish Holiday Dances.* Music by Trudi Rittman. New York: Behrman House, 1948.

Citron, Atay. "Pageantry and Theatre in the Service of Jewish Nationalism in the United States, 1933–1946," Ph.D. diss., New York University, 1989.

Cohen, Naomi. *American Jews and the Zionist Idea.* New York: Ktav Publishing, 1975.

Cohen, Selma Jeanne. *Doris Humphrey: An Artist First.* Middletown, Conn.: Wesleyan University Press, 1972.

Coleman, Martha. "Modern Dance: Its Role in the Curriculum of the 92nd Street Y.M.-Y.W.H.A. in New York, under Dance Director Doris Humphrey." *Dance Magazine* 22 (January 1948): 40–41.

Crowley, Alice Lewisohn. *The Neighborhood Playhouse: Leaves from a Theatre Scrapbook.* New York: Theatre Arts Books, 1959.

De Mille, Agnes. *Martha: The Life and Work of Martha Graham.* New York: Vintage Books, 1992.

———. *Portrait Gallery.* Boston: Houghton Mifflin, 1990.

Friedland, Nancy. "The 92nd St. Y and Anglo-Jewish Theatre." Master's thesis, New York University, 1993.

Goldsmith, Emanuel S., Mel Scult, and Robert M. Seltzer, eds. *The American Judaism of Mordecai M. Kaplan.* New York: New York University Press, 1990.

Graff, Ellen. "Dancing Red: Art and Politics," *Studies in Dance History,* 5(1) (spring, 1994): 1–13.

———. "Stepping Left: Dance and Politics in New York City 1928 –1942." Ph.D. diss., New York University, 1992.

———. *Stepping Left: Dance and Politics in New York City, 1928–1942.* Durham, N.C.: Duke University Press, 1997.

Hart, Joseph. *Adult Education.* New York: T. Y. Crowell, 1927.

Hirsch, David H. *The Deconstruction of Literature: Criticism after Auschwitz.* [Providence, R.I.]: Brown University Press, 1991.

Hobsbawm, Eric, and Terence Ranger, eds. *The Invention of Tradition.* New York: Cambridge University Press, 1983.

Hopkins, C. Howard. *History of the Y.M.C.A. in North America.* New York: Association Press, 1951.

Ingber, Judith Brin. "Shorashim: The Roots of Israeli Folk Dance,*" Dance Perspectives,* no. 59 (1974).

———. *Victory Dances: The Story of Fred Berk, a Modern Day Jewish Dancing Master.* Tel Aviv: Israel Dance Library, 1985.

Janowsky, Oscar I. *The JWB Survey.* New York: Dial Press, 1948.

Johnson, Elmer L. *The History of YMCA Physical Education.* Chicago: Association Press, 1979.

Joselit, Jenna. *New York's Jewish Jews: The Orthodox Community in the Interwar Years.* Bloomington: Indiana University Press, 1990.

Kadman, Gurit. *Am Roked* (The nation dances: History of Israeli folk dance). Tel Aviv: Schocken Publishing, 1969.

Kalas, John W. *The Grant System.* Albany: State University of New York Press, 1987.

Kaplan, Mordecai. *Judaism as a Civilization: Toward a Reconstruction of American-Jewish Life.* Philadelphia: Jewish Publication Society of America and the Reconstructionist Press, 1981.

Kaufman, David. *Shul with a Pool: The "Synagogue-Center" in American Jewish History.* Hanover, N.H.: University Press of New England, 1999.

Kendall, Elizabeth. "Katherine Litz: Daughter of Virtue," *Ballet Review,* 7(2–3) (1978 –1979): 1– 9.

Kirshenblatt-Gimblett, Barbara. Introduction to *Life Is with People.* Edited by Mark Zborowski and Elizabeth Herzog. New York: Schocken Books, 1995.

———. "Theorizing Heritage," *Ethnomusicology,* 39 (fall 1995): 367 – 81.

Kolodney, William. "History of the Educational Department of the YM-YWHA." Ed.D. diss., Teachers College, Columbia University, 1950.

Koner, Pauline. *Solitary Song/Pauline Koner.* Durham, N.C.: Duke University Press, 1989.

Kriegsman, Sali Ann. *Modern Dance in America: The Bennington Years.* Boston: G. K. Hall, 1981.

Lanes, Doreen. "The Ninety Second Street YM-YWHA: 1934–1953." *Dance Research Annual* 10 (1979):251–66.

Liebman, Arthur. *Jews and the Left.* New York: John Wiley & Sons, 1979.

Lifson, David S. *The Yiddish Theatre in America.* New York: Thomas Yoseloff, 1965.

Lindeman, Eduard C. *The Meaning of Adult Education.* New York: New Republic, 1926.

Lloyd, Margaret. *The Borzoi Book of Modern Dance.* New York: A. A. Knopf, 1949.

Manning, Susan. *Ecstasy and the Demon: Feminism and Nationalism in the Dances of Mary Wigman.* Berkeley: University of California Press, 1993.

Martin, Everett Dean. *The Meaning of a Liberal Education.* New York: W. W. Norton & Co., 1926.

Martin, John. *America Dancing: The Background and Personalities of the Modern Dance.* New York: Dodge Publishing Co., 1936.

———. *The Modern Dance.* New York: A. S. Barnes, 1933.

McDonagh, Don. *The Rise and Fall and Rise of Modern Dance.* Pennington, N.J.: A Capella Books, 1990.

Moore, Deborah Dash. *At Home in America: Second Generation New York Jews.* New York: Columbia University Press, 1981.

Novack, Cynthia. *Sharing the Dance: Contact Improvisation and American Culture.* Madison: University of Wisconsin Press, 1990.

Perpener, John O., III. "The Seminal Years of Black Concert Dance." Ph.D. diss., New York University, 1992.

Prevots, Naima. "Benjamin Zemach: From Darkness to Light." In *Israel Dance.* Tel Aviv: Israel Dance Society and Friends of the Dance Library of Israel, 1986, 22–30.

———. "Benjamin Zemach: Social Content." *Proceedings of the 8th Annual Conference, Society of Dance History Scholars,* February 1985, 166–75.

———. *Dancing in the Sun: Hollywood Choreographers 1935–1937.* Ann Arbor, Mich.: UMI Research Press, 1987.

Rabinowitz, Benjamin. *The Young Men's Hebrew Associations, 1854–1913.* New York: National Jewish Welfare Board, 1948.

Rosen, Lillie. "The What of the Y." *Eddy,* no.6 (spring 1975): 22–28.

Rutkoff, Peter M., and William B. Scott. *New School: A History of the New School for Social Research.* New York: Free Press, 1986.

Sandrow, Nahma. *Vagabond Stars: A World History of Yiddish Theater.* Syracuse, N.Y.: Syracuse University Press, 1996.

Schein, Eugenie. "The Dance, the Y.M.H.A. and Mr. Kolodney." *Dance Observer* 8 (December 1941): 133.

Schurman, Nona, and Sharon Leigh Clark. *Modern Dance Fundamentals.* New York: Macmillan, 1972.

Siegel, Marcia B. *Days on Earth: The Dance of Doris Humphrey*. New Haven, Conn.: Yale University Press, 1987.

Stern, Alfred, ed. *Building Character for 75 Years: 1874–1949, Y.M.&Y.W.H.A.* New York: Robin Hood Press, 1949.

Stout, Helen R. "The Y.M.H.A. and the Modern Dance." *Dance Observer* 4 (October 1937): 95 – 96.

———. "The Y.M.H.A. and the Modern Dance," *Dance Observer* 6 (April 1939): 207 – 08.

Taylor, Paul. *Private Domain*. New York: Knopf, 1987.

Tomko, Linda J. "The Settlement House and the Playhouse: Cultivating Expressive Dance in Early Twentieth-Century New York City." In *Conference Papers,* 5th Hong Kong International Dance Conference. July 15 – 28, 1990, vol. 2. Hong Kong: Hong Kong Academy for Performing Arts.

Warren, Larry. *Anna Sokolow: The Rebellious Spirit*. Princeton, N.J.: Princeton Book Company, 1991.

———. *Lester Horton: Modern Dance Pioneer*. Princeton, N.J.: Princeton Book Company, 1977.

Wenger, Beth. *New York Jews and the Great Depression.* New Haven, Conn.: Yale University Press, 1996.

INDEX

About the author:
Naomi Jackson is Associate Professor in
the Department of Dance at
Arizona State University.